Houghton Mifflin Science
DISCOVERYWORKS

 HOUGHTON MIFFLIN

Boston • Atlanta • Dallas • Denver • Geneva, Illinois • Palo Alto • Princeton

Authors

William Badders
Elementary Science Teacher
Cleveland Public Schools
Cleveland, OH

Lowell J. Bethel
Professor of Science Education
The University of Texas at Austin
Austin, TX

Victoria Fu
Professor of Child Development
and Early Childhood Education
Virginia Polytechnic Institute and
State University
Blacksburg, VA

Donald Peck
Director (retired)
The Center for Elementary Science
Fairleigh Dickinson University
Madison, NJ

Carolyn Sumners
Director of Astronomy and Physical Sciences
Houston Museum of Natural Science
Houston, TX

Catherine Valentino
Author-in-Residence, Houghton Mifflin
West Kingston, RI

Acknowledgements appear on page H39, which
constitutes an extension of this copyright page.

Printed in the U. S. A.

ISBN 0-618-00633-8

4 5 6 7 8 9 10 RRD 08 07 06 05 04 03 02 01 00

CONTENTS

THINK LIKE A SCIENTIST

How to Think Like a Scientist S2
Practice Thinking Like a Scientist S4
Using Science Process Skills S10
Reading to Learn S12
Safety S14

UNIT A Earth's Land

THINK LIKE A SCIENTIST
NATURE'S ARTWORK

A2

CHAPTER 1 The Shape of the Land

A4

Investigation 1 **How Does Moving Water Shape the Land?** . . . A6
Activity: Hills and Valleys A6
Activity: At the Beach A8
Resource: Carving the Land A10
Resource: The Changing Shoreline A13

Investigation 2 **How Do Wind and Ice Shape the Land?** A16
Activity: Blowin' in the Wind A16
Activity: Gigantic Frozen Sandpaper A18
Resource: Sand Blasted A20
Resource: Glaciers—Nature's Bulldozers A22

Reflect and Evaluate **A25**

CHAPTER 2

The Importance of Natural Resources   A26

Investigation 1

Why Is Soil an Important Resource? A28
Activity: Little Ones From Big A28
Activity: Saving Soil A29
Resource: Gully! It's Soil Erosion A30

Investigation 2

Why Are Rocks and Minerals Important? . . . A34
Activity: Exploring Minerals A34
Activity: Being Polite About Resources A36
Resource: Minerals Through the Ages A38
Resource: From Rocks to Riches A40

Investigation 3

Why Are Energy Resources So Important? . . A44
Activity: Sun-Toasted Marshmallows A44
Resource: Fuels Around the World A46
Resource: Coal, Gas, and Black Gold A48

Reflect and Evaluate **A51**

The Problem With Trash A52

Investigation 1

What Do People Throw Away, and Where Does It Go? **A54**
Activity: Looking at Trash A54
Activity: Making a Landfill A56
Resource: Trashing Trash A58

Investigation 2

How Can Trash Affect Resources? **A62**
Activity: A Litter Walk A62
Activity: Clean It Up! A63
Resource: Don't Teach Your Trash to Swim! A64
Resource: Trashing Resources A65

Investigation 3

How Can You Help Solve the Trash Problem? **A68**
Activity: A New Life for Trash A68
Activity: The Rethink Link A69
Resource: Conserving Resources A70
Resource: Recycling A72
Resource: The Wrap Trap A75

Reflect and Evaluate **A77**

Using Reading Skills **A78**

Using Math Skills **A79**

Unit Wrap-up! **A80**

UNIT B Properties of Matter

THINK LIKE A SCIENTIST

ROCKETS' RED GLARE   B2

CHAPTER 1 Describing Matter   B4

Investigation 1 **How Can Matter Be Described?** **B6**
Activity: Describing Things B6
Activity: Similar but Different. B8
Activity: Layers of Liquids B9
Resource: Matter, Matter Everywhere. B10
Resource: Making Materials Useful B12

Investigation 2 **How Can Matter Be Measured?**. **B14**
Activity: A Balancing Act B14
Activity: Wider or Taller? B16
Activity: How Much? B17
Resource: Making Measurements B18
Resource: The Metric System B19

Reflect and Evaluate **B23**

CHAPTER 2
Observing States of Matter   B24

Investigation 1

What Is Matter Like? **B26**
   Activity: States of Matter. B26
   Activity: Invisible Matter B28
   Resource: More About Matter. B29
   Resource: A Precious Metal B32
   Resource: Compounds: They're Elementary B33

Investigation 2

How Can Matter Change State? **B36**
   Activity: From State to State B36
   Activity: Liquid From Thin Air B37
   Resource: Cool It B38
   Resource: Causing Change. B39

Reflect and Evaluate **B43**

CHAPTER 3
Causing Changes in Matter   B44

Investigation 1

What Are Physical Changes? **B46**
   Activity: Same Stuff B46
   Activity: All Mixed Up B47
   Resource: A Change for the Better? B48
   Resource: Magnificent Mixtures. B50
   Resource: A Valuable Mixture B52

Investigation 2

What Are Chemical Changes? **B54**
   Activity: Different Stuff B54
   Resource: Changed for Good B56
   Resource: Get the Picture? B59

Reflect and Evaluate **B61**

Using Reading Skills **B62**

Using Math Skills **B63**

Unit Wrap-up! **B64**

UNIT C Classifying Living Things

THINK LIKE A SCIENTIST
SCHOOL'S OUT   C2

CHAPTER 1 All Kinds of Living Things   C4

Investigation 1

How Can Living Things Be Classified? **C6**
Activity: Animals Are Different C6
Resource: Variety of Life on Earth C8
Resource: Classifying—Past and Present C12
Resource: Classification of Animals C14

Investigation 2

How Do Vertebrates Differ? **C16**
Activity: Cold Fish C16
Resource: Swim, Leap, and Slither C18
Resource: Fly, Dive, and Gallop C21

Investigation 3

**How Do the Groups of
    Invertebrates Differ?** **C24**
Activity: Worming Their Way Home. C24
Resource: Lifesaving Leeches C26
Resource: Nothing Much in Common C27

Investigation 4

How Are Plants Classified?. **C32**
Activity: Looking at Leaves C32
Resource: Plants to the Rescue C34
Resource: All Kinds of Plants C35

Reflect and Evaluate **C39**

CHAPTER 2

The Survival of Living Things C40

Investigation 1

**What Are the Basic Needs
of Living Things?** **C42**
Activity: Needs in Common C42
Resource: The ABCs of Survival C44
Resource: The African Savanna C48

Investigation 2

How Do Living Things Meet Their Needs? . . **C50**
Activity: Feather Feats C50
Activity: Tap, Tap, Tap C52
Resource: The Survival Game C54
Resource: Is It Ever Too Late? C58

Reflect and Evaluate **C61**

Using Reading Skills **C62**

Using Math Skills **C63**

Unit Wrap-up! **C64**

Magnetism and Electricity

THINK LIKE A SCIENTIST
POLAR LIGHT SHOW **D2**

CHAPTER
1

Magnetism   **D4**

Investigation
1
What Are Magnets?. **D6**
Activity: Make a Magnet. D6
Activity: A Magnet's Ends D8
Activity: Pulling Through D10
Resource: Properties of Magnets. D11
Resource: Maglev Trains D14

Investigation
2
What Are Magnetic Force Fields? **D16**
Activity: Getting Directions D16
Activity: Picture a Magnet's Force D18
Resource: Force Fields. D19
Resource: Earth as a Magnet D22

Reflect and Evaluate. **D25**

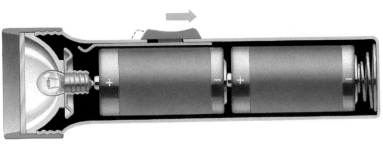

Electrical Energy   D26

Investigation
1
What Is Static Electricity? **D28**
Activity: Charge! D28
Resource: Static Electricity D30
Resource: Lightning D34

Investigation
2
What Is Current Electricity? **D36**
Activity: On or Off? D36
Activity: Stop or Go? D38
Resource: Electric Current D40

Investigation
3
How Do Electric Circuits Differ? **D44**
Activity: One Type of Circuit. D44
Activity: Another Type of Circuit D46
Resource: The Light Bulb D48
Resource: Series and Parallel Circuits D50

Reflect and Evaluate **D53**

CHAPTER 3   Electricity at Work   D54

Investigation 1   **What Are Some Sources**
                       of Electric Current? D56
                       Activity: Detect a Current .D56
                       Activity: A Magnetic Source D57
                       Resource: Producing Electric Current D58
                       Resource: From Power Plant to You D62
                       Resource: Electricity From Sunlight D64

Investigation 2   **How Is Electricity Useful?** D66
                       Activity: Make It Move .D66
                       Resource: Long Distance, Short Time D68
                       Resource: Electric Magnets D70
                       Resource: A Car That Plugs In D73
                       Resource: Safety Around Electricity D74

Reflect and Evaluate **D77**

Using Reading Skills **D78**

Using Math Skills **D79**

Unit Wrap-up! **D80**

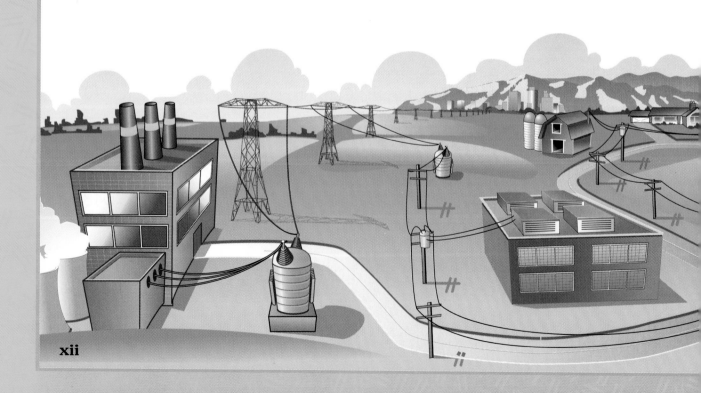

Weather and Climate

THINK LIKE A SCIENTIST
TORNADO WARNING **E2**

CHAPTER 1
The Air Around Us   **E4**

Investigation 1

What Is Air? **E6**
Activity: An Empty Cup E6
Activity: An Ocean of Air E8
Resource: It's Got Us Covered E10
Resource: Not Too Warm, Not Too Cold E14

Investigation 2

Why Does Air Move? **E16**
Activity: Warming the Air E16
Activity: Making an Air Scale....................... E18
Resource: Hot-Air Balloon E20
Resource: Feeling the Air E21

Reflect and Evaluate **E23**

Chapter 2 — Observing Weather E24

Observing Weather   **E24**

Investigation **1**

What Is Air Pressure? **E26**
Activity: It's a Pressing Problem E26
Activity: Measuring Air Pressure. E28
Resource: Torricelli's Barometer E30
Resource: All About Pressure E31

Investigation **2**

**How Can You Find Wind Speed
and Direction?** **E34**
Activity: A Windy Day E34
Activity: How Fast the Wind Blows. E36
Resource: Which Way Is the Wind Blowing? E38
Resource: Wind Power. E40

Investigation **3**

**How Does Water in the Air
Affect Weather?** **E42**
Activity: Make a Rain Gauge E42
Resource: Snow Around the World E44
Resource: The Water Cycle E46

Reflect and Evaluate **E49**

Weather Patterns E50

Investigation 1

What Can Clouds Tell You About the Weather?. **E52**
Activity: Kinds of Clouds E52
Activity: Cloudy Weather. E53
Resource: The Weather From Space E54
Resource: Watching the Clouds Go By E55

Investigation 2

How Can Maps Help You Predict Weather?. **E58**
Activity: Weather Maps. E58
Resource: Weather Wisdom E60
Resource: Weather in the News. E61

Investigation 3

How Can You Stay Safe During Dangerous Weather? **E64**
Activity: Storm Safety. E64
Activity: Tornado Tube E65
Resource: Light and Sound Show E66
Resource: Staying Safe in a Storm E68
Resource: The Fiercest Storms on Earth. E70

Reflect and Evaluate **E73**

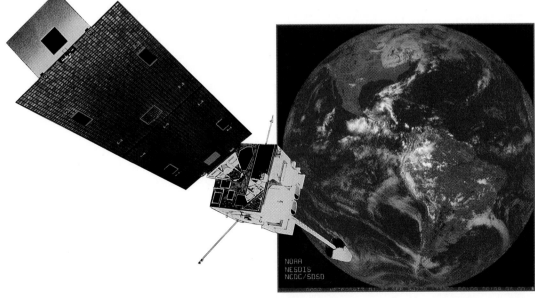

Seasons and Climate E74

Investigation 1 **What Causes the Seasons?** **E76**
Activity: Sunshine Hours E76
Resource: Changing Seasons E78

Investigation 2 **What Factors Affect Climate?** **E82**
Activity: Microclimates Everywhere! E82
Resource: Florida Is Not North Dakota E84
Resource: Clues to Earth's Climate E88
Resource: Weather Records E90

Reflect and Evaluate **E93**

Using Reading Skills **E94**

Using Math Skills **E95**

Unit Wrap-up! **E96**

SCIENCE and MATH TOOLBOX

Using a Hand Lens H2
Making a Bar Graph H3
Using a Calculator H4
Finding an Average H5
Using a Tape Measure or Ruler H6
Measuring Volume H7
Using a Thermometer H8
Using a Balance H9
Making a Chart to Organize Data H10
Reading a Circle Graph H11
Measuring Elapsed Time H12
Measurements H14

Glossary **H16**

Index **H34**

Credits **H39**

Extra Practice **R1**

How to Think Like a Scientist

How to Think Like a Scientist S2

Practice Thinking Like a Scientist

Off to the Races

Make Observations S4

Ask a Question S5

Make a Hypothesis S6

Plan and Do a Test S7

Record and Analyze S8

Draw Conclusions S9

Using Science Process Skills S10

Reading to Learn S12

Safety S14

HOW TO THINK LIKE A SCIENTIST

Make Observations

To think like a scientist, learn as much as you can by observing things around you. Everything you hear, smell, taste, touch, and see is a clue about how the world works. As you test your ideas, you'll continue to make careful observations.

Make Observations

Ask a Question

Look for patterns. You'll get ideas. For example, you know that there are more hours of daylight in summer than there are in winter. Ask questions such as this.

How does the time that the Sun sets change from day to day?

Make a Hypothesis

If you have an idea about why something happens, make an educated guess, or hypothesis, that you can test. For example, suppose that your hypothesis about sunset time is that it changes by one minute each day.

Make Observations

Plan and Do a Test

Plan how to test your hypothesis. Your plan would need to consider some of these problems.

How will you measure the time that the Sun sets?

Will you measure the time every day? For how long?

Then test your hypothesis.

Record and Analyze

When you test your idea, you need to observe carefully and record, or write down, everything that happens. When you finish collecting data, you may need to do some calculations with it. For example, you might calculate how much the sunset time changes in a week.

Make Observations

Draw Conclusions

Whatever happens in a test, think about all the reasons for your results. Sometimes this thinking leads to a new hypothesis. If the time of the sunset changes by one minute each day, think about what else the data shows you. Can you predict the time that the Sun will set one month from now?

Make Observations

Now read "Off to the Races" to see scientific thinking in action.

S3

THINK LIKE A SCIENTIST

PRACTICE THINKING LIKE A SCIENTIST

Off to the Races

Make Observations

Sarah and her parents piled into the family car and drove to the auto races. Sarah enjoyed everything about the races—the sounds, the smells, and the excitement. She watched the cars whiz by. She loved the beauty and sleek design of the race cars. Sarah noticed that the cars all had the same basic shape. They looked very different from her family's car, a sport utility vehicle (SUV).

To learn about the world, you observe it. **Observations** can be made with any of the senses—sight, hearing, touch, taste, or smell.

Ask a Question

First Sarah thought about the shape of race cars. Then she thought about the different shapes of family cars. She wondered why some cars were faster than others. "Suppose two cars weighed the same and had the same kind of engine. Would their shapes affect how fast they could go?" wondered Sarah. Sarah asked a question that she wanted to answer.

How does a car's shape affect its speed?

Sarah decided to try to answer the question as part of a school science project. She had an idea about what the answer might be.

Scientific investigations usually begin with ideas that you're not sure about. Such ideas can help you ask a question that you really want to answer.

Make a Hypothesis

To find out how a car's shape affects its speed, Sarah began looking at model cars. At a hobby shop she saw that model cars come in many shapes.

Sarah thought that a sleek-shaped car, such as a race car, would travel faster than a boxy car, such as her family's car. So she chose this idea as her hypothesis. A hypothesis is a possible answer to a question.

When you use what you've observed to suggest a possible answer to your question, you're making a hypothesis. Make sure that your hypothesis is an idea that you can test. If you can't test your hypothesis, try changing it.

a Test • Record and Analyze • Draw Conclusions • Make Observations • Ask a Question • Make a Hypothesis • Plan and Do a Test

Ask a Question • Make a Hypothesis • Plan and Do a Test • Record and Analyze • Draw Conclusions • Make Observations • Ask a Question • Make a Hypothesis

Plan and Do a Test

At school Sarah and some friends worked together to plan an experiment that would test her hypothesis. They decided to test the speed of model cars. At the hobby shop they found three cars that had the same mass but different shapes. A blue car was low, sleek, and had a sloping roof. A gold car had a high roof and a boxy shape but with some curved parts. A red car looked like Sarah's family's car—a boxy SUV.

The students used a balance to check the mass of each model car. Then they set up a ramp to race the cars. They got a stopwatch with which to time each race. They planned to race each car three times. Then they would find the average time for each car.

One way to try out your hypothesis is to use a **test** called a **controlled experiment**. The setups in this kind of experiment are identical in all ways except one. The one difference is the **variable**. In Sarah's experiment the variable is the shape of the cars.

Record and Analyze

Sarah released each car, one at a time, at the top of the ramp. Another student used a stopwatch to time how long it took for each car to reach a line drawn near the end of the ramp. A third student recorded the times in a chart like the one shown.

When you do an experiment, you make observations so that you can obtain information called data. You need to write down, or record, this data and then organize it. Graphs and tables are ways to organize data. Analyze the information that you collect by looking for patterns. To see if your results are reliable, repeat the experiment several times.

MODEL CAR RACES

Shape of Model Car	Time (in seconds)			
	Trial 1	Trial 2	Trial 3	Average
High body, boxy shape (red car)	3.33	3.23	3.56	3.37
Low, sleek with sloped roof (blue car)	2.98	2.88	3.03	2.96
Low, boxy shape, some curves (gold car)	3.02	3.18	3.10	3.10

Draw Conclusions

The students decided that their data supported Sarah's hypothesis. They looked at the average of the races. They saw that the blue car traveled down the ramp the fastest. The students concluded that a car's shape affects its speed. They also concluded that a low, sleek-shaped car is faster than a high, boxy-shaped car.

The students wondered if there were other things that might affect how fast the cars would go. They wanted to test cars that all had the same sleek shape but that had different masses. Now the group had a new question and new hypothesis to explore.

After you have analyzed your data, you should use what you learned to draw a conclusion. A **conclusion** is a statement that sums up what you learned. The conclusion should be about the hypothesis you made. A hypothesis supported by a lot of evidence may be called a **theory**.

USING SCIENCE PROCESS SKILLS

Observing involves gathering information about the environment through your five senses—seeing, hearing, smelling, touching, and tasting.

Classifying is grouping objects or events according to common properties or characteristics. Often you can classify in more than one way.

Measuring and using numbers involves the ability to make measurements (including time measurements), to make estimates, and to record data.

Communicating involves using words, both speaking and writing, and using actions, graphs, tables, diagrams, and other ways of presenting information.

Inferring means coming to a conclusion based on facts and observations you've made.

Predicting involves stating in advance what you think will happen based on observations and experiences.

Collecting, recording, and interpreting data

all involve gathering and understanding information. This skill includes organizing data in tables, graphs, and in other ways. Interpretation includes finding patterns and relationships that lead to new questions and new ideas.

Identifying and controlling variables involves

determining the effect of a changing factor, called the variable, in an experiment. To do this, you keep all other factors constant, or unchanging.

Defining operationally means to describe an object, an

event, or an idea based on personal observations. An operational definition of a plant might be that it is a green living thing that is attached to soil and that does not move around.

Making a hypothesis is suggesting a possible

answer to a question or making an educated guess about why something happens. Your hypothesis should be based on observations and experiences.

Experimenting is testing your hypothesis

to collect evidence that supports the hypothesis or shows that it is false.

Making and using models includes

designing and making physical models of processes and objects, or making mental models to represent objects and ideas.

READING TO LEARN

Before You Read

1. **Scan** each page.
   - titles
   - subheads
   - highlighted words
   - captions
   - photos and illustrations

2. **Identify** the main topic.

3. **Ask** yourself what you know about the topic.

4. **Predict** what you will learn by turning subheads into questions.

Not Too Warm, Not Too Cold

Reading Focus How is Earth's atmosphere like the glass of a greenhouse?

Have you ever visited a gardener's greenhouse? A greenhouse is usually made of glass. The glass lets in sunlight, which warms the ground and other surfaces inside the greenhouse. As these surfaces warm, they release heat into the air. The glass keeps this heat from escaping. This is similar to the way the inside of a car heats up when sunlight shines through closed windows. The air inside the greenhouse stays warm enough for plants to grow throughout the year.

Earth's Greenhouse

In some ways, Earth's atmosphere acts like the glass of a greenhouse. It allows the Sun's rays to pass through and heat Earth's land and water. Some of the heat from the warmed Earth then goes back into the atmosphere a invisible rays. Some of these heat ray escape into space. But most are trapped by water vapor, carbon dioxid and other gases of Earth's atmospher So the atmosphere warms up.

The gases send some of this heat back toward Earth's surface, as show

Plants are grown in a greenhouse like this one. ▼

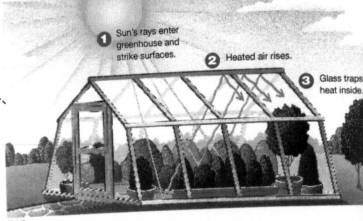

1 Sun's rays enter greenhouse and strike surfaces.

2 Heated air rises.

3 Glass traps heat inside.

E14

Scientists use scientific methods when they do experiments. They also use special methods when they read to learn. You can read like a scientist, too. Just follow the steps below.

in the diagram below. So the air in the lower atmosphere stays warm enough for life to exist. This process in which heat from Earth is trapped by the atmosphere is called the **greenhouse effect**.

Without the greenhouse effect, Earth would be a much colder place. For example, the Moon has no atmosphere. Without an atmosphere, there is no greenhouse effect. So the Moon's

surface gets much colder than any place on Earth, as low as −173°C (−278°F). The atmosphere keeps Earth's average surface temperature at about 14°C (57°F).

The amount of carbon dioxide in the air is increasing. Because of this fact, some scientists think that the greenhouse effect may be increasing, raising Earth's average surface temperature. ■

The greenhouse effect on Earth ▼

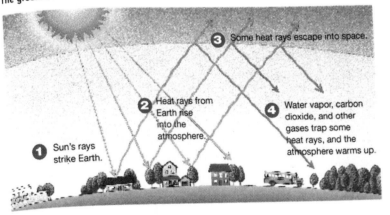

1 Sun's rays strike Earth.

2 Heat rays from Earth rise into the atmosphere.

3 Some heat rays escape into space.

4 Water vapor, carbon dioxide, and other gases trap some heat rays, and the atmosphere warms up.

THINK IT
WRITE IT

—— INVESTIGATION 1 WRAP-UP ——

REVIEW

1. What is air made of? -

2. Which gas makes up about 78% of air?

CRITICAL THINKING

3. Give evidence to show one way in which the atmosphere is like other matter.

4. Could there be life on Earth without the greenhouse effect? What might happen if Earth lost its atmosphere?

E15

While You Read

1. Look for words that signal cause and effect and sequence.

2. Make inferences and draw conclusions.

3. Ask questions when you don't understand and then reread.

After You Read

1. Say or **write** what you've learned.

2. Draw, **chart**, or **map** what you've learned.

3. Share what you've learned.

SAFETY

The best way to be safe in the classroom and outdoors is to use common sense. Prepare for each activity before you start it. Get help from your teacher when there is a problem. Always pay attention.

Stay Safe From Stains

- Wear protective clothing or an old shirt when you work with messy materials.
- If anything spills, wipe it up or ask your teacher to help you clean it up.

Stay Safe From Flames

- Keep your clothes away from open flames. If you have long or baggy sleeves, roll them up.
- Don't let your hair get close to a flame. If you have long hair, tie it back.

Make Wise Choices About Materials

- Use only the amount of material you need.
- Recycle materials so they can be reused.
- Take care when using valuable tools so they can be used again.

Stay Safe From Injuries

- Protect your eyes by wearing safety goggles when you are told that you need them.
- Keep your hands dry around electricity. Water is a good conductor of electricity, so you can get a shock more easily if your hands are wet.
- Be careful with sharp objects. If you have to press on them, keep the sharp side away from you.
- Cover any cuts you have that are exposed. If you spill something on a cut, be sure to wash it off immediately.
- Don't eat or drink anything unless your teacher tells you that it's okay.

Stay Safe During Cleanup

- Wash up after you finish working.
- Dispose of things in the way that your teacher tells you to.

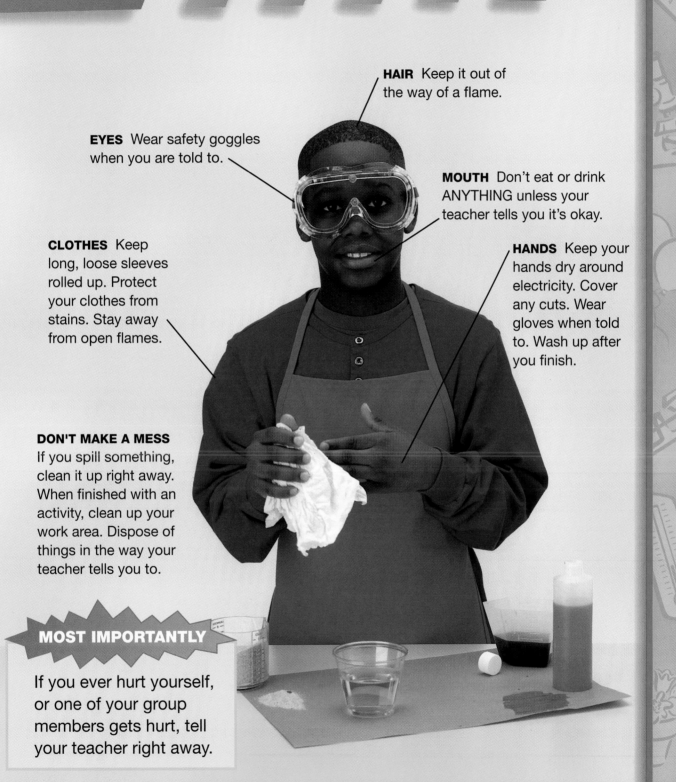

HAIR Keep it out of the way of a flame.

EYES Wear safety goggles when you are told to.

MOUTH Don't eat or drink ANYTHING unless your teacher tells you it's okay.

CLOTHES Keep long, loose sleeves rolled up. Protect your clothes from stains. Stay away from open flames.

HANDS Keep your hands dry around electricity. Cover any cuts. Wear gloves when told to. Wash up after you finish.

DON'T MAKE A MESS If you spill something, clean it up right away. When finished with an activity, clean up your work area. Dispose of things in the way your teacher tells you to.

MOST IMPORTANTLY

If you ever hurt yourself, or one of your group members gets hurt, tell your teacher right away.

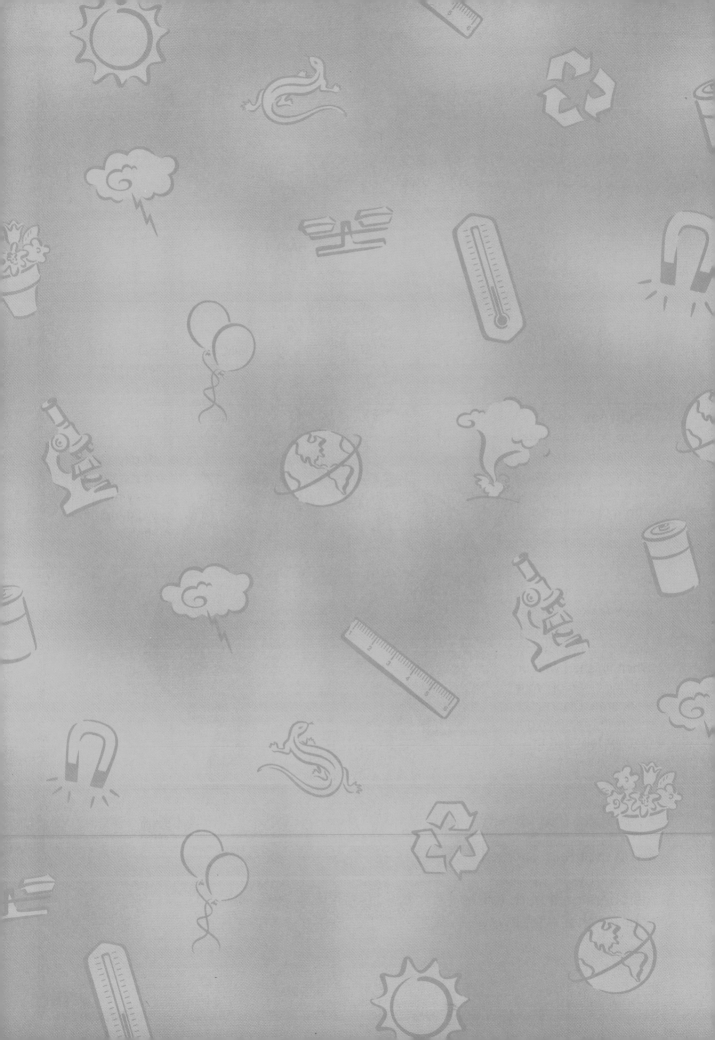

UNIT A

Earth's Land

Theme: Constancy and Change

THINK LIKE A SCIENTIST
NATURE'S ARTWORK A2

CHAPTER 1
The Shape of the Land A4

Investigation 1   How Does Moving Water
                       Shape the Land? A6

Investigation 2   How Do Wind and Ice
                       Shape the Land? A16

CHAPTER 2
The Importance of Natural Resources A26

Investigation 1   Why Is Soil an Important Resource? . . .A28

Investigation 2   Why Are Rocks and Minerals
                       Important? A34

Investigation 3   Why Are Energy Resources So
                       Important? A44

CHAPTER 3
The Problem With Trash A52

Investigation 1   What Do People Throw Away,
                       and Where Does It Go? A54

Investigation 2   How Can Trash Affect Resources? A62

Investigation 3   How Can You Help Solve the
                       Trash Problem? A68

Using Reading Skills A78
Using Math Skills A79
Unit Wrap-up! A80

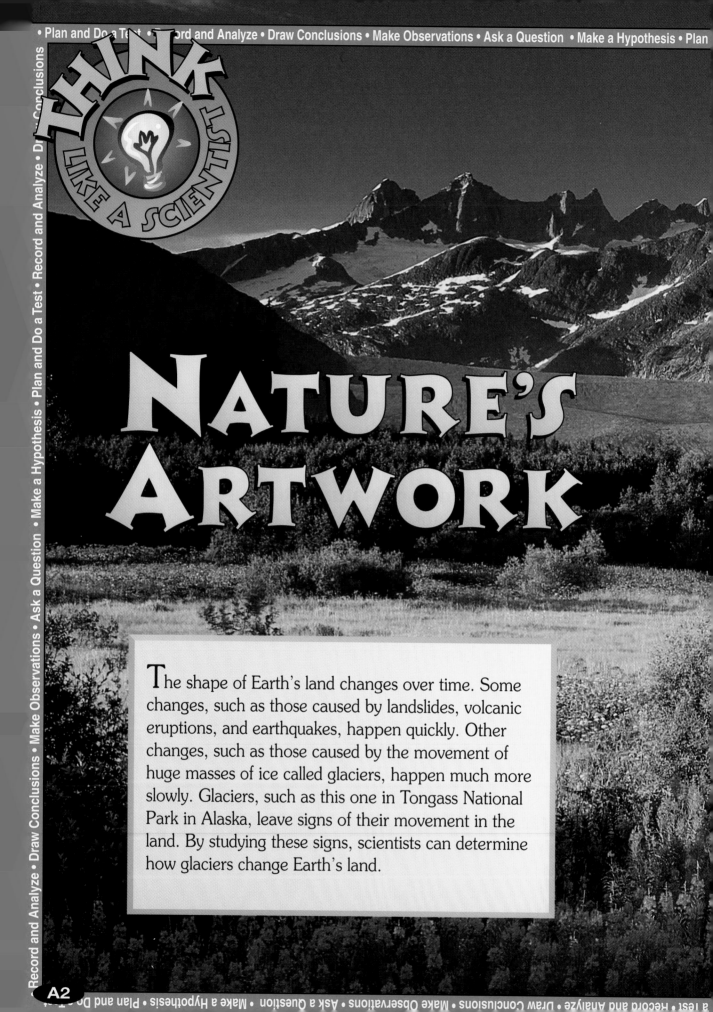

THINK LIKE A SCIENTIST

NATURE'S ARTWORK

The shape of Earth's land changes over time. Some changes, such as those caused by landslides, volcanic eruptions, and earthquakes, happen quickly. Other changes, such as those caused by the movement of huge masses of ice called glaciers, happen much more slowly. Glaciers, such as this one in Tongass National Park in Alaska, leave signs of their movement in the land. By studying these signs, scientists can determine how glaciers change Earth's land.

THINK LIKE A SCIENTIST

Questioning In this unit you'll study glaciers and other forces that shape the land. You'll investigate questions such as these.

- How Do Wind and Ice Shape the Land?
- Why Is Soil an Important Resource?

Observing, Testing, Hypothesizing In the Activity "Gigantic Frozen Sandpaper," you'll make observations about the effect of a model glacier on a rock's surface. You'll also hypothesize about the effect of a real glacier on Earth's surface.

Researching In the Resource "Glaciers—Nature's Bulldozers," you'll gather more information about how glaciers change the land.

Drawing Conclusions After you've completed your investigations, you'll draw conclusions about what you've learned—and get new ideas.

CHAPTER 1

THE SHAPE OF THE LAND

Have you seen pictures or movies that show white-water rafting? Were the riders paddling wildly in a crashing, speeding river? You know that rivers can be very powerful forces. But did you know that such forces help to shape the land?

PEOPLE USING SCIENCE

Landscape Photographer Miriam Romais got her first camera from her father while on an outing in Central Park in New York City. He paid one dollar for the camera. It was, as she recalls, "old and very used." Miriam Romais was eight years old at the time. From that day to the present, she has been "taking pictures." At an early age she was, in her own words, "fascinated with the idea of taking a moment of time and saving it for later. . . ."

Today Miriam Romais is a highly regarded photographer. She travels a great deal, always taking at least one camera with her to record on film the landscapes and natural formations that capture her eye. In this chapter you will find out what forces of nature work to shape Earth's surface, creating these landscapes.

Coming Up

INVESTIGATION 1

HOW DOES MOVING WATER SHAPE THE LAND?
.... A6

INVESTIGATION 2

HOW DO WIND AND ICE SHAPE THE LAND?
.... A16

◀ Forces of nature help shape the mountains and valleys shown in these photographs taken by Miriam Romais.

HOW DOES MOVING WATER SHAPE THE LAND?

A gentle rain falls. You watch puddles form and water trickle along the ground. How can these small streams of water affect the land? In this investigation you'll find out how Earth's land is shaped by water.

Activity

Hills and Valleys

Hills and valleys don't look as if they'd ever change. But they do. Find out how moving water can change them.

Procedure

1. Spread newspaper over your work area. Pile damp sand in one end of a baking pan. Shape the sand so that it forms a hillside with a steep slope near the top. The slope should gradually level out to form an area that is nearly flat. Shape the sand down to a thin edge a short distance from the other end of the pan. With your finger, make a small hole near the top of the hill and fill it with salt to model a mineral.

2. Use a coffee can with holes in the bottom as your rain-maker. Have a group member hold the rainmaker a few centimeters above the top of the hill. Fill a container with water. **Predict** what will happen to the sand and salt if you make the "rain" fall on the top of the hill. **Record** your prediction in your *Science Notebook*.

MATERIALS
- goggles
- newspaper
- large baking pan
- sand
- salt
- coffee cans with holes in the bottom
- metric ruler
- large container
- water
- *Science Notebook*

SAFETY //////
Wear goggles during this activity. Clean up spills immediately.

A6

3. Then **test** your prediction. Pour the water into the rainmaker. **Observe** the water as it flows down the hill. **Describe** where the water makes a "stream," a "river," and an "ocean."

4. **Make a drawing** of what you observe. Draw arrows to point out the stream, river, and ocean areas. Then add the labels *stream, river,* and *ocean* to your drawing.

5. With your group, **experiment** with different-shaped hills. Try using more than one rainmaker. **Make drawings** of what you observe.

Analyze and Conclude

1. How do your observations compare with your prediction? What happened to the salt? How does your model hillside differ from a real hillside?

2. **Compare** the shape of the valley that the stream made near the top of the hill with the shape of the valley that the river made near the bottom of the hill.

3. Study the drawing you made. What can you **infer** about how moving water changes the shape of the land over which it moves?

UNIT PROJECT LINK

In this project you will plan, prepare, and present an exhibit about your state's natural resources, including scenic places. With your group, make a list of scenic places in your state. Collect pictures of them if you can and make a display of the pictures.

Technology Link

For more help with your Unit Project, go to **www.eduplace.com**.

A7

Activity

At the Beach

Where does sand on a beach come from?
Where does it go? Find out how moving
water affects sand on a beach.

Procedure

1. Spread newspaper over your work area. Pile damp sand in one side of a baking pan. Shape the sand into a beach.

2. Fill a container with water. Slowly pour water into the side of the pan opposite the sand until the water is about 3 cm deep.

See **SCIENCE** and **MATH TOOLBOX** page H6 if you need to review *Using a Tape Measure or Ruler.*

3. Place a ruler in the water. Make waves by carefully moving the ruler back and forth.

4. **Observe** what happens to the beach. **Record** your observations in your *Science Notebook*.

5. Make a jetty by piling up pebbles in a line that extends from the middle of the shoreline into the water about 5 cm, as shown.

Step 3

Step 5

A8

6. With your group, **predict** what will happen to the waves and the beach if you make waves that hit the jetty. Explain your prediction.

7. Use the ruler again to make waves. **Observe** what happens when waves strike the jetty. **Record** your observations.

Analyze and Conclude

1. From your observations in step 4, **infer** how ocean waves can change a shoreline.

2. **Compare** the changes you observed in step 4 with those you observed in step 7. How did your prediction compare with your observations?

3. **Hypothesize** how a jetty changes the movement of sand. **Give evidence** to support your hypothesis.

INVESTIGATE FURTHER!

EXPERIMENT

Hypothesize whether the direction from which the waves come makes a difference in what happens to a beach. Make a plan to find out, and then carry it out. Share your findings with your class.

Science in Literature

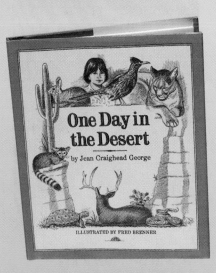

One Day in the Desert
by Jean Craighead George
Illustrated by Fred Brenner
HarperCollins, 1983

FLASH FLOOD

"Water came bubbling and singing down the arroyo. It filled the riverbed from bank to bank, then rose like a great cement wall, a flash flood that filled the canyon. It swept over the embankment, over the hut, over the old saguaro cactus."

Deserts are normally dry places. But water can and does change the shape of a desert floor. In *One Day in the Desert*, by Jean Craighead George, you'll learn how Bird Wing, a young Papago Indian, and plants and animals of the desert face the power of a wall of water.

A9

Carving the Land

Reading Focus How does erosion, with weathering, shape the land?

You may have watched water flow along the ground after a rainstorm. Gravity causes the water to flow downhill until it finds a low spot. There the water forms a puddle. Often a puddle is muddy from soil that the rainwater picked up and carried with it. The process just described takes place on a much larger scale all over the world. It is called erosion (ē rō′zhən).

Partners That Shape the Land

Erosion is the process by which rock material is broken down and carried from one place to another by moving water, wind, or moving ice. Water causes more erosion on Earth than wind and moving ice combined.

Have you ever scraped your knee in a fall? Land can also be scraped—by materials that are carried by water. Over time, erosion and weathering—part of the process of erosion—work to wear away the land. **Weathering** is the process by which rock is broken into smaller pieces. The small pieces of rock in soil are formed by weathering.

OVER STEEP LAND
Fast-moving rivers can carve deep valleys. Rivers often join before reaching the ocean.

ACROSS A VALLEY FLOOR
As a river approaches the ocean, it winds in a string of S-curves across a valley floor. On the inside of each curve, the river deposits, or drops, some of the material it is carrying.

ON A FLOOD PLAIN
Melting snow often causes rivers to overflow and deposit silt on the valley floor, producing rich soil. The land formed from this silt is called a flood plain.

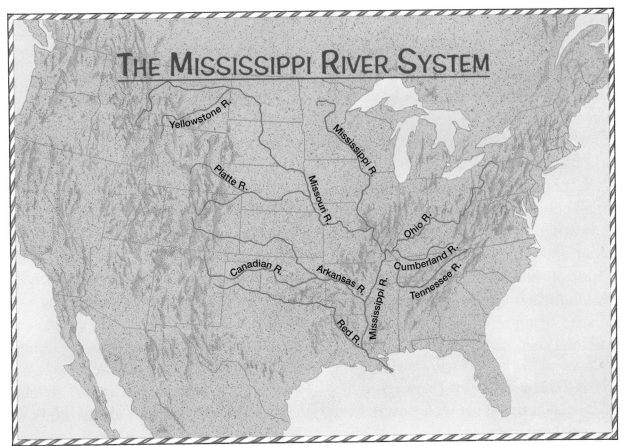

THE MISSISSIPPI RIVER SYSTEM

(Map labels: Yellowstone R., Mississippi R., Platte R., Missouri R., Ohio R., Canadian R., Arkansas R., Cumberland R., Tennessee R., Mississippi R., Red R.)

Using Math *The longest part of the Mississippi River system is 5,970 km (3,582 mi) long. How much longer is that than the Mississippi River itself, which is 3,766 km (2,260 mi) long?*

Breaking Up, Wearing Down

Rocks are changed all the time. Some rocks contain minerals that dissolve in water. When the minerals dissolve, the rocks are made weaker. Sometimes certain gases in the air mix with water, making a weak acid. This acid also can dissolve minerals in the rocks, causing the rocks to weaken.

Once a rock is weakened, cracks form in the rock. Water can seep into the cracks. Plant roots can also force their way into the cracks. Over time the freezing and thawing of the water and the growth of plant roots can cause weathering of the rock, breaking it into smaller pieces.

From Trickle to River

When rain falls on a hill or mountain-side, some soaks into the ground. The rest of the rainwater trickles down the slope. Several trickles may join to form a brook. Several brooks may join to form a stream. Streams join to form a river. Small rivers join larger ones.

A river and the waterways that drain into it are referred to as a **river system**. The map above shows some rivers of the Mississippi River system. It's the largest river system in the United States.

Moving water causes more erosion than any other factor. Think of a stream or river rushing down a slope.

A11

Either can move soil, sand, gravel, and rocks. The materials carried by moving water are called **sediments**. The activity on pages A6 and A7 shows how moving water carries away sand and minerals.

Fast-flowing rivers can even move small boulders. As boulders and rocks are carried along, they crash into each other and into rocks along riverbanks. Chips of rock break off. Over time moving water grinds rocks into grains of sand or tiny particles of rock material called clay, or silt.

How River Valleys Form

Just as a metal file wears away hard material, a fast-moving river can carve a deep, steep-sided valley. Over time the river valley deepens and widens.

As water batters the sides of the valley, the water breaks up rock and soil and carries them away. At some point the soil above the eroded sides of the valley caves in. This widens the river valley even more.

When Water Slows Down

When a river reaches the ocean, the water slows down. Then the water loses energy and can no longer carry all its sediments. The river deposits, or drops, the sediments. They build up along the banks and bottom of the river. As you can see below, when a river empties into the ocean, sediments form a flat plain called a **delta** (del'tə). The formation of a delta is just one way that weathering and erosion reshape the land. ■

The Mississippi Delta ▼

A SATELLITE VIEW OF THE DELTA
Look for a clue to why deltas are named after the triangle-shaped Greek letter *delta*.

The Changing Shoreline

Reading Focus How do the actions of wind and water change shorelines?

When you look at a map of the world, you can see the thousands of kilometers of shoreline, the boundary where the ocean meets the land. Coastal areas are among the most beautiful places in the world. However, these areas are under constant attack by water and wind.

Wearing Away the Shoreline

Moving water and wind are the major causes of weathering and erosion. Nowhere on Earth is the land more exposed to moving water and wind than along shorelines.

Waves are driven onto the shore by wind. Along rocky shorelines, sand and small rocks carried by the waves grind against large rocks. This grinding breaks down the rocks and wears them away. It produces the sand that forms coastal beaches. It also helps to form interesting shapes and formations along rocky shorelines.

The water brought in by a wave rushes back toward the ocean. Along sandy shorelines, waves remove sand from some places and deposit it in other places, often very far away.

Using Math *Much of the Pacific Ocean's shoreline erodes at a rate of about 1 m (3 ft) a year. Estimate how much shoreline erodes in one month.*

A13

In fact, sand can be deposited hundreds of kilometers from where it was removed. Some sandy beaches change with the seasons. During the winter, strong winds produce waves that are steep and close together. These waves remove more sand from the shore than they deposit. In summer, gentler waves deposit more sand on beaches than they remove.

Building Up the Shoreline

Sometimes, sand carried by a current along the shoreline moves past a headland. A **headland** is a natural piece of land that extends out into the water. The headland may be at the mouth, or opening, of a bay. A **bay** is a body of water that is partly enclosed by land but has an opening, called a mouth, connecting the water to the ocean.

Sand is washed along an ocean shore by waves. When the sand reaches a headland, the headland directs the sand across the mouth of the bay. Over time the sand may build up and form features such as the barrier island shown. Such narrow islands stretch for hundreds of kilometers along the Atlantic and Gulf coasts of the United States.

A Tug of War at the Shore

As the ocean and land interact, movement and change are normal. This is especially true for beach areas. Beaches can change a lot—almost overnight. If no people lived in these areas, the natural changes would go almost unnoticed. However, people do live in these areas. Some of the world's largest cities are found near the shore.

Headland and bay ▼

Barrier island ▼

▲ **Sea wall and jetty**

In the United States, many people live and work on many of the barrier islands along the Atlantic and Gulf coasts. In addition, millions of tourists visit these beaches each year. These areas can be greatly damaged or even destroyed by the erosion of sand caused by the strong winds and huge waves produced by severe storms.

People have thought of different ways to protect shore areas, such as building jetties and sea walls. The activity on pages A8 and A9 shows how to build a jetty out of pebbles. A jetty, shown above, is a structure built to stop the erosion of sand. Water that strikes a jetty slows and drops the sand it is carrying.

The different methods of saving or restoring beaches are costly. Most of them will not work over a long period. And none can completely protect people or property from fierce storms, such as hurricanes. What is your answer, then, to this question: Who's winning the tug of war at the shore—people or nature? ■

Internet Field Trip

Visit **www.eduplace.com** to learn more about weathering and erosion.

INVESTIGATION 1 WRAP-UP

REVIEW

1. Describe two ways that water can help to weaken or break up rocks.

2. What causes moving water to drop sediments it is carrying?

CRITICAL THINKING

3. How is weathering related to the process of erosion?

4. Suppose you planned to build a house at the shore. Would you build it on a rocky shore or a sandy beach? Give reasons for your answer.

HOW DO WIND AND ICE SHAPE THE LAND?

When you're hot and sweaty, wind and ice can cool you off. In winter they may keep you from playing outdoors. But wind and ice can do something more. They can shape the land. In this investigation you'll find out how.

Activity

Blowin' in the Wind

The word desert can make you think of huge dry areas and hills of sand called sand dunes. What part does wind play in shaping a desert landscape? Find out in this activity.

MATERIALS

- goggles
- newspaper
- tray or pan
- dry sand
- ruler
- cardboard box
- hair dryer
- timer
- craft sticks
- *Science Notebook*

SAFETY //////

Wear goggles during this activity. Be careful not to burn yourself when using the hair dryer. Use the coolest setting.

Procedure

1. Spread newspaper over your work surface. **Make a model** of a desert. Use a ruler to spread an even layer of sand about 2 cm deep in a tray.

2. Set one end of the tray in a cardboard box as shown. The box is to keep the sand from blowing around the room.

3. Use a hair dryer as a source of wind. Use the settings for the coolest temperature and lowest air speed. Hold the dryer far enough from the tray so that the "wind" *gently* blows across the surface of the sand, as shown. Allow the wind to blow for 15 to 20 seconds.

4. **Observe** the surface of the sand. **Record** your observations in your *Science Notebook*.

5. Spread the sand out evenly again. Lay several sticks on top of the sand, as shown below. **Talk with your group** and together **predict** what the surface of the sand will look like if you repeat step 3.

6. **Record** your prediction and give reasons for predicting as you did. Then **test** your prediction and **record** what you observe.

Analyze and Conclude

1. **Compare** the surface of the desert produced in step 3 with the surface produced in step 6.

2. How did your prediction compare with what you observed in step 6?

3. What role do the sticks play in helping to shape a desert surface? **Infer** what must happen in order for a sand dune to form.

INVESTIGATE FURTHER!

EXPERIMENT

Smooth out your desert sand. Put plants in the desert. Then use the hair dryer to blow wind along the surface of the sand for 15 to 20 seconds. Record your observations. Infer the effect that plants have on the erosion of sand in desert areas.

Activity

Gigantic Frozen Sandpaper

Have you ever seen what sandpaper can do to a piece of wood? In nature a huge mass of ice called a glacier (glā'shər) *can do the same thing to rock. Find out how ice shapes the land.*

Procedure

1. **Make a model** of a glacier. Scatter a handful of sand and pebbles in a small pan. Add water to the pan until it is two-thirds full. Then carefully place the pan in a freezer.

Math Hint *To fill the pan two-thirds full with water, measure the height of the pan. Fill two of three parts with water.*

2. After the water has frozen solid, remove the block of ice from the pan. The ice is your "glacier."

Step 1

Step 4

3. Use a hand lens to examine the surface of a smooth flat rock.

See **SCIENCE** and **MATH TOOLBOX** page H2 if you need to review **Using a Hand Lens.**

4. Using a towel to protect your hands, place the glacier, sandy-side down, on the flat rock. **Talk with your group** and **predict** what will happen if you press down on the glacier and move it back and forth over the rock. **Record** your predictions in your *Science Notebook*.

5. Holding the glacier with the towel, move the glacier back and forth over the rock. Then **observe** the rock's surface with a hand lens. **Record** your observations.

Analyze and Conclude

1. **Compare** your observations with your prediction.

2. In what ways is your model glacier different from a real glacier?

3. **Hypothesize** what a real glacier would do to Earth's surface as the glacier moves over it. **Give reasons** to support your hypothesis.

Technology Link CD-ROM

INVESTIGATE FURTHER!

Use the **Best of the Net—Science CD-ROM**, Earth Sciences, *Glaciers of Blackcomb Mountain* site to find out some cool facts about glaciers and how to make model glaciers. You can also learn about the only animals known to live inside glaciers.

Sand Blasted

Wind is not as powerful as moving water. But, like water, wind can change the shape of land. Have you ever had wind blow sand into your eyes? Then you know that wind can carry sediment.

Wind Blows Away the Land

The stronger the wind, the more sediments it can carry. Wind must blow at least 18 km/h (11 mph) just to move sand along the ground. Stronger winds are needed to lift sand and carry it less than a meter above the ground.

In areas with loose sand and fine soils, wind can blow these materials away. The wind is even more likely to erode materials during dry periods, when most of the plants in an area may die off. In some areas, wind erosion can be prevented or reduced by windbreaks. Windbreaks may be fences, shrubs, grass, or trees— anything that can slow down the wind.

Wind Carves the Land

Wind erodes Earth's surface by removing sand and silt from one place and depositing them in another. The sediments that wind carries also weather Earth's surface. As windblown grains of sand move along the ground, they act as sandblasters—chipping, cutting, and polishing.

DUNES THAT MOVE Where winds blow steadily in the same direction, dunes migrate, or move, as much as 30 m (100 ft) a year. Dunes can even bury towns and forests. ▼

Sand dunes are formed on desert floors, on dry sandy flood plains, and along shorelines. Dunes vary in size. In the Sahara Desert, in North Africa, sand dunes cover an area larger than the state of Texas. Small beach dunes may be 1–2 m (3–7 ft) high. Some sand dunes in the Sangre de Cristo Mountains, in Colorado, are nearly 300 m (1,000 ft) high.

To carve buttes, polish rock, and make sand dunes move, wind has to attack, wear down, and carry away pieces of Earth's surface. Then the pieces have to be deposited somewhere else. All of these activities take a lot of sandblasting! ■

BUTTE Erosion by windblown sand can help shape the surfaces of rock formations such as this butte (byo͞ot). A butte is a narrow-topped hill with very steep clifflike sides. ▼

Wind Builds Up the Land

The sediments that wind picks up from one surface are deposited on another. The surface on which the sand is deposited is then built up.

Wind will carry its load of sediments until an object such as a boulder, a bush, or a fence slows it down. In the activity on pages A16 and A17, a hair dryer is used to model wind blowing across sticks on a desert. When an object in a desert slows down the wind, the wind deposits some of the sediments it carries. Piles of sand are often deposited in one place, forming hills called **sand dunes**.

◀ **Desert sand dunes**

Glaciers— Nature's Bulldozers

Reading Focus How do glaciers change the land over which they move?

A bulldozer pushes soil, trees, stumps, and rocks ahead of it as it moves. Nature has its own "bulldozers." They are called glaciers. A **glacier** is a huge mass of slow-moving ice that forms over land. Glaciers form in cold regions, where more snow falls in winter than melts in summer. In such places the snow piles up, becomes heavy, and turns to ice. As shown in the pictures below, there are two kinds of glaciers— continental and valley.

How Glaciers Move

As unlikely as it may seem, glaciers do move. The great weight of the ice causes a continental glacier to flow outward in all directions from its center. Gravity is the main force that makes valley glaciers flow.

Some glaciers move only a few centimeters a day. Others move a few meters a day. No matter how slowly a glacier moves, the surface beneath the glacier is changed by the weight of the ice and the material carried by the ice.

CONTINENTAL GLACIERS   Also called ice sheets, these gigantic masses of ice are found only in Greenland and Antarctica. ▼

VALLEY GLACIER   Also called alpine (al′pīn) glaciers, these thick "rivers" of ice form in high mountain ranges. ▼

MORAINE As a valley glacier flows, it carries rock material called moraine (mə rān′). A glacier stops moving forward when temperatures get warm enough to melt the ice as fast as the ice flows.

TERMINAL MORAINE As a glacier melts, it deposits its moraine. The moraine deposited at the farthest point to which the glacier has moved is known as terminal moraine. Terminal moraine is usually a glacier's largest deposit.

GLACIER GROOVES Material that is carried on the bottom of a glacier carves out the surface under the glacier. Grooves left in rock show the direction of a glacier's path and give some idea of the glacier's size.

ERRATICS These large boulders dropped by a glacier as it melts are called erratics (er rat′iks).

Often two or more valley glaciers move down a mountain at the same time. The glaciers grind away at the rocky structure between them, producing narrow ridges. The activity on pages A18 and A19 uses a piece of ice to show how a glacier grinds away rock. Around the mountain near its top, the glaciers carve out bowl-shaped holes. This action produces a pyramid-shaped peak, called a horn. Perhaps the most famous horn is the Matterhorn, located in the Alps between Switzerland and Italy.

Like wind and moving water, glaciers shape the land in two ways. As a glacier moves across the land, it carries away tons of material. Later, when the glacier stops moving and begins to melt, it deposits its load of sediments.

A glacier does more than just push materials from one place to another. Its action shapes mountains, carves valleys, and leaves huge boulders and piles of rocks along its path. Some of the most beautiful landscapes in the world have been produced by the actions of nature's bulldozers. ■

Using Math *The Matterhorn was carved by glaciers. It has four triangular faces that are each about the same size. What space shape is this peak most like?*

What Ice Leaves Behind

In places where a huge mass of ice once moved, signs of its presence and its power are left behind. These signs include U-shaped valleys, pointed peaks, sharp ridges, steep cliffs, lakes, and waterfalls.

INVESTIGATION 2 WRAP-UP

THINK IT WRITE IT

REVIEW

1. Name and describe two types of glaciers.

2. What are some signs that show that a giant ice sheet once covered an area?

CRITICAL THINKING

3. How do sediments that are deposited by wind compare with those deposited by glaciers?

4. Glaciers move very slowly, yet they can transport huge amounts of sediments. Explain.

REFLECT & EVALUATE

Word Power

Write the letter of the term that best matches the definition. *Not all terms will be used.*

1. Process by which rock is broken into smaller pieces
2. Body of water partly enclosed by land
3. Material carried by moving water
4. Flat plain formed where a river empties into the ocean
5. Mass of slow-moving ice
6. Movement of weathered rock materials by water, wind, or ice

a. bay
b. delta
c. erosion
d. glacier
e. headland
f. sand dune
g. sediment
h. weathering

Check What You Know

Write the term in each pair that best completes each sentence.

1. A horn is formed by the action of (wind, glaciers).
2. Materials carried by moving water are called (sediments, dunes).
3. A structure built to save sand beaches is a (headland, jetty).
4. Land that forms near the mouth of a river is a (delta, bay).

Problem Solving

1. You plan to build a rock wall in an area that receives a lot of rainfall. Would you use rocks that contain a high percentage of salt crystals? Explain your answer.

2. Think about what happens to sediments carried by water when the flow of water slows down. How does this explain why a barrier island might form near a headland?

BUILD YOUR PORTFOLIO

Study the drawing, which shows grooves, or scratches, in bedrock. Infer what could cause such scratches. Record your inferences. Then tell what information you could infer about the object that produced the scratches.

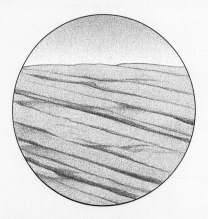

CHAPTER 2

THE IMPORTANCE OF NATURAL RESOURCES

Many natural resources come from the land. One of the most important is soil. Why is soil important? One reason is that plants, the world's food source, can grow in it. What other natural resources come from the land? Why are they important?

PEOPLE USING SCIENCE

Soil Scientist Dr. Thanh Dao is a scientist who is interested in the conservation, or wise use of, soil. If soil is conserved, it can be used a long time for the raising of livestock or for the production of crops.

Dr. Dao conducts laboratory and field experiments in his study of soil. According to him, the work he is doing in the picture deals with "protecting soil particles and plant nutrients from being washed away by rainwater." He uses a rainmaking machine to make rain. Then he collects and studies the chemical makeup of the rain that runs off the soil.

A soil scientist must know a great deal about the resource soil. In this chapter you'll find out more about this and other natural resources of the land.

Coming Up

INVESTIGATION 1

WHY IS SOIL AN IMPORTANT RESOURCE? A28

INVESTIGATION 2

WHY ARE ROCKS AND MINERALS IMPORTANT? A34

INVESTIGATION 3

WHY ARE ENERGY RESOURCES SO IMPORTANT? A44

◄ Soil scientist Dr. Thanh Dao uses a pump to collect water that runs off the soil following a rainstorm.

WHY IS SOIL AN IMPORTANT RESOURCE?

Soil is a valuable natural resource. A natural resource is any material from Earth that can be used by people. Where does soil come from? How do we use it? How can we make sure we'll always have enough? Find out in this investigation.

Activity

Little Ones From Big

You can make soil the way a mountain stream does. Find out how.

Procedure

Wash some rock chips with water. Fill a plastic jar one-third full of chips. Cover them with water. Screw the lid on tightly. With a partner, take three 1-minute turns each, shaking the jar hard to model a mountain stream.

Place filter paper in a funnel. Stand the funnel in a second plastic jar. Predict what you would see if you poured the water through the filter. Then test your prediction. Use a hand lens to observe the material on the paper. Record your observations in your *Science Notebook*.

Analyze and Conclude

Compare your prediction with what you observed. Infer how mountain streams help to make soil.

Activity

Saving Soil

Do plants help to keep soil from being washed away? Find out in this activity.

MATERIALS
- goggles
- 2 baking pans
- topsoil
- piece of sod
- 2 wooden blocks
- 2 coffee cans, each with holes in their bottoms
- 2 large containers
- water
- *Science Notebook*

SAFETY //////
Wear goggles during this activity. Clean up spills immediately.

Procedure

1. Place soil in one baking pan and sod in another. Sod is soil with grass growing in it. Set one end of each pan on a wooden block so that the pans are sloped.

2. Predict how rain might affect the soil in each pan. Record your prediction in your *Science Notebook*.

3. Use coffee cans with holes in their bottoms as rain-makers. Hold the rainmakers over the pans.

4. Have two other members add equal amounts of water into each rainmaker as shown. Be careful not to add too much "rain" to the pans, causing them to overflow. Observe each pan. Record your observations.

Analyze and Conclude

1. Compare your observations with your predictions.

2. Infer how soil might be kept from washing away during a rainstorm.

Step 4

Gully! It's Soil Erosion

Reading Focus Why is soil important, and how can it be conserved?

The word *soil* means different things to different people. A construction worker sees soil as material that can be moved by digging. To a farmer, soil is the loose surface material in which plants with roots can grow.

To a person doing laundry, soil is dirt that needs to be washed from clothing.

Soil—A Limited Resource

Geologists (jē äl'ə jists) are scientists who study Earth materials. To a geologist, **soil** is loose rock material such as that produced in the activity on page A28. Soil covers much of Earth's land surface. If you've ever

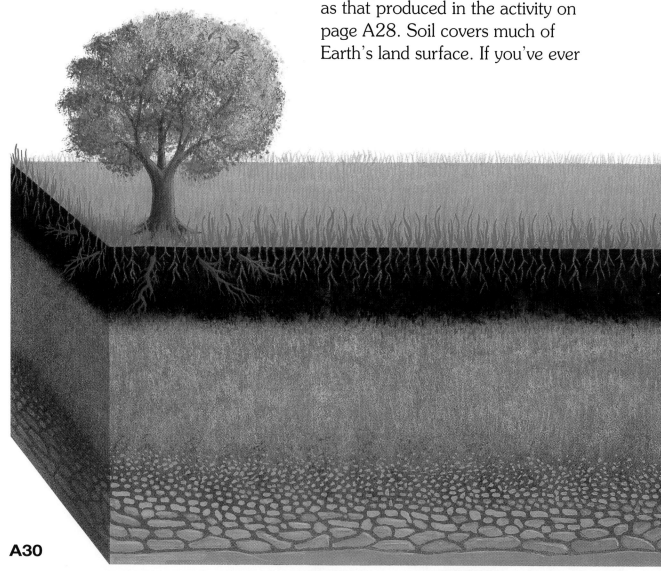

watched a building crew dig a deep hole, it may seem that the soil goes on forever. Actually, the layer of soil that covers the land is very thin compared with the thick layer of rock that's under the soil.

Soil is a natural resource. A **natural resource** is any useful material from Earth. Some other natural resources are trees, coal, air, and water.

The most important thing about soil is that plants can grow in it. Without plants, life as we know it couldn't exist. That's because plants are the source of food for all living things on Earth.

Soil doesn't just happen. A well-developed soil is made up of layers that take many years to form. A side view of the different layers, called a soil profile, is shown below.

Using Soil Wisely

The greatest cause of soil loss is erosion by running water. When rain falls on bare soil, it runs across the surface, carrying soil with it. Gullies, or miniature river valleys, are formed in the soil. With each new rainfall, the gullies get bigger and deeper, and more soil is carried away.

Conservation (kän sər vā′shən) is the wise use of natural resources. There are many things people can do to conserve soil. The most important is to leave plants growing where they are whenever possible.

A SOIL PROFILE

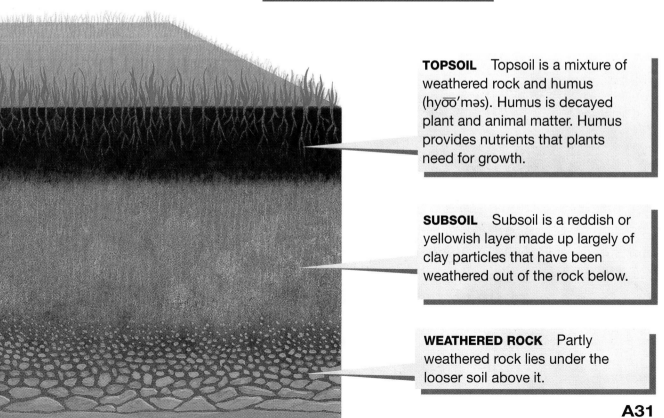

TOPSOIL Topsoil is a mixture of weathered rock and humus (hyoo′məs). Humus is decayed plant and animal matter. Humus provides nutrients that plants need for growth.

SUBSOIL Subsoil is a reddish or yellowish layer made up largely of clay particles that have been weathered out of the rock below.

WEATHERED ROCK Partly weathered rock lies under the looser soil above it.

CONTOUR PLOWING Contour plowing is plowing hilly land in a way that follows the shape of the land. This practice slows rainwater as it runs downhill, giving it time to sink into the soil. ▶

◀ **STRIP CROPPING** Strip cropping is planting a cover crop in strips between rows of crops. A cover crop is a crop, such as clover, that grows quickly. The closely planted cover crop absorbs rainfall. Then the rainfall will not run off the land and erode the soil.

Plants, such as trees and grass, provide protection against soil erosion. The activity on page A29 shows how rain affects sod and how it affects bare soil. When "rain" falls on both samples, less soil erodes from the sod, which has grass growing in it. Plant roots hold soil in place. Some of the ways to protect soil from erosion are described on these two pages.

Conserving soil is hard work. But it's worth the effort. Soil is important. The word *soil* has different meanings. But probably the one most important to you is that soil is a natural resource that helps to produce food. ■

DAM BUILDING   Dam building helps slow or stop the formation of gullies. Dams may be built with boulders, small trees, tree branches, bushes, or boards. Water that would have run into a gully, thus carrying soil away, is stopped by a dam. ▶

▲ **TERRACING**   Terracing is the building of terraces, or steplike ridges, in hilly areas to prevent or slow down water runoff.

INVESTIGATE FURTHER!

EXPERIMENT

Collect samples of soils with different textures. Plan experiments to test each sample for its ability to absorb water and to support plants. If your teacher approves your plans, conduct your experiments.

INVESTIGATION 1 WRAP-UP

THINK IT WRITE IT

REVIEW

1. What is the most important role of soil?

2. In what ways are terracing and contour plowing similar?

CRITICAL THINKING

3. In addition to providing food, what other important functions do plants serve?

4. How do the processes of weathering and erosion relate to soil?

WHY ARE ROCKS AND MINERALS IMPORTANT?

Below the layers of soil exists a wealth of materials that we use to build everything from computers to roads. What are these materials? Rocks and minerals! In this investigation you'll learn how we get and use these materials.

Activity

Exploring Minerals

You can explore the different properties of minerals, natural solids found in Earth. Then decide how these properties make the minerals useful.

Procedure

1. Observe the labeled minerals your teacher has displayed—magnetite (mag′nə tīt), hematite (hem′ə tīt), chalcopyrite (kal kō pī′rīt), gypsum (jip′səm), sphalerite (sfal′ər īt), and quartz (kwôrts). In your *Science Notebook*, **make a chart** like the one shown. In the first column, write the names of the minerals.

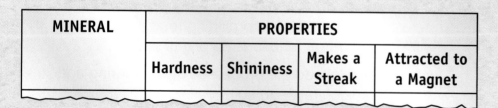

MINERAL	PROPERTIES			
	Hardness	Shininess	Makes a Streak	Attracted to a Magnet

2. A softer mineral can be scratched by a harder one. With your group, handle the minerals and **predict** their hardness, from softest to hardest. Then rub the minerals together to test them. Under *Hardness* in your chart, write a letter from *A* to *F* to tell each mineral's hardness, with *A* representing the softest and *F* the hardest.

Step 2

3. Minerals that are shiny, like a coin, are said to have metallic luster. **Observe** each of the minerals. Under *Shininess*, write *yes* if the mineral has a metallic luster. Write *no* if it doesn't.

4. Some minerals leave a colored streak when they are rubbed on a hard tile. Rub each mineral on a hard tile. Under *Makes a Streak*, write *yes* if the mineral makes a streak. Write *no* if it doesn't.

5. **Test** each mineral with a magnet. Under *Attracted to a Magnet*, write *yes* if the mineral is attracted to the magnet. Write *no* if it isn't.

6. Go on a scavenger hunt. Use reference books to find out what materials come from the minerals. **Record** your findings.

Analyze and Conclude

1. Which of the minerals is hardest? Which is softest? **Compare** your results with your predictions.

2. **Infer** which property might be common to all minerals.

3. Use what you learned in this activity to **infer** how the different properties of mineral resources make them useful for different things.

UNIT PROJECT LINK

As you study this chapter, write and design a class newsletter that informs others about the need to conserve natural resources, such as soil. Choose natural resources that are important in your own community. Distribute the newsletter locally.

Technology Link

For more help with your Unit Project, go to **www.eduplace.com**.

Activity

Being Polite About Resources

MATERIALS
- small plastic bowl
- paper clips to represent the total supply of a natural resource
- 3 role cards
- *Science Notebook*

Suppose at dinner your favorite food is passed. To be polite, you must take only your fair share. In this activity you'll find out why being polite about mineral resources is important, too.

- -

Procedure

1. You will play a game in which a bowl of paper clips at your work station represents the total supply of a metal resource that is present in Earth's crust today. Place the role cards face down on the table. Each group member selects one card. Hold up your card so that the other group members can read it. The card tells you the name of your generation group—parent, children, or grandchildren—and how many people are in that group.

Step 1

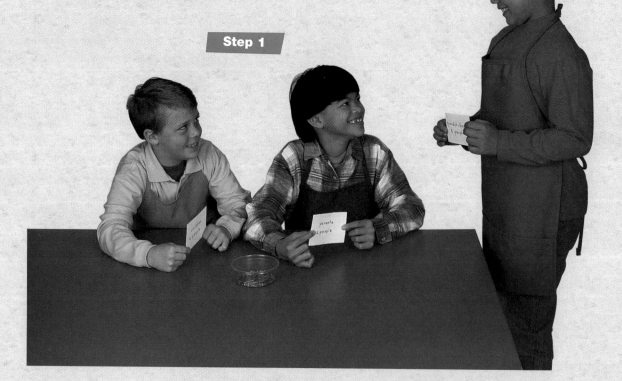

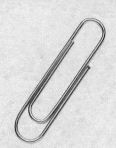

2. When your turn comes, take five paper clips for each person in your generation group. The student with the "Parent" card goes first.

Step 2

3. The student with the "Children" card goes next, followed by the student with the "Grandchildren" card.

4. In your *Science Notebook*, **record** the results of this activity.

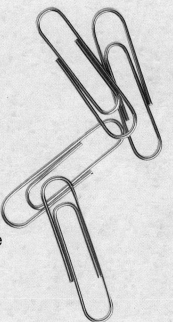

Analyze and Conclude

1. Based on the results, what can you **infer** about the number of paper clips that represents a fair share of the world's present supply of this metal?

2. **Hypothesize** about what would happen to the supply of the metal in several more generations.

INVESTIGATE FURTHER!

TAKE ACTION

Make a list of items that you use that are made of metals—for example, paper clips. Brainstorm with members of your group to think of some ways that you can help to make sure that people in future generations will have their fair share of metal resources. Record your ideas in your *Science Notebook* and share them with your classmates.

Minerals Through the Ages

Reading Focus How did the understanding of minerals and their uses develop over time?

People have always found ways to use materials that are taken from the ground. Some of these materials are called minerals. Metals come from a group of minerals that contain metal ore, or rock that can be mined to obtain metals.

Suppose no one had ever found out how to use metals. You wouldn't be sitting at a desk. There would be no desks because there would be no metal tools for making desks. Look at the time line to discover some things that people have learned about minerals over time.

THE STONE AGE
2 million years ago to 4000 B.C.

58,000 B.C.
People in what are now Europe, the Middle East, and North Africa shape flint, a mineral, into spear points for hunting. They shape other rocks into tools for scraping hides.

7000 B.C.
In what is now China, people make stone spades for digging up plants and roots. In what is now North America, people use stone tools for woodworking.

THE BRONZE AGE
4000 B.C. to 1000 B.C.

4000 B.C.
The Egyptians and Sumerians find that gold and silver are easy to hammer and shape. They also use copper alloys (al′σiz). An alloy is a mixture of metals. Bronze, for example, is an alloy of copper and tin.

1000 B.C.
The use of bronze for weapons, armor, and tools is widespread. Better ways to make bronze are developed.

THE INDUSTRIAL AGE
1700 to the 1900s

1770s
The Industrial Revolution begins in the textile, or cloth, industry in Great Britain and later spreads to the rest of Europe and to America. Machines replace hand methods. Factories are built. In 1789, Samuel Slater, a British textile worker, opens the first factory in the United States.

1800
The first copper-and-zinc battery is invented.

1874
A steel bridge that spans the Mississippi River is built at St. Louis, Missouri. This bridge is the first major steel structure in the United States.

1912
Stainless steel is invented. Its ability to resist rusting makes it an ideal material for surgical instruments and kitchen utensils.

THE IRON AGE
1000 B.C. to A.D. 1700

350 B.C.
In China, ironworks produce better tools for farming and stronger weapons. At ironworks, iron is separated from the rock it's in.

1452
Metal plates are used for printing. These plates are usually made of copper.

1668
The first cast-iron pipeline is used in Versailles, France, to supply water to the city.

THE INFORMATION AGE
1960 to the 1990s

1960s
Computers help guide spacecraft to the Moon and back.

1981
The silicon chip is invented and used in computers.

1990s
Scientists are finding newer and better ways to use metals and other minerals. For example, gold is used in making very small computers called microcomputers.

RESOURCE

From Rocks to Riches

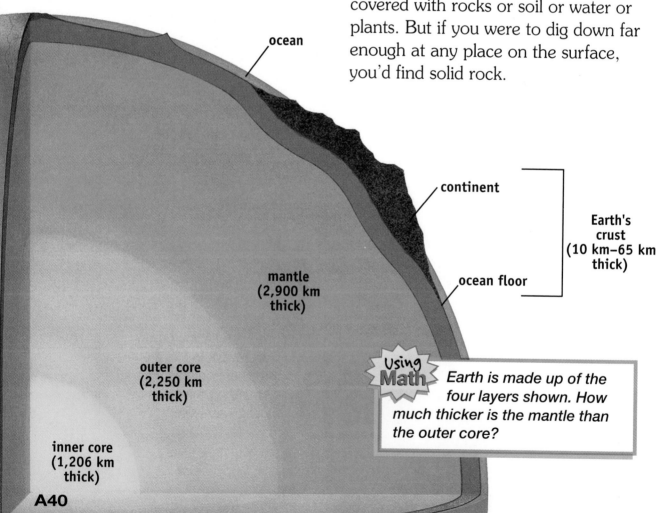

Reading Focus Why are minerals important, and why should they be conserved?

The next time you look at jewelry, pick up a coin, or pedal away on your bicycle, think a minute. Where did the materials that were used to make those objects come from? The materials came from rocks. The next time you pick up a rock, look at it carefully. It may contain a little iron, copper, lead, or even gold!

Where Rocks Are Found

Earth is made up of layers as you can see in the drawing below. The thinnest, outermost layer is called Earth's crust. It is made mostly of rock. The thickest parts of the crust are the continents (kän'tə nənts). The thinnest parts are the ocean floors.

The surface of Earth's crust may be covered with rocks or soil or water or plants. But if you were to dig down far enough at any place on the surface, you'd find solid rock.

ocean

continent

Earth's crust
(10 km–65 km thick)

mantle
(2,900 km thick)

ocean floor

outer core
(2,250 km thick)

Using Math Earth is made up of the four layers shown. How much thicker is the mantle than the outer core?

inner core
(1,206 km thick)

A40

▲ Many items you use came from or are minerals.

An Inside Look at Rocks

Rock is a solid material made up of one or more minerals. A **mineral** is a natural solid that has a definite chemical makeup, found in Earth's crust. Just as different foods can make up a cookie, different minerals can make up a rock. Most rocks are made up of at least two kinds of minerals.

Uses of Rocks & Minerals

The way rocks are used depends on their properties. For example, granite (gran'it) is a very hard rock. Because granite doesn't weather easily, it's commonly used as a building material. Marble is a rock used for its beauty. Many of the most famous statues are carved from marble.

Rocks may be valuable because of the minerals they contain. If you tried to list all the uses of minerals, your list couldn't fit on all the pages in this book. In fact, you might need a whole sheet of paper just to list the things in your classroom that are made from minerals. In the activity on pages A34 and A35, different minerals are examined to determine how they could be useful.

The pictures at the top of the page show some familiar minerals. The lead in your pencil is made from the mineral graphite (graf'īt). Chalk is a mineral called calcite (kal'sīt). The salt you sprinkle on food is a mineral called halite (hal'īt).

Minerals in Ore

All the metals in your classroom come from minerals found in ores. An **ore** is a rock that can be mined for the minerals it contains.

If you look closely at a rock, you may see specks of different minerals. ▶

Most minerals come from ores. Some rocks are made up of a single mineral. Rock salt, for example, is rock made up of the mineral halite. Rock salt is an ore that is mined for its one mineral—salt.

Metals are perhaps the most valuable substances that come from ores. Iron, copper, aluminum, gold, and tin are some metals found in ores. Obtaining pure metals from ores is a long and costly process. The first step in this process is to find an ore deposit, or place where there is a large amount of ore. The pictures on page A43 show what is done after a metallic ore deposit is found.

Resources Worth Saving

Some natural resources can be replaced fairly easily. For example, an area that once had trees can be replanted with trees that grow quickly. A resource that can be replaced is called a **renewable resource**.

Many natural resources, such as metallic ores, can't be replaced. A natural resource that can't be replaced is called a **nonrenewable resource**. Nonrenewable resources should be conserved, or people someday will have to do without them. What happens to the paper clip "resource" in the activity on pages A36 and A37 could happen to actual mineral resources.

Science in Literature

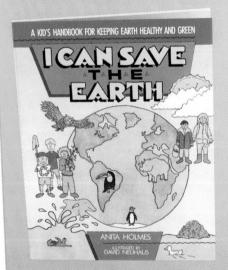

I Can Save the Earth
by Anita Holmes
Illustrated by David Neuhaus
Julian Messner, 1993

YOU-ME-ALL-OF-US

"Help! There's a monster on the rampage! This monster eats up the earth's resources. Then it spits them out all over the land. Do you know the name of this monster? It is You-Me-All-of-Us."

This passage is part of the introduction to Chapter 4 of *I Can Save the Earth* by Anita Holmes. This book is filled with ideas about small things you, your family, and your neighbors can do to save Earth's natural resources.

1 First a metallic ore is mined, or dug out of the ground.

2 The ore is taken from the mine to a crusher.

3 The ore is crushed and the valuable metal is collected.

4 The pure metal is taken away to be used.

INVESTIGATION 2 WRAP-UP

THINK IT WRITE IT

REVIEW

1. What does the chalk in your classroom have in common with the salt you put on your food?

2. Why is it important to conserve Earth's mineral resources?

CRITICAL THINKING

3. Pretend you have discovered a new mineral. Name the mineral and describe one property that makes the mineral especially useful.

4. Write a short paragraph explaining why rocks are important natural resources.

WHY ARE ENERGY RESOURCES SO IMPORTANT?

People need energy for many things—to move things, to make things, and to keep themselves warm or cool. In this investigation you'll explore how people get energy to meet their current needs, and you'll think about what fuels might be used in the future.

Activity

Sun-Toasted Marshmallows

You can feel the energy from the Sun on a hot, sunny day. Can you make this energy work for you? Find out as you try to make a Sun-powered marshmallow toaster.

MATERIALS

- goggles
- 3 pieces of aluminum foil
- glue
- scissors
- 3 sheets of cardboard
- several books
- 3 thermometers
- 4 wooden dowels
- tape
- marshmallows
- *Science Notebook*

SAFETY
Wear goggles during this activity.

Procedure

1. Glue a sheet of aluminum foil, shiny side out, to a cardboard square to make a sun reflector. Repeat this procedure to make two more reflectors.

2. Carefully bend one reflector into a V shape and another into a U shape. Use stacks of books as shown to help these reflectors hold their shapes. Keep the third reflector flat. Tape a thermometer to one end of each of three wooden dowels.

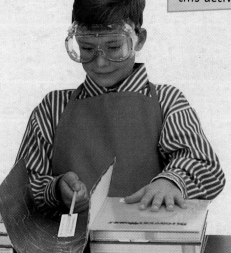

3. Talk with your group and predict which thermometer will show the highest temperature if held in the center of each reflector placed in direct sunlight. Also predict whether the time of day will affect the temperature readings. In your *Science Notebook*, record your predictions and explain why you made them.

4. Test your predictions and record your observations.

See **SCIENCE** *and* **MATH TOOLBOX** page H8 if you need to review *Using a Thermometer.*

5. Use your results from step 4 to design a solar cooker that will toast a marshmallow.

6. After getting your teacher's approval, test your design. Carefully put a marshmallow on the end of a wooden dowel. Use the dowel to hold the marshmallow in or over your solar cooker. Observe the marshmallow and record your observations.

Analyze and Conclude

1. Which reflector produced the highest temperature? How did the time of day affect the temperature? Compare your results with your prediction.

2. What kind of energy was used to heat the marshmallow? How did you apply what you learned in step 4 to design and use your cooker?

Technology
Link
CD-ROM

INVESTIGATE
FURTHER!

Use the **Best of the Net—Science CD-ROM**, Physical Sciences, *Energy Quest: California... Discover Its Energy!* to learn more fascinating facts about fossil fuels.

Step 4

Fuels Around the World

Reading Focus How does the use of fossil fuels in the United States compare with that of other nations?

What is happening when a car engine starts up and when hamburgers sizzle on a grill? Fuel is being burned to produce energy. People around the world burn different kinds of fuels to produce energy.

Fuel From Living Things

Wood has been used as a fuel for thousands of years. It's still a very important fuel in some parts of the world. Wood, of course, comes from trees. A tree stores energy from the Sun. This energy is released when wood is burned.

In some areas solid animal waste, called dung, is burned as fuel. The energy in dung comes from energy stored in plants that are eaten by animals. Dung is used, in a limited way, in the United States. An electric power plant in California uses cow manure as fuel!

WORLD SOURCES OF FOSSIL FUELS

Oil
Natural Gas
Coal

Fossil Fuels

Much of the energy that people use comes from burning fossil fuels. **Fossil fuels** —natural gas, coal, and petroleum, also called crude oil—are fuels made from the remains of once-living things. Peat, another fuel, comes from the remains of ancient swamp plants. In time and with enough pressure, peat can change into coal.

Supply and Demand

As you can see from the map and graphs, the world's fossil fuels are not shared equally. What country today uses the most petroleum? the most natural gas? the most coal?

Fossil fuel use per person is even less equal. The average person in the United States uses about 47 times as much petroleum as the average person in India. And the United States uses more than three times as much coal per person as does China.

Fossil fuels are nonrenewable resources. Suppose all people used as much fossil fuel as do people in the United States. Imagine how quickly fossil fuels would disappear. In the future more people might use solar energy, the kind used in the activity on pages A44 and A45. ■

Using Math *China's population is about four times that of the United States. Explain how the graph shows that the United States uses three times as much coal per person as does China.*

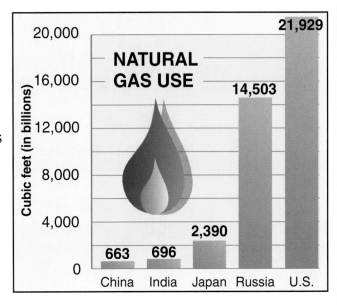

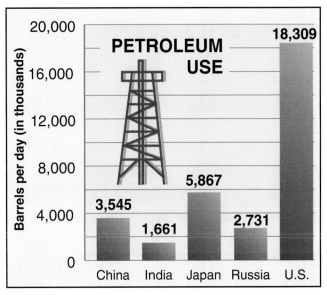

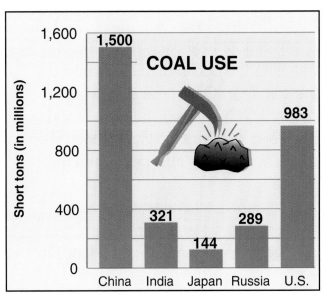

Coal, Gas, and Black Gold

Reading Focus What are the major drawbacks of using fossil fuels as the main source of energy?

It's hard to imagine what life would be like without fossil fuels—fuels made from once-living things. And fossil fuels are valuable. In fact, petroleum is sometimes called black gold.

Energy From Ancient Sunlight

All fossil fuels contain energy that was once stored in the cells of living things. In turn, those living things—plants and animals—got their energy from the Sun. As today, plants used the Sun to make food. Animals ate the plants to get the energy they needed to carry out their life activities. So the energy stored in fossil fuels can be traced back to the Sun, the major source of energy for Earth.

Fuel From Fossils

Millions of years ago tiny living things in the ocean died and sank to the sea floor. Over time they were covered with layers of mud and sand. Heat and pressure slowly changed the once-living things into petroleum and natural gas.

While these changes were taking place on the ocean floor, other changes were taking place on land. In swampy areas giant ferns and trees were dying. The plants were then covered by sand and mud. Over time they changed into a type of fuel called peat. If peat is buried long enough, it changes into coal.

Bad News About Fossil Fuels

Fossil fuels that we use today cannot be replaced in our lifetime. Natural gas and petroleum take millions of years to form. Today people are using these fuels at an alarming rate. Just think about all the car motors running and homes being heated. Once a gallon of oil or cubic meter of gas is burned, it is gone forever!

Coal is more plentiful than oil or natural gas, and it isn't being used up as quickly. However, even Earth's supply of coal won't last forever.

Even if supplies of fossil fuels were plentiful, there would still be problems. For example, mining coal destroys huge areas of land. And even though mine operators try to repair the damage, the process is very costly and takes many years.

Burning fossil fuels adds carbon dioxide and other harmful gases to air.

Land that is strip-mined (*left*) is ripped up by power shovels. The same land can be restored (*right*).

Carbon dioxide traps and holds heat close to Earth's surface, much like the glass in a greenhouse. Some scientists fear that too much carbon dioxide in the air will cause climates on Earth to change.

Good News About Fossil Fuels

We know how fast we are using our supplies of fossil fuels. So it's possible to estimate when the supplies might run out long before that ever happens. That's part of the good news—fossil fuel supplies are dependable.

Because fossil fuels are formed and stored in the ground, they can be removed as they are needed. Fossil fuels can also be transported from where they are formed to where they are needed.

Coal is made from the remains of plants that lived long ago. ▼

▲ To find coal buried deep underground, miners dig hundreds of meters into Earth's crust.

A49

▲ **A windmill farm uses the wind as a source of energy.**

A small amount of a fossil fuel has a great deal of energy. This energy can be used to warm rooms or heat water or power machines.

New Energy Sources

In the activity on pages A44 and A45, it may take a very long time to cook the marshmallow in the solar cooker. The cooker uses **solar energy**, or energy from the Sun.

Sunlight is a cheap, clean energy. Solar energy is being used more today than ever before. Over half the homes in Israel, and nearly all the homes in Cyprus, use solar energy to heat water.

As Earth's supply of fossil fuels runs low, people will continue to search for cleaner and better sources of energy. New energy sources include the wind, energy from inside Earth, and sea water. Chances are that sea water might become an important source of energy in the future. ■

Internet Field Trip
Visit **www.eduplace.com** to learn more about energy sources.

INVESTIGATION 3 WRAP-UP

REVIEW

1. Why are petroleum, natural gas, and coal known as fossil fuels?

2. Why are fossil fuels nonrenewable resources?

CRITICAL THINKING

3. Cars are being designed to use less fuel and burn fuel more cleanly. Why is this important?

4. Choose one of these kinds of energy—solar energy, wind energy, or energy from inside Earth. Explain why using that kind of energy might be better than using energy from fossil fuels.

REFLECT & EVALUATE

Word Power

Write the letter of the term that best completes each sentence. *Not all terms will be used.*

1. Any useful material from Earth is called a (an) ——.
2. Rock that can be mined for its minerals is called a (an) ——.
3. Loose material that covers much of Earth's surface is ——.
4. Wise use of natural resources is called ——.
5. Energy from the Sun is ——.

a. conservation
b. fossil fuel
c. natural resource
d. ore
e. rock
f. soil
g. solar energy

Check What You Know

Write the word in each pair that correctly completes each sentence.

1. Decayed plant and animal matter in soil is (subsoil, humus).
2. Ores are valuable because they contain (marble, minerals).
3. Peat is an early stage in the formation of (coal, natural gas).

Problem Solving

1. As in the past, living things today are dying and being covered by mud and soil. Why can't people count on these changes to meet fossil fuel needs in the future?

2. Suppose you're on a mission to discover new elements in space. What special properties would you look for? Explain your choices.

Using the picture shown here, make a sketch of a soil profile. Label each of the layers in your sketch. Briefly describe each layer. Then in a short paragraph, discuss the importance of soil and some ways to conserve it.

CHAPTER 3

THE PROBLEM WITH TRASH

Trash—it's what becomes of many of our land resources. In fact, Americans throw out enough trash every day to fill 63,000 garbage trucks. Where does all the trash go? And how does trash affect our natural resources?

· ·

PEOPLE USING SCIENCE

Garbologist William Rathje is an unusual kind of archaeologist (är kē äl'ə jist). An archaeologist is a scientist who digs up buried objects and studies them to learn about the people who left them. Rathje is sometimes called a gar- bologist. He is part of a team that digs up, sorts, and catalogs garbage from old landfills and dumps. In garbage that had been buried for 40 years, the team made these two discoveries. Newspapers were still readable, and hot dogs were still recognizable.

These and other discoveries have led people to think about new ways to dispose of, or get rid of, wastes. As you explore this chapter, think about how you dispose of wastes. Can you make some changes?

Coming Up

INVESTIGATION **1**

WHAT DO PEOPLE THROW AWAY, AND WHERE DOES IT GO?
.... A54

INVESTIGATION **2**

HOW CAN TRASH AFFECT RESOURCES?
.... A62

INVESTIGATION **3**

HOW CAN YOU HELP SOLVE THE TRASH PROBLEM?
.... A68

◀ Dr. Rathje is a scientist who studies garbage.

WHAT DO PEOPLE THROW AWAY, AND WHERE DOES IT GO?

Think of a 13-story building the size of a football field. Americans produce enough trash to fill 10,000 of these buildings every year. Where do we put it all? In Investigation 1 you'll find out!

Activity

Looking at Trash

Think about the trash your family throws away. What materials make up the trash most people throw away? Find out!

Procedure

1. Your teacher will give your group a bag of trash that a family might dispose of. Before the bag is opened, **talk with your group** and **predict** what material most items will be made of. **Record** your prediction in your *Science Notebook*.

2. Make a chart like the one shown.

Group (Material Item Is Made Of)	Item of Trash

3. Carefully empty the bag onto newspaper and **examine** the trash. **Classify** the trash into groups based on the material each item is made of. **Count** and **record** the number of trash items in each group.

4. **Analyze the data** in your chart. Then **make a bar graph** to show your data.

 See **SCIENCE** and **MATH TOOLBOX** page H3 if you need to review *Making a Bar Graph.*

Analyze and Conclude

1. Which material was most of the trash made of?

2. How did your prediction compare with what you found out?

3. Resources were used to make the materials in the trash. What resources were being thrown away?

Step 3

Activity

Making a Landfill

Many towns dispose of trash in a landfill. What happens to trash buried in a landfill? Build a model and find out!

- - - - - - - - - - - - - - - - - - - -

Procedure

1. Look at different items of trash. **Predict** what will happen to each kind of waste after it has been buried for two weeks.

2. Spread newspaper on your work surface. Work with your group to **build a model** landfill as shown in the cutaway drawing. Press down the layers. End with a layer of soil on top. Set the landfill on a tray where it won't be disturbed.

Step 2

3. Each day, sprinkle the landfill with 60 mL of "rain" as shown.

 See **SCIENCE** *and* **MATH TOOLBOX** page H7 if you need to review **Measuring Volume**.

plastic wrap

soil

trash

shoebox

▲ Cutaway view

4. At the end of two weeks, dump the wastes onto newspaper. **Record** in your *Science Notebook* any changes you observe.

Analyze and Conclude

1. **Compare** your results with your predictions.

2. **Infer** what happens to the different items of trash buried in a landfill.

3. What material served as a liner in your model landfill? **Hypothesize** what would happen if wastes were buried in the ground without a liner.

INVESTIGATE FURTHER!

EXPERIMENT

Bury trash in a model landfill for three months. Predict what will happen. Check your predictions. Infer what happens to trash in a landfill over long periods of time.

Trashing Trash

Reading Focus What are some good points and bad points of using landfills and burning to dispose of trash?

"It's time to take out the trash!" Do you ever hear that reminder? People produce a lot of trash. The average American produces 1.8 kg (4 lb) of trash each day.

Look at the circle graph below. It shows the kinds of trash a town produces and how much space each kind takes up. What kind of trash is missing from the graph?

Trash can be a problem. It's ugly, smelly, and can be harmful to living things. Let's take a look at where trash goes, what problems it can cause, and how people try to prevent those problems.

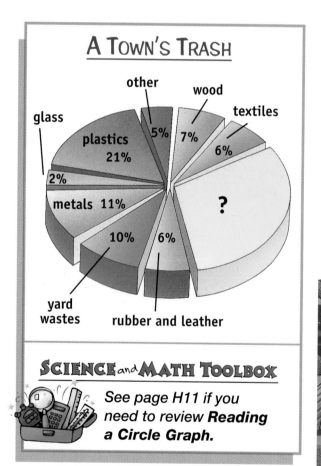

A TOWN'S TRASH

- other 5%
- wood 7%
- textiles 6%
- plastics 21%
- glass 2%
- metals 11%
- yard wastes 10%
- rubber and leather 6%
- ?

SCIENCE and MATH TOOLBOX

*See page H11 if you need to review **Reading a Circle Graph**.*

TRASH Trash is brought to the landfill by trucks. The trash is spread in a layer and squeezed together to take up less room.

A58

Trashing Trash in the Past

Until recently, most trash was put in dumps far away from people. These dumps were usually holes in the ground that were covered over when they were filled. Such dumps have many drawbacks. The wastes in uncovered dumps attract birds, rats, mice, flies, and other disease-carrying animals. Dumps also smell bad, and rainwater moving through a dump picks up harmful chemicals. If this water reaches underground drinking water supplies, the water becomes unsafe to drink.

Today most places have laws against simply dumping trash. Instead the Environmental Protection Agency (EPA) suggests four ways of dealing with trash—bury it, burn it, make new things out of it, or make less of it.

The activity on pages A56 and A57, shows how landfills are made. A **landfill**, like a dump, is a large hole that is filled with trash over time. But landfills are built to keep trash from harming the environment. Examine the layers in the landfill pictured below. How is the trash kept from getting outside the landfill? How is this landfill like the model?

When a landfill is full, the area can be covered over, planted with grass, and made into a park or used for other purposes. Some cities build recreational areas on old landfills.

BURYING TRASH IN A LANDFILL

SOIL Each layer of trash in the landfill is covered with soil. The soil helps reduce odors and keep animals away.

CLAY OR PLASTIC LINER In a sealed landfill, a waterproof liner of plastic or clay keeps liquids in the trash from leaking out of the landfill and into the surrounding soil.

The Problem With Landfills

Landfills aren't the perfect solution to the trash problem. There are strict laws about how landfills should be built and run. These laws make it costly to run a landfill. People don't like to live near landfills. So it's hard to find places to put new landfills.

There's another problem with land-fills. For many years, people thought that trash in a landfill decayed, or rotted, very fast. But think back to Dr. Rathje and his team of garbologists. They found out that trash in a landfill doesn't decay quickly at all.

In a landfill the trash is squeezed together so tightly that there is very little air or water around it. Without air and water, little decay occurs. Dr. Rathje found that the products thought to rot first—paper products—are very slow to rot. Would anyone have ever predicted this without his research? He also found that paper products take up the most space in landfills.

Look back at the circle graph on page A58. Did you think that paper makes up the largest amount of trash?

What About Burning Trash?

Getting rid of trash by burning it is called **incineration** (in sin ər ā′shən). Burning trash reduces the amount of material that needs to be disposed of.

Science in Literature

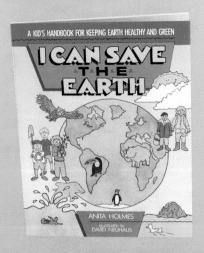

A KID'S HANDBOOK FOR KEEPING EARTH HEALTHY AND GREEN

I CAN SAVE THE EARTH

ANITA HOLMES
ILLUSTRATED BY
DAVID NEUHAUS

I Can Save the Earth
by Anita Holmes
Illustrated by David Neuhaus
Julian Messner, 1993

WASTE NOT, WANT NOT

"Every person on earth uses natural resources. They are nature's gift to us. People in the United States use more than most. But sadly, much of what we use is thrown away soon after we buy it. Did you know that every person in the United States throws away about four pounds of trash every day?"

This passage in *I Can Save the Earth*, by Anita Holmes, is part of an article titled "A Word About Resources." It leads to an activity you can do dealing with household trash.

INCINERATION

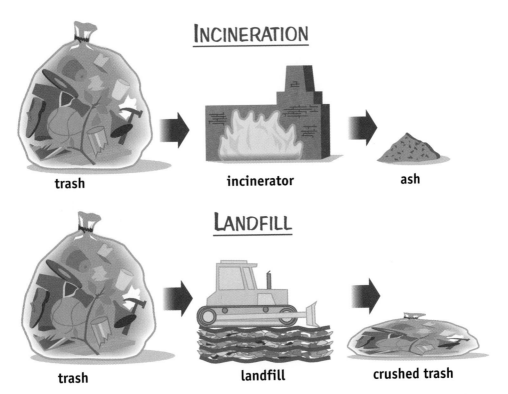

trash   incinerator   ash

LANDFILL

trash   landfill   crushed trash

And the heat produced by burning the trash can be used to make electricity. But today less than one tenth of all the trash in the United States is burned. That's because burning causes smoke. The smoke can contain harmful materials that make the air dirty. The ash itself may also contain harmful materials and must be disposed of carefully.

▲ **Here are two ways to get rid of trash. What are some problems with each?**

What Else Can We Do?

As you can see, burning and burying trash offer some solutions, but they aren't perfect. Remember the EPA's other ideas? In Investigation 3 you'll explore how you can make new things out of trash and how you can make less trash. ■

=== **INVESTIGATION 1 WRAP-UP** ===

REVIEW

1. What are four ways the EPA suggests for dealing with trash?

2. What are two drawbacks to incinerating trash?

CRITICAL THINKING

3. Imagine that you are in charge of getting rid of your town's trash. If you had to choose between burning it and burying it, which method would you choose? Give reasons for your choice.

4. If you examined the contents of a town's garbage bags, what type of trash would you expect to find most of? Explain your answer.

HOW CAN TRASH AFFECT RESOURCES?

Some trash isn't "lucky" enough to end up in a landfill or incinerator. It's thrown out of car windows, dropped on city streets, or piled up in illegal dumps. Find out in Investigation 2 what effects this trash has on our environment.

Activity

A Litter Walk

Trash thrown on the ground is litter. How does litter affect your school's environment?

- -

Procedure

Take a walk outdoors to look for litter. In your *Science Notebook*, **make a list** of the kinds of litter you see. When you return to the classroom, work with your group to decide how you would like to classify the litter. Using the categories your group decides on, **classify** the litter on your list. **Make a chart or bar graph** to help you **analyze your data**. Share your results with the class.

Analyze and Conclude

1. What material was most litter made of? What else did you learn about litter?

2. How was the litter affecting the environment? **Infer** how litter can waste resources.

A62

Activity

Clean It Up!

Find out why oil spills present special problems for the environment.

MATERIALS
- goggles
- clear plastic cup
- sand
- metric measuring cup
- vegetable oil
- clean-up materials of your choice
- *Science Notebook*

SAFETY /////
Wear goggles during this activity.

Procedure

1. Half-fill a plastic cup with sand. Pour 20 mL of vegetable oil on the sand. The vegetable oil represents motor oil.

2. After an hour, observe the oily sand. Discuss with your group ways to remove the oil from the sand. Predict which method will best clean up the oil.

3. Make a plan to test one of your ideas. Show the plan to your teacher and then carry it out. Note how long you work to remove the oil. Record all your results in your *Science Notebook*.

Step 1

Analyze and Conclude

1. How well did your plan work? Hypothesize whether your plan would work on a real oil spill on land. Explain.

2. Motor oil is made from crude oil, a vital natural resource. How does improper disposal of used motor oil affect the environment and Earth's limited supply of crude oil?

INVESTIGATE FURTHER!

RESEARCH

Find out about the methods used to clean up oil spills. Research one of the following: the 1993 *Braer* tanker spill off the Shetland Islands into the North Sea; the 1996 *Sea Empress* oil spill near the southwest of Wales; or another spill.

Don't Teach Your Trash to Swim!

Reading Focus What are some harmful effects of dumping trash into the ocean?

You might think that litter is only a problem on land. But littering is a big problem in the ocean, too. For centuries, sailors have thrown their garbage over the sides of their boats. And for a long time, trash produced in coastal cities was taken out to sea and dumped.

Ocean dumping does more than make the water dirty. Trash that's dumped at sea washes up on beaches, making them unsafe areas for swimming. Animals that live in or near the ocean can become ill from the trash or can become trapped in broken fishing nets that have been discarded in the ocean.

Some fishers are trying very hard to change their habits. In Newport, Oregon, fishers bring their garbage back to land. There it is sorted and disposed of properly. Some fishers are even picking up trash they see floating in the ocean. They are hoping that their motto—Don't teach your trash to swim!—catches on. ■

◀ **These plastic objects were found in the nest of this albatross. Birds are attracted to colorful plastics, which are harmful if eaten.**

Trashing Resources

Reading Focus How does the improper disposal of trash affect the environment and waste resources?

Earth is full of treasures. Soil, rocks, minerals, water, and petroleum are all natural resources that people get from the land. Sometimes people add unwanted materials to the environment, causing **pollution** (pə lōō′shən). These unwanted materials are called **pollutants**.

People cause pollution when they improperly dispose of trash. Look at the picture below. It shows how pollutants can seep into the ground from oil cans that have been disposed of improperly. Trace the oil as it moves through the ground and into the water. What will happen to the soil in this area? How will the environment of the stream change?

The activity on page A63 shows how difficult it can be to clean up the oil from the soil.

Hazardous Wastes

There are many materials that can harm soil or water supplies. They include motor oil, paint, pesticides, many cleaning supplies, and chemicals from the inside of batteries. These pollutants are called hazardous wastes. **Hazardous wastes** are wastes that can pollute the environment even when they are in very small amounts.

The improper disposal of trash can pollute the environment. ▼

A65

▲ **Littering reduces natural resources and harms the environment.**

PETROLEUM Plastics are made from petroleum, or crude oil. Since this is a non-renewable resource, every time you throw away a plastic bottle the amount of available petroleum is reduced. How does throwing away plastic harm the environment? ▶

Hazardous wastes in soil or drinking water can cause diseases.

Litter—An Ugly Trash Problem

Litter is solid waste, or trash, that is discarded on the ground or in water. Littering can hide the beauty of the land and be harmful to living things.

Some animals are attracted to and collect litter to feed to their young. This can cause serious health problems in the young animals.

Internet Field Trip

Visit **www.eduplace.com** to learn more about protecting your environment.

◄ **PAPER** Paper is made from trees. Even though we can plant more trees, it takes time for them to grow. And processing trees into paper produces many pollutants.

◄ **METALS** Aluminum cans are made from metal. This picture shows what aluminum ore looks like when it is mined. Mining aluminum is expensive and uses energy. How would reusing the aluminum in cans reduce pollution?

Littering also wastes available resources. In the activity on page A62, students take a walk outdoors to look for litter. What resources do you think are being thrown away? Look at the pictures on these pages to see some other ways that littering wastes resources. ■

INVESTIGATION 2 WRAP-UP

THINK IT
WRITE IT

REVIEW

1. What are hazardous wastes? Name some.

2. What natural resource is used to produce plastics?

CRITICAL THINKING

3. Look for evidence of land pollution in your community. Record your observations. Then suggest the cause of the pollution and how it might be prevented.

4. Describe two ways that trash can affect available natural resources.

INVESTIGATION 3

HOW CAN YOU HELP SOLVE THE TRASH PROBLEM?

"Please take out the trash!" How many times a week do you hear that? How can your family reduce the amount of trash it produces? Find out in Investigation 3.

Activity

A New Life for Trash

MATERIALS
- street map of your community
- telephone directory
- colored markers
- *Science Notebook*

Make a map that shows places to take items for recycling and reuse.

Procedure

With your group, use a telephone directory to identify recycling centers and stores that sell used items. Using a street map, mark the location of each place you identify. In your *Science Notebook*, **make a chart** like the one below. **Record** information about places you marked on your map.

WHERE TO RECYCLE AND REUSE			
Name and Address	**Telephone Number**	**Kinds of Items Accepted**	**Payment Given for Items**

Analyze and Conclude

What kinds of items can be accepted for recycling or reuse? How does recycling or reusing help conserve resources?

Activity

The Rethink Link

You've heard of the three R's—reading, 'riting, and 'rithmetic. Now you'll learn about the four R's—reduce, reuse, recycle, and rethink. They can help you find ways to save resources.

Procedure

1. The pictures on this page show some ways to save resources. Think of a way to save resources that you would like to try. **Make a plan** for what you'll do and show it to your teacher.

2. **Predict** how your plan will work. **Record** your prediction in your *Science Notebook*. Carry out the plan. Then share your results.

Analyze and Conclude

1. **Compare** your results with your prediction.

2. How will your plan help save resources?

▲ Collect leaves and grass clippings for compost.

▲ Have a yard sale to sell items that you no longer use.

▲ Use a sponge or cloth instead of paper towels.

▲ Start a recycling center in your home.

Conserving Resources

Reading Focus What are some different reasons people have recycled materials over the ages?

Have you ever given away clothing that you've outgrown or toys that you no longer play with? If you have, you were conserving resources. Using materials that otherwise would be thrown away is one important method of conserving valuable natural resources.

Today many communities recycle paper, aluminum cans, glass, and plastic items. They try to save resources and reduce the amount of trash going into landfills.

Study the time line shown here. As you can see, conserving resources by recycling and reusing materials is not a new idea at all.

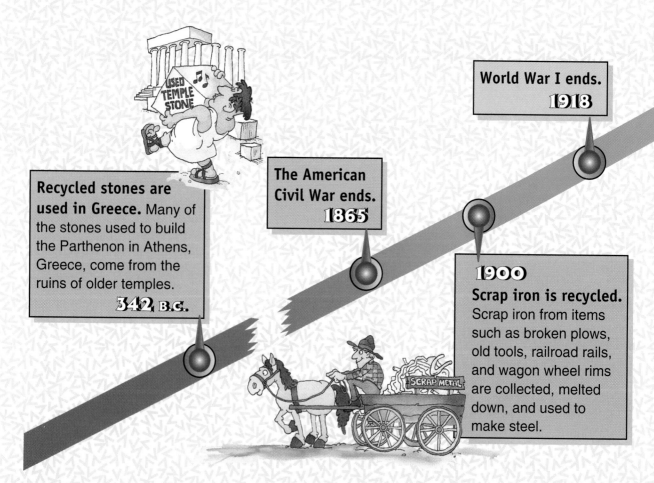

Recycled stones are used in Greece. Many of the stones used to build the Parthenon in Athens, Greece, come from the ruins of older temples.
342 B.C.

The American Civil War ends.
1865

1900
Scrap iron is recycled. Scrap iron from items such as broken plows, old tools, railroad rails, and wagon wheel rims are collected, melted down, and used to make steel.

World War I ends.
1918

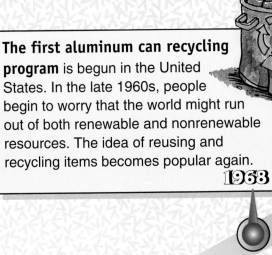

The first aluminum can recycling program is begun in the United States. In the late 1960s, people begin to worry that the world might run out of both renewable and nonrenewable resources. The idea of reusing and recycling items becomes popular again.
1968

1970
The first Earth Day is held.

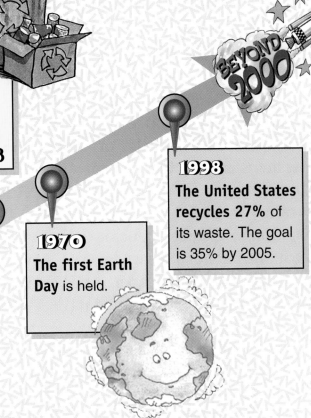

1998
The United States recycles 27% of its waste. The goal is 35% by 2005.

1942
Rubber, metal, and paper are recycled during World War II. Resources are needed to build ships, tanks, and planes. Even children collect scrap metal, old rubber tires, tin foil, and tin cans for recycling.

UNIT PROJECT LINK

Choose one resource in your state. Use the information in Investigation 1 to figure out how much of this resource is thrown away. Make a plan for reducing this amount. Then carry out your plan.

Technology Link
For more help with your Unit Project, go to **www.eduplace.com**.

Recycling

Reading Focus What steps are common to the recycling processes of plastics, glass, and aluminum?

Each day, Americans make enough trash to fill two football stadiums. This trash could be reduced by half if people would **recycle**, or process items and use them again.

Recycling Paper

As you learned earlier, paper makes up about one third of a typical town's trash. So the recycling of paper, especially newspapers, is a very important part of any recycling program.

Paper to be recycled is first ground up and mixed with water to form a mushy pulp. The pulp is treated with chemicals to remove ink and other impurities. Then bleach is added to make it white. Finally the pulp is processed in different ways to make a variety of paper products, from egg cartons to greeting cards.

Recycling Plastic

The diagram below shows the stages in recycling plastics. Although many plastic bottles look alike, they may contain different materials. That's why the plastics industry created a number code that shows what kind of plastic an item is made of. As you can see in the picture on the next page, the code is stamped on the bottom of plastic containers.

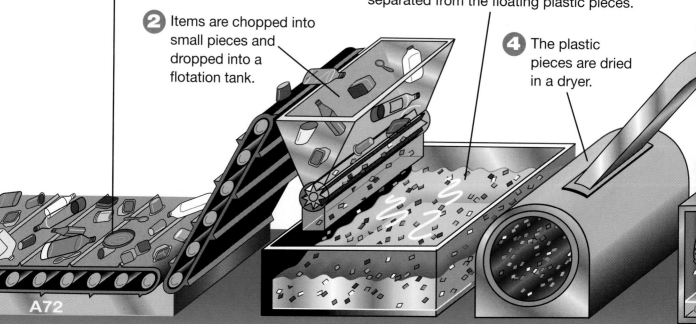

1 Recyclable plastic items are carried along a belt.

2 Items are chopped into small pieces and dropped into a flotation tank.

3 The pieces of plastic are washed in the tank. Dirt and nonplastic items, which sink, are separated from the floating plastic pieces.

4 The plastic pieces are dried in a dryer.

Recycling Plastics

Code	Original Plastics	New Products
1	soft-drink bottles, peanut-butter jars, frozen-food trays	surfboards, film, skis, carpets, soft-drink bottles
2	detergent bottles, milk and water jugs, toys	flowerpots, trash cans, stadium seats, toys
3	shampoo bottles, clear food wrap	floor mats, pipes, hoses, mud flaps on trucks
4	bread bags, frozen-food bags, grocery bags	grocery and other types of bags
5	ketchup bottles, yogurt cups, other food containers	food trays, car battery parts
6	videocassette cases, plastic spoons, food trays, foam cups	trash cans, egg cartons, hangers
7	packages with many layers of materials	plastic lumber

The plastic coded 1 is called PET or PETE. PET is used to make plastic soda bottles. It is the easiest plastic to recycle. The plastic coded 2, called HDPE, is also easy to recycle. Look at the table above to find out what products are made from the plastics you recycle.

▲ **Number code on plastic container**

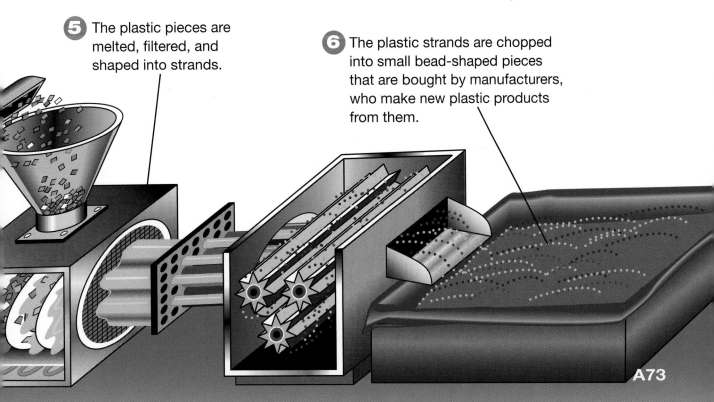

5 The plastic pieces are melted, filtered, and shaped into strands.

6 The plastic strands are chopped into small bead-shaped pieces that are bought by manufacturers, who make new plastic products from them.

A73

Recycling Glass

1. Used glass bottles are sorted by color and checked for metal caps.

2. The bottles are crushed into small pieces.

3. The glass pieces are cleaned and mixed with sand, soda ash, and limestone.

4. The mixture is melted, and the melted glass is shaped and cooled.

Recycling Aluminum

1. Aluminum cans are crushed.

2. The crushed cans are melted.

3. The liquid aluminum is poured into molds and cooled.

Recycling Glass

Some types of glass—such as that used in light bulbs, windows, and auto headlights—can't be recycled. These types of glass can cause damage to a glass furnace when they're mixed with glass bottles. Study the process used to recycle glass bottles.

Recycling Aluminum

Aluminum cans may be melted down to make new cans. The steps above show the process of recycling aluminum cans. How does it compare with recycling glass and plastics?

Recycling materials helps save resources. However, recycling is not free. It takes energy resources to collect the materials and run the machines used in recycling. But the energy used to recycle materials is usually less than what is needed to make the same materials from scratch. ■

Using Math *Each person in the United States produces about 87 pounds of glass waste per year. A glass bottle weighs about 8 ounces. About how many glass bottles is that per person per year?*

The Wrap Trap

Reading Focus What are some of the unwanted effects of overpackaging products?

In the activity on page A69, a plan is made to reduce, reuse, or recycle. All the methods shown in the activity help solve the problem of too much trash. And they help conserve natural resources. But one of the most important things that can be done to help reduce the amount of trash is to rethink. Rethinking is making choices before you buy or use a product.

Wrap Rap

Packaging is the wrappings and containers of items for sale. Think about the trash and litter discussed earlier in this chapter. How many of those items are wrappings or containers? In the United States about one third of the trash in landfills comes from packaging. Think about the many products for sale and their wrappings. Could less wrapping have been used? Why not just stop making packaging? The answer is that packaging serves many purposes.

Look at the diagram. It shows some of the purposes for packaging and an example of each. What other examples can you think of?

▲ Layers of packaging keep products fresh, safe, and unbroken. They also add to the trash problem.

Technology Link
CD-ROM

INVESTIGATE FURTHER!

Use the **Best of the Net— Science CD-ROM**, Physical Sciences, *Energy Quest: Saving Energy* site, to find out more about conserving energy and recycling. You can also learn how to start an "Energy Patrol" in your school.

A75

You Decide

Many of the items people buy are wrapped several times. Some bags of snack food come packed within larger bags. Fruit is often put on paper or plastic-foam trays and then covered with plastic wrap.

How can you help with the "wrap trap" of overpackaging? You have a choice of products when you go shopping. What type of packaging will you look for? If you choose products wisely, you can help reduce the amount of trash in landfills.

PURPOSES FOR PACKAGING

protect from breaking

make convenient

keep fresh

give product information

make safe

advertise and display

INVESTIGATION 3 WRAP-UP

REVIEW

1. Why is the recycling of paper an important part of any recycling program?

2. What are the first two "steps" in the recycling of certain materials?

CRITICAL THINKING

3. Name and describe four ways that you can help reduce trash.

4. Most people agree that reducing the amount of packaging would help conserve natural resources. Why is it difficult to reduce packaging?

REFLECT & EVALUATE

Word Power

Write the letter of the term that best matches the definition. *Not all terms will be used.*

1. Burning of trash
2. Process items and reuse them
3. Wrappings and containers of items for sale
4. Trash discarded on the ground or in water
5. Wastes that can pollute even in small amounts
6. Large hole filled with trash over time

a. hazardous wastes
b. incineration
c. landfill
d. litter
e. packaging
f. pollutant
g. recycle

Check What You Know

Write the term in each pair that best completes each sentence.

1. The addition of unwanted materials to the environment is called (packaging, pollution).
2. Trash discarded along a roadside is (litter, landfill).
3. Keeping an item fresh is one purpose of (incineration, packaging).
4. Each layer of trash in a landfill is covered with (plastic, soil).

Problem Solving

1. Suppose your town found it was more expensive to recycle certain materials than it was to dump them in a landfill. As a voter, what would you choose to do? Explain your choice.

2. A town has a problem with unsafe drinking water. Draw a map showing how the location of the town dump might be related to the problem with the drinking water.

Copy the drawing shown here. Then use the drawing to write a paragraph that describes how newspapers are recycled.

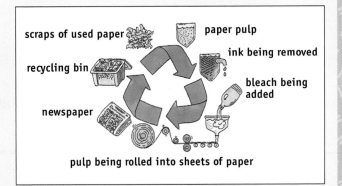

scraps of used paper
paper pulp
recycling bin
ink being removed
bleach being added
newspaper
pulp being rolled into sheets of paper

Main Idea and Details

When you read science, it's important to recognize which facts and details support or explain the main idea. First identify the main idea by looking for clues such as a title, or a topic sentence that states the main idea. Then look for statements that support that idea.

> Look for clues to find the main idea.
>
> Look for statements, facts, and details that support the main idea.

Read the paragraphs below. Then complete the exercises.

Partners That Shape the Land

Erosion is the process by which rock material is broken down and carried from one place to another by moving water, wind, or moving ice. Water causes more erosion on Earth than wind and moving ice combined.

Have you ever scraped your knee in a fall? Land can also be scraped—by materials that are carried by water. Over time, erosion and weathering—part of the process of erosion—work to wear away the land. **Weathering** is the process by which rock is broken into smaller pieces. The small pieces of rock in soil are formed by weathering.

1. Write the letter of the sentence that states the main idea of the paragraphs.

   a. Weathering breaks rocks into small pieces.

   b. Most of the land's erosion is caused by water.

   c. Erosion, with weathering, works to change the land.

   d. Erosion moves rock from one place to another.

2. What clue helped you find the main idea?

3. List the most important facts and details that support the main idea.

A78

Circle Graph

People in the United States use energy in many ways. The circle graph shows the main purposes for which crude oil products, such as gasoline and heating oil, are used.

Use the data in the circle graph to complete the exercises that follow.

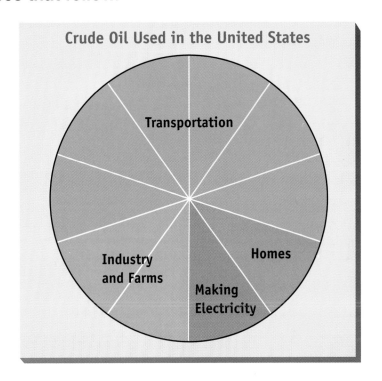

Crude Oil Used in the United States

1. For what purpose is the greatest amount of crude oil used? the least amount?

2. What uses twice as much crude oil as homes do?

3. Which two groups, added together, use $\frac{8}{10}$ of the crude oil used in the United States?

4. How much more crude oil is used for industries and farms than is used for making electricity?

5. Is more crude oil used for transportation or for all of the other purposes combined? Tell how you know.

On your own, use scientific methods to investigate a question about Earth and its resources.

THINK LIKE A SCIENTIST

Ask a Question

Pose a question about Earth and its resources that you would like to investigate. For example, ask, "What effect does contour plowing have on soil?"

Make a Hypothesis

Suggest a hypothesis that is a possible answer to the question. One hypothesis is that contour plowing helps to hold soil in place.

Plan and Do a Test

Plan a controlled experiment to find the effect that contour plowing has on soil. You could start with two pans, soil, a craft stick, a coffee can with holes in the bottom, and a pitcher of water. Develop a procedure that uses these materials to test the hypothesis. With permission, carry out your experiment. Follow the safety guidelines on pages S14–S15.

Record and Analyze

Observe carefully and record your data accurately. Make repeated observations.

Draw Conclusions

Look for evidence to support the hypothesis or to show that it is false. Draw conclusions about the hypothesis. Repeat the experiment to verify the results.

WRITING IN SCIENCE
Persuasive Letter

Write a letter that persuades farmers to plant cover crops to help stop erosion. Follow these guidelines for writing a persuasive letter.

- State your opinion about what you want to persuade the farmer to do.
- Include facts and reasons that support your opinion.
- End with a strong conclusion.

UNIT B

Properties of Matter

Theme: Scale

THINK LIKE A SCIENTIST
ROCKETS' RED GLARE B2

Describing Matter B4

CHAPTER 1

Investigation 1   How Can Matter Be Described? B6
Investigation 2   How Can Matter Be Measured? B14

Observing States of Matter B24

CHAPTER 2

Investigation 1   What Is Matter Like? B26
Investigation 2   How Can Matter Change State? B36

Causing Changes in Matter B44

CHAPTER 3

Investigation 1   What Are Physical Changes? B46
Investigation 2   What Are Chemical Changes? B54

Using Reading Skills B62
Using Math Skills B63
Unit Wrap-up! B64

THINK LIKE A SCIENTIST

ROCKETS' RED GLARE

Fireworks displays like this one in Detroit, Michigan, can fill the air with brilliant bursts of color and sudden deafening booms. When these displays occur, matter changes rapidly from one kind to another kind. Scientists describe the matter used to produce fireworks by that matter's ability to change and produce the brillant effects you see. Such an ability is called a property. Scientists use properties to describe all matter. The properties of matter help scientists know how matter can be used.

THINK LIKE A SCIENTIST

Questioning In this unit you'll study properties of matter and you'll learn some of the ways that matter changes. You'll investigate questions such as these.

- How Can Matter Be Measured?
- How Can Matter Change State?

Observing, Testing, Hypothesizing In the Activity "Different Stuff," you'll make observations about how one kind of matter can change into a different kind of matter. You'll also infer what caused the change.

Researching In the Resource "Changed for Good," you'll gather more information about changes in matter and find out one thing you can't do to matter!

Drawing Conclusions After you've completed your investigations, you'll draw conclusions about what you've learned—and get new ideas.

CHAPTER 1

DESCRIBING MATTER

What do a snowflake, a flower, a dinosaur skeleton, and the Moon have in common? They are all made up of the same stuff—matter. It's the stuff the universe is made of. It's the stuff that we see. Sometimes it's the stuff we *don't* see.

Connecting to Science
ARTS

Creative Matters The work of art shown here is called mixed media, or collage (kə lazh'). Different kinds of matter, or materials, are used to form collages. The materials that artist Martina Johnson-Allen uses include paper, beads, fabric, stones, yarn, buttons, ribbon, seeds, wire, and wood. What materials did she use in this collage? Martina Johnson-Allen believes that art ". . . . is a way to communicate with other people." Like other collage artists, she studies matter and considers the color, texture, shape, and size of each piece of material used. In this chapter you'll study matter and learn how different kinds of matter can be described.

Coming Up

INVESTIGATION 1

How Can Matter Be Described?
.... B6

INVESTIGATION 2

How Can Matter Be Measured?
.... B14

◀ Artist Martina Johnson-Allen uses many different kinds of matter to create her collages.

HOW CAN MATTER BE DESCRIBED?

Did you know that you and this page are made of the same stuff? That stuff is called matter. Everything around you, even air, is made of matter. In this investigation you'll find out what matter is and how it can be described.

Activity

Describing Things

What features of a baseball bat would you use to describe it? Anything that can be used to describe an object is called a property of that object. In this activity you'll use properties to describe and classify objects.

- -

Procedure

1. Your teacher will give your group a bag with several objects in it. Without touching the objects, empty the bag onto your desk.

2. **Observe** the objects and decide what you can tell about them just by looking at them. In your *Science Notebook*, **make a chart** like the one shown. **Record** the name of each object and what you can tell about it.

Object	Description

See **SCIENCE** *and* **MATH TOOLBOX** page H10 if you need to review *Making a Chart to Organize Data.*

3. Now pick up each object and study it. Think of new information that you can **infer** about the object by handling it. Add the new information to the description of that object in your chart.

4. Find out if some of the objects share certain properties. To do this, you can **classify** the objects—divide the objects into groups based on shared properties. **Record** the properties you chose to classify the objects.

Analyze and Conclude

1. What properties could you describe by just looking at the objects?

2. What other properties were you able to describe after handling the objects?

3. **List** some other properties that you might use to describe objects. **Hypothesize** what objects or materials might have these properties.

INVESTIGATE FURTHER!

EXPERIMENT

The ability of an object to float in water is a property called buoyancy (boi′ən sē). Predict which of the objects used in the activity have buoyancy. Test your predictions by placing each object in a bucket of water. Compare your results with your predictions.

Activity

Similar but Different

MATERIALS
- assortment of numbered balls
- *Science Notebook*

A baseball bat and a toothpick are both made of the same matter—wood. But the bat contains more wood than the toothpick. How do you know? Can you always tell how much matter is in an object from its size?

Step 3

Procedure

1. Look at the numbered balls. Using the numbers, rank the balls in order of size, from largest to smallest, in your *Science Notebook*.

2. Now make inferences about the amounts of matter in the balls. Predict the order of the balls, from the one having the most matter to the one having the least. Record your prediction, using the numbers.

3. Check your prediction by picking up the balls and comparing how heavy they are. Using the numbers, rank the balls in order, from heaviest to lightest. Repeat step 3 several times to check your ranking.

Analyze and Conclude

1. What properties do all the balls have in common? What can you tell about the different balls just by looking at them? What did you learn by lifting them?

2. What property did you use in making your prediction about which ball contains the most matter and which contains the least matter?

3. Compare your prediction with your observations. What property did you use to infer the amount of matter each object contains?

Activity
Layers of Liquids

Matter can be described by how much is in a given space. Do equal amounts of different liquids contain the same amount of matter? Find out in this activity.

Procedure

1. Use a metric measuring cup to **measure** 50 mL of vegetable oil. Pour the oil into a clear plastic jar.

2. Use a paper towel to wipe the cup dry. **Measure** 50 mL of water. Add one drop of blue food coloring and stir to mix. Rinse and dry the stirrer.

3. Tilt the jar and slowly pour the blue water into it. Set the jar on a flat surface. **Observe** the liquids. **Record** what you see in your *Science Notebook*.

4. Wipe the cup dry. **Measure** 50 mL of corn syrup. Add one drop of red food coloring and stir to mix.

5. With your group, **predict** the order of liquids, from bottom to top, if you add corn syrup to the jar. **Record** your prediction.

6. **Test** your prediction. Tilt the jar and slowly pour the red corn syrup into it. Set the jar on a flat surface. **Observe** the liquids. **Record** what you see.

Step 3

Analyze and Conclude

1. In what order did you add the liquids to the jar? What was their final order, from bottom to top? **Compare** your prediction in step 5 with your result.

2. The property that describes how much matter is in a given space, or volume, is called **density** (den′sə tē). All of these liquids have the same volume. From your results, order their density from greatest to least.

Matter, Matter Everywhere

Reading Focus What two things describe every type of matter?

Suppose you're home alone at night and all the lights go out. You hear a strange creaking sound and grab a flashlight to investigate.

In the beam of light, different things come into view. You even see dust in the air. Finally, the light reveals a cabinet door swinging slowly back and forth on rusty hinges. You can relax. You've found the source of the strange creaking sound.

What Is Matter?

Everything you saw in the beam of light was matter—even the dust in the air. **Matter** is anything that has mass and takes up space. Look back at the different kinds of matter that are described in the activity on pages B6 and B7. If you can see it, smell it, or taste it, it's matter. Matter can also be invisible, as air is.

A Matter of Mass

The many different things around you are all matter. But they don't all contain the same *amount* of matter. In the activity on page B8, some balls feel heavier than others because they contain different amounts of matter. They have different masses.

Mass is a measure of the amount of matter something contains. The more matter an object or material contains, the greater its mass will be.

A Matter of Volume

In addition to having mass, matter also takes up space. The amount of space that matter takes up is called **volume**. Even the smallest bit of matter that you can think of has volume.

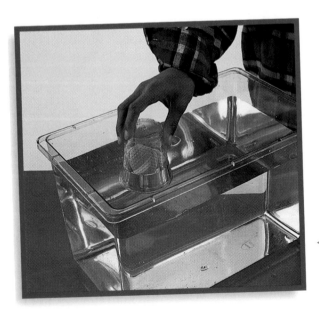

◄ Air in the glass keeps the paper towel from getting wet. What does this tell you about air?

B10

▲ **How many objects in this picture are made of wood? Do they all have the same mass? How do you know?**

Look at a piece of chalk. You can see that it takes up space. You could measure its volume quite easily. Now think about the chalk dust in the tray that is at the bottom of the chalkboard. Does a single speck of this dust have volume? Does it have mass? The answer is yes, even though these properties are hard to measure because of the tiny size of the specks.

A Matter of Volume and Mass

Suppose several samples of matter have the same volume but different masses. You can compare these samples by a property called density. **Density** is the amount of matter in a given space.

In the activity on page B9, each of the three liquids has a different density. The corn syrup stays on the bottom, and the oil stays on top. This layering shows that corn syrup has a greater density than water and that water has a greater density than oil.

Oil in a jar, dust in a beam of light, even you—it's all matter. And where is matter found? It's on a faraway star and high atop a mountain peak. It's deep inside the darkest cave and at the bottom of the sea. Matter is, indeed, everywhere. ■

UNIT PROJECT LINK

For this Unit Project you will make Matter Mysteries displays. Collect several objects. Make up a question that challenges visitors to your museum to order the objects by mass or volume (size). Describe the materials used in each object. Name the property or properties that make each material useful.

Technology Link
For more help with your Unit Project, go to **www.eduplace.com**.

Making Materials Useful

RESOURCE

Reading Focus How do physical properties and chemical properties differ?

You are probably familiar with the story of Cinderella. One of the most important parts of the story deals with a glass slipper.

Useful Properties

How would you describe glass? You might use such words as *hard*, *solid*, *clear*, and *breakable*. All of these words describe properties of glass. A **property** is something that describes matter.

The idea of making a slipper out of glass is silly. The kind of matter used to make an object is chosen for its useful properties. Slippers and other kinds of footwear are made from materials that are flexible, or easy to bend.

Kinds of Properties

There are two kinds of properties that describe matter—physical (fiz′i kəl) and chemical (kem′i kəl). The **physical properties** of a material are those characteristics that can be seen or measured without changing the material.

You can identify the physical properties of a material by using your five senses. Odor, color, shape, and texture are physical properties.

What's wrong with this picture? ▼

▲ Name the materials used in each object. Describe properties that make each material useful for the purposes shown.

The **chemical properties** of a material are characteristics that can only be seen when the material changes and new materials are formed. A chemical property of wood is its ability to burn. This property makes wood a useful fuel. As wood burns, it changes. It is no longer wood. The wood is "gone," and other materials are left.

So the next time you put on your sneakers or look through a window, think about the materials those objects are made of. Ask yourself what properties made those materials right for the job. ■

INVESTIGATION 1 WRAP-UP

REVIEW

1. What are four examples of matter?

2. Name four physical properties that can describe matter.

CRITICAL THINKING

3. Look at this list: hammer, ice cube, mirror, rubber balloon. What property or properties make the material each object is made of useful?

4. Suppose you are going on a trip to the South Pole. Name two nonfood items you might take with you. Tell why each would be useful.

INVESTIGATION 2

HOW CAN MATTER BE MEASURED?

Do you know how tall you are? You probably do, because you've been measured. Measuring is one way to describe matter. In Investigation 2 you'll learn how to make measurements of matter, using different measuring tools.

Activity

A Balancing Act

A rock contains matter—but how much matter? How can you measure the amount of matter in an object?

MATERIALS

- balance
- small rock
- clear plastic bag *A*, containing a number of different objects
- clear plastic bag *B*, containing a number of identical objects
- *Science Notebook*

Procedure

1. Place a small rock in the pan on the left side of a balance. **Observe** what happens. Add objects from bag *A* to the other pan until both pans contain the same amount of matter. **Infer** how you will know when this happens. **Record** your inference and your results in your *Science Notebook*.

See **SCIENCE** *and* **MATH TOOLBOX** page H9 if you need to review *Using a Balance.*

2. Leave the rock in its balance pan. Remove the objects from the other pan. Replace them in bag *A*.

B14

3. Look at the objects in bag *B*. **Talk with your group.** Then **predict** how many of the objects it will take to balance the rock. Be sure you can give reasons for your prediction. **Record** your prediction.

4. Use objects from bag *B* to **measure** the amount of matter in the rock. **Measure** the amount several times to check your results. **Record** your results.

Step 3

Analyze and Conclude

1. Name the objects used in step 1 to find the amount of matter in the rock.

2. How many objects from bag *B* were used to equal the amount of matter in the rock? **Compare** your results with your prediction.

3. Which measurement is easier for telling about the amount of matter in the rock, the one made in step 1 or the one made in step 4? Explain your answer.

Science in Literature

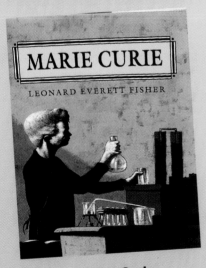

Marie Curie
by Leonard Everett Fisher
Macmillan, 1994

WHAT'S THE MATTER?

"In 1896, Antoine Henri Becquerel, a French physicist, saw an unusually strong glow in a brown lump of uranium ore . . . . Marie began testing chemical elements to identify the substance . . . and by the end of the year she had concluded that the mysterious substance was an unknown 'radiant' element."

This story is from *Marie Curie* by Leonard Everett Fisher. The book tells about the discovery of a property never before identified. Read this book to find out the property that caused this glow.

Activity

Wider or Taller?

MATERIALS
- assorted objects
- chalk
- *Science Notebook*

With arms outstretched, are people wider than they are tall, or taller than they are wide? Measure to find out.

- - - - - - - - - - - - - - - - - - - -

Procedure

1. Work with a partner. One of you will be the model. The other will be the marker. The model will stand, arms outstretched, with his or her back against the chalkboard. The marker will use a piece of chalk to mark the model's height and arm span, as shown. Arm span is the width from the tip of one hand to the tip of the other.

Step 1

2. Select an object to use as a measuring tool. Don't select the same tool that your partner does. Using the floor and the chalk marks, **measure** the model's height and arm span. To check your measurements, repeat them several times. **Record** your results in your *Science Notebook*. **Compare** your results with those of your partner.

Math Hint

To compare results means to decide if one result is greater than (>), less than (<), or equal to (=) another result.

3. Repeat step 2, this time using the *same* measuring tool that your partner does. **Predict** how your measurements will compare with those of your partner. **Record** your prediction and then **test** it.

Analyze and Conclude

1. Which was greater, the model's height or arm span?

2. Which measurements were easier to compare, those made in step 2 or those in step 3? Explain your answer.

Activity

How Much?

Suppose that you could have as much gold dust as you could carry in a single container. If you had three containers, how could you find out which would hold the most? Could you tell by just looking?

MATERIALS

- goggles
- newspaper
- 3 plastic containers of different sizes and shapes
- grease pencil
- small plastic cup
- sand
- *Science Notebook*

SAFETY /////

Wear goggles during this activity. Clean up spills immediately.

Procedure

1. Spread newspaper on your work area. Place three containers on the newspaper. Use a grease pencil to label the containers *A, B, C,* with a different letter for each container.

2. Study the containers. **Infer** which can hold the most matter. **Record** your inference in your *Science Notebook.*

3. The amount of sand that each container can hold is the volume of that container. **Write a plan** to find the volume of each container. Show the plan to your teacher. Carry out your plan and **record** your results.

Analyze and Conclude

1. Which container can hold the most sand? How did your results compare with your inference?

2. Which container has the greatest volume? How do you know?

Step 2

Making Measurements

Reading Focus What are two measuring tools that were developed before 1900?

You may not realize it, but you measure things every day. How do you know when it's time to go to school or go home? You look at a clock. How can you know what day it is? You can see it on a calendar— another way for you to measure time.

Whenever you weigh yourself or check your height, you're measuring.

You measure ingredients when you make lemonade or cocoa. How did people of long ago measure things? You'll have to go back in time to see for yourself.

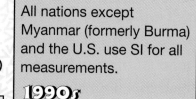

All nations except Myanmar (formerly Burma) and the U.S. use SI for all measurements.

1990s

The first sundial is set up in Rome. Sundials are used to tell time.

290 B.C.

The mercury themometer is invented.

1714

1300
A British inventor makes the first mechanical clock.

1960
Scientists worldwide agree to use the International System (SI) of measurement. This system is based on the number 10.

1600 B.C.
The Egyptians intro- duce the cubit, a unit of measure. A cubit is the distance from the elbow to the end of the middle finger.

The Metric System

Reading Focus What are some differences between the English and metric systems of measurement?

Suppose that you and a group of friends are planning to build a clubhouse. You receive permission from your parents, draw up your plans, and collect your materials.

On the first day of work, each member of your group shows up with a homemade ruler. Nobody's units match anybody else's units! How will your clubhouse look if measurements are made with these rulers?

The activities on pages B14–B16 show the importance of using standard units to make measurements. A **standard unit** is one that is agreed on and used by *everyone*. When all members of a group use the *same* objects to make measurements, they are using standard units.

Measuring Systems

To accurately describe matter, it is necessary to use a set of standard units to measure such properties as size, mass, volume, and temperature. Such a set of standards is known as a system of measurement.

At the present time, there are two widely used systems of measurement—the metric system and the English system. The metric system is used in just about *every* country. But it is not used in Myanmar, formerly Burma. And almost everyone in the United States uses the English system.

How Many Inches in a Mile?

The English system of measurement includes such units as feet and inches,

Why is the clubhouse so crooked? ▼

English System Units

Length	Weight (mass)	Volume
mile (1,760 yards)	ton (2,000 pounds)	gallon (4 quarts)
yard (3 feet)	pound (16 ounces)	quart (2 pints)
foot (12 inches)	ounce	pint (16 ounces)

pounds and ounces, quarts and pints, and degrees Fahrenheit.

The problem with the English system is the way its units vary. The table above lists some units used to measure length (or distance), weight, and volume in the English system.

As the table shows, there is no logical relationship between units, even for measurements of the same property. For example, suppose you want to find out how many inches are in one mile. You must know how many feet are in one mile and how many inches are in one foot. Then you need to do a lot of multiplying.

The Metric System

The **metric system** is a system of measurement that is based on the number 10 and multiples of 10. In other words, it is a decimal system.

The metric system of measurement was introduced in France during the 1790s and is used by most people in the world today. In 1960, scientists worldwide agreed to use a modern version of the metric system. This system is known as the International System of Units, abbreviated SI.

BALANCE Balances are used to measure mass. An object of unknown mass placed in one pan is balanced by objects of known mass placed in the other pan. ▼

METRIC RULER AND METERSTICK Metric rulers and metersticks are used to measure length, or distance. The scale of this meterstick is divided into centimeters. Each centimeter is divided into millimeters. ▼

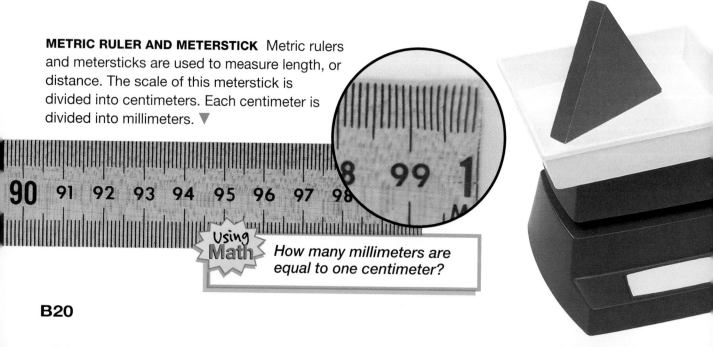

Using Math *How many millimeters are equal to one centimeter?*

Because the metric system is a decimal system, it's easy to learn. And it's easier to use than the English system. The table below shows some basic units of measurement in the metric system and their symbols. The pictures show some measuring tools. You can learn more about these tools in the Science and Math Toolbox, which begins on page H1.

A set of prefixes make the metric system easy to use. A *prefix* is a syllable added to the beginning of a word to give the word a new meaning.

Metric System Units

Measurement	Unit	Symbol
length	meter	m
mass	gram	g
volume	liter	L
temperature	degree Celsius	°C

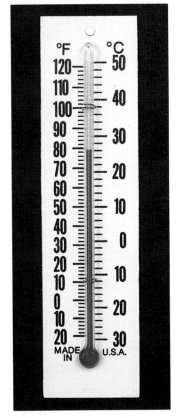

▲ **THERMOMETER** Thermometers are used to measure temperature. The thermometer shown here has two temperature scales.

GRADUATED CYLINDER Graduated cylinders, or graduates, are used to measure volumes of liquids. The scale of a graduate is divided into milliliters. ▶

Metric Prefixes

Prefix	Meaning	Symbol	Example
kilo-	one thousand	k	1 kilometer (km) = 1,000 m
deci-	one tenth	d	1 decimeter (dm) = 0.1 m
centi-	one hundredth	c	1 centimeter (cm) = 0.01 m
milli-	one thousandth	m	1 millimeter (mm) = 0.001 m

Think of the word *triangle*. The prefix *tri-* means "three." So *triangle* means "three angles."

The table above lists the prefixes used in the metric system. It gives their meanings, their symbols, and examples of how they are used.

How do the prefixes help to make using the metric system easy? The same prefixes are used with all the basic units. So you know that a kilogram is equal to 1,000 grams and that a kiloliter is equal to 1,000 liters. You also know that 5 kilograms is equal to 5,000 grams. Similarly, a centimeter is equal to $\frac{1}{100}$ of a meter, or 0.01 meter. How many centimeters are in 5 meters?

Scientists have chosen the metric system because it's simple, it's accurate, and it's known worldwide. Much of a scientist's time is spent making observations and measurements. By using the same system of measurement—SI—scientists can easily compare their work with that of other scientists, no matter what nation they're from. ■

Internet Field Trip

Visit **www.eduplace.com** to find out more about the properties and measurement of matter.

INVESTIGATION 2 WRAP-UP

REVIEW 1. Which measuring system is based on the number 10, the English system or the metric system?

2. What does the prefix *kilo-* mean?

CRITICAL THINKING 3. Suppose you want to move a desk into your bedroom. What properties of the desk will you have to measure?

4. You need enough punch to fill a large bowl. What property of the bowl should you measure? How would you make the measurement?

REFLECT & EVALUATE

Word Power

Write the letter of the term that best completes each sentence. *Not all terms will be used.*

1. The amount of matter that a container holds is its ——.
2. Corn syrup has a greater —— than does oil.
3. Mass is a measure of the amount of —— something contains.
4. An object's color is one —— of that object.
5. The prefix *kilo-* is used in the —— of measurement.
6. If everyone uses the same size paper clip to measure an object, the paper clip can be called a ——.

a. mass
b. matter
c. metric system
d. density
e. property
f. standard unit
g. volume

Check What You Know

Write the term in each pair that best completes each sentence.

1. The more matter an object contains, the greater will be its (length, mass).
2. A tool used to measure volume is a (graduated cylinder, balance).
3. A liter is a unit of (mass, volume).
4. The ability to burn is a (physical property, chemical property).
5. Mass can be measured in (grams, centimeters).

Problem Solving

1. Suppose you want to find the length and mass of your science textbook. What measuring tools will you use? In what units will you record your measurements?

2. Suppose you need to find the mass of a jar of paste. You have a balance and washers to use as masses. Each washer has a mass of 2 g. It takes 41 washers to balance the jar. What is its mass?

Study and record the names of the materials in the photograph shown here. List as many properties of each material as you can. Tell how the properties make each material useful for the purpose shown.

CHAPTER 2

OBSERVING STATES OF MATTER

Have you ever wanted to catch a cloud? Did you ever wonder how water turns to ice? Are you curious about what a rainbow is made of? In this chapter you'll investigate the forms of things around you and how those forms can change.

PEOPLE USING SCIENCE

Physicist In the 1930s a boy named Fred roamed the land of his ancestors. His family lived the way Navajos had for hundreds of years. They hunted, fished, and picked wild herbs. Practicing Navajo medicine was their work.

As he traveled, young Fred wondered about the world around him. He wondered how mountains form and what lightning is. He questioned how things work. Though he didn't know it, Fred was already a scientist.

Today, Dr. Fred Begay still asks questions about how the world works. That is his job as a physicist (fiz´ə sist). A physicist is a scientist who studies matter and energy.

As you move through this chapter, be a scientist like young Fred Begay. Think about the way things are made and how they work. Explore the mysteries of matter and energy.

Coming Up

INVESTIGATION

WHAT IS MATTER LIKE?
. . . . B26

INVESTIGATION

HOW CAN MATTER CHANGE STATE?
. . . . B36

◀ Dr. Fred Begay, physicist

WHAT IS MATTER LIKE?

Your friend is having a birthday party. There are cookies, juice, and balloons. These things are all made of matter, but each is different. In this investigation you'll find out about the states of matter and what kinds of matter exist.

Activity

States of Matter

Does juice change shape when poured from a carton into a glass? Do all kinds of matter change in the same way? Compare the property of shape in three states of matter.

MATERIALS
- 5 objects of different shapes and sizes, labeled *A–E*
- 3 plastic containers of different shapes, labeled 1–3
- plastic soda bottle filled with water
- small inflated balloon
- *Science Notebook*

SAFETY
Clean up spills immediately.

Procedure

1. **Observe** objects *A* through *E*. Press down on each object with your thumb. **Observe** what happens to the object. Pick up each object, handle it, and describe its properties. **Record** your descriptions in your *Science Notebook*.

Step 1

2. Place each object, one at a time, into each of the containers. Each time, gently shake the container and its contents. **Observe** and **record** any changes in the objects. Remove the objects from the containers.

3. Pour water from the bottle into the containers to fill them, one at a time. **Observe** what happens to the shape of the water in each container. **Record** your findings.

Step 3

4. **Observe** and **record** what happens to the matter inside an inflated balloon when you press on it with your hand and when you stop pressing on it. **Predict** what will happen to the air inside the balloon when you untie the balloon. **Record** your prediction.

5. Hold the balloon and slowly undo the twist tie on the neck of the balloon. **Observe** and **record** what happens to the air inside the balloon.

Analyze and Conclude

1. The objects used in steps 1 and 2 are all solids. Based on your observations, what can you **infer** about the shape and volume of a solid?

2. From your observations of liquid water, what can you **infer** about the shape and volume of a liquid?

3. Air is a mixture of gases. From your observations in steps 4 and 5, what can you **infer** about the shape and volume of a gas?

UNIT PROJECT LINK

With your group, brainstorm a list of materials that can be presented in a form or state different from that in which they are normally found. Prepare a display of three of the materials (either pictures or actual materials) in their unusual form or state. Make signs inviting visitors to identify the materials.

TechnologyLink

For more help with your Unit Project, go to **www.eduplace.com**.

Activity

Invisible Matter

Did you ever enter a front doorway and know what was cooking in the kitchen? How did the odor get from the kitchen to your nose? Find out how one state of matter behaves.

MATERIALS
- goggles
- small plastic bottle (stoppered) containing vanilla extract
- large wide-mouthed plastic jar
- timer
- *Science Notebook*

SAFETY //////
Wear goggles during this activity. Clean up spills immediately.

Procedure

1. Put your nose over the opening of a large plastic jar to find out if you smell any odor. Record your observations in your *Science Notebook*.

2. Remove the stopper from a bottle of vanilla extract. Put your nose over the bottle to see if you smell any odor. Record your observations.

Step 2

3. Place the opened bottle of vanilla extract at arm's length on your desktop. Have a group member quickly place the large jar upside down over the bottle of vanilla.

4. Leave the jar undisturbed over the bottle for about one minute.

> See **SCIENCE** and **MATH TOOLBOX** page H12 if you need to review **Measuring Elapsed Time.**

5. Pick up the jar and put your nose to the opening to see if you smell any odor. Record your observations.

Step 3

Analyze and Conclude

1. How did the jar smell before it was placed over the bottle of vanilla extract?

2. How did the jar smell after it was placed over the bottle? Compare your observations from steps 2 and 5. Talk with your group and hypothesize about what happened. Give evidence to support your hypothesis. What weaknesses can you identify in your hypothesis?

More About Matter

Reading Focus In what ways do the states of matter differ?

Can you identify the kind of matter being described in this riddle?

You can see it and skate on it, but you can't pour it.

You can see it and pour it, but you can't skate on it.

You can't see it or pour it or skate on it, but it can fog up a mirror.

Did you answer "water"? If you did, you're correct.

States of Matter

The riddle describes some properties of water in three different forms. These forms—solid, liquid, and gas—are called **states of matter**. The state of a sample of matter is a physical property of that sample.

The activities on pages B26–B28 show the properties of the three different states of matter. Look at the pictures below of the three states and read about each one.

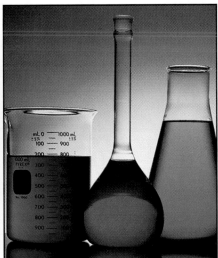

SOLIDS A **solid** is matter that has a definite volume and a definite shape.

LIQUIDS A **liquid** is matter that has a definite volume but no definite shape. A liquid takes the shape of its container.

GASES A **gas** is matter that has no definite volume or shape. A gas spreads out to fill its container.

A Closer Look at Matter

Scientists have discovered much of what is known about matter by studying gases. In the activity on page B28, the odor of vanilla spreads out from its container when the stopper is removed. Such observations have led scientists to the theory (thē'ə rē), or idea, that all matter is made up of tiny bits, or particles.

The particles that make up matter are much too small to be seen, even with a powerful microscope. Although scientists can't see them, they know that the particles are always moving. This explains how vanilla particles can move out of a bottle and spread through a jar to a person's nose. The drawings on these pages show the arrangement of particles in each state of matter.

Back to Basics

Think of all the different kinds of matter there are in the world. It might surprise you to learn that there are only 112 basic kinds of matter, called elements (el'ə mənts). An **element** is any material made up of a single kind of matter.

Elements are made up of very tiny particles called atoms. An **atom** is the smallest part of an element that has the properties of that element. All of the atoms in a given element are the same. For example, all the atoms in a piece of iron are iron atoms. Iron atoms are different from the atoms that make up any other element.

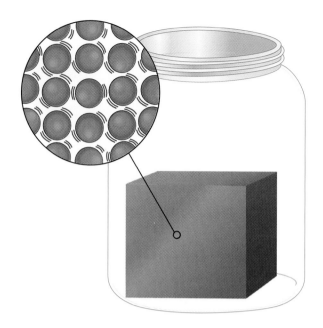

▲ Particles in a solid, such as this block, are packed closely together. Forces of attraction between the particles hold them in place. The particles can only vibrate, or move back and forth, in a very small space.

Symbols for Elements

To save time and space when recording their observations, scientists use chemical symbols. A **chemical symbol** is one or two letters that stand for the name of an element. The table shows the names and symbols of some elements.

Element & Symbol		Element & Symbol	
oxygen	O	iron	Fe
hydrogen	H	gold	Au
iodine	I	carbon	C

Internet Field Trip

Visit **www.eduplace.com** to see examples of different kinds of matter.

▲ Particles in a liquid are slightly farther apart than those in a solid. They can move past each other, allowing the liquid to take the shape of its container.

▲ Particles in a gas are farther apart and move much more freely than particles in a liquid or solid. As the particles move, they spread out in all directions, filling their container.

Science in Literature

STRANGE SCIENCE

"Strictly speaking, glass is not a solid. It is actually a very slow-moving liquid. . . .

At a fashion show in London in 1991, clothes were modeled that change color as they become warmer."

From Glasses to Gases: The Science of Matter
by Dr. David Darling
Dillon Press, 1992

These strange facts are found in the book *From Glasses to Gases: The Science of Matter* by Dr. David Darling. Dr. Darling also tells what makes raindrops stick to windows and why ketchup is often hard to get out of a bottle. He also describes how sunlight can dispose of plastic. You'll find lots of other facts and many fun-filled experiments about matter in this book.

A Precious Metal

Reading Focus What are three locations where the element gold has been discovered?

Babies and children are often described as *precious*, meaning "dear" or "beloved." Some elements—particularly metals such as gold—are also said to be precious. The term is used to describe certain elements because they are valuable, not because they're beloved.

Gold is valuable because it's beautiful, easy to mold, and rare. Only a few places in the world have large deposits of gold. In the past, people have gone to great lengths to obtain some of that gold. The map below shows the location of some of the best-known gold discoveries in history.

The discovery of gold has changed many places. Tiny towns and remote villages have been turned into bustling communities just because gold was found nearby. In 1886 the discovery of gold in South Africa led to war between the British and a group of Dutch settlers called the Boers.

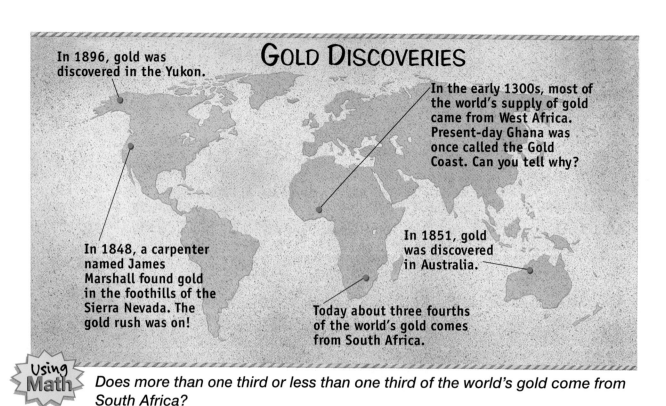

GOLD DISCOVERIES

In 1896, gold was discovered in the Yukon.

In the early 1300s, most of the world's supply of gold came from West Africa. Present-day Ghana was once called the Gold Coast. Can you tell why?

In 1848, a carpenter named James Marshall found gold in the foothills of the Sierra Nevada. The gold rush was on!

In 1851, gold was discovered in Australia.

Today about three fourths of the world's gold comes from South Africa.

Using Math

Does more than one third or less than one third of the world's gold come from South Africa?

Compounds: They're Elementary

Reading Focus What can you learn about a compound from its chemical formula?

Picture yourself on a spaceship headed for a planet in a distant solar system. When you arrive, you discover that all matter is in the form of elements—the same elements found on Earth. Would you want to live there, even if you could?

You possibly could breathe the air, because there would be oxygen present. You might find a lot of gold or silver, but you wouldn't find soil or rubber or cloth.

Most importantly, you wouldn't find many of the things you need to live.

No water and no living things! So even though all the natural elements were there, you wouldn't want to stay around very long.

Building Blocks

As you may have guessed, not many things on Earth are made of a single element. Rather, you can think of elements as the building blocks of matter. Most kinds of matter are compounds. A **compound** is a kind of matter made up of two or more elements that are joined together.

A planet of elements ▼

Elements and compounds make up a large class of matter that is known as **substances**.

Let's look at the common compound salt. The salt that you sprinkle on food is made up of two elements: sodium and chlorine (klôr′ēn). Look at the picture of salt grains as seen through a magnifying glass. Each grain looks like a tiny cube.

As Small as It Gets

Suppose you were to cut a grain of salt in half. You would then have two smaller grains of salt. If you continued to cut the smaller pieces in half, you would finally end up with a tiny piece of salt made up of two very tiny particles. What do you think those particles would be? They wouldn't be salt. They would be atoms—one sodium atom and one chlorine atom.

Of course, all of this is make-believe. A single grain of salt is made up of millions of sodium atoms and chlorine atoms. The drawing below shows how the sodium and chlorine atoms are arranged in salt.

▲ Grains of salt

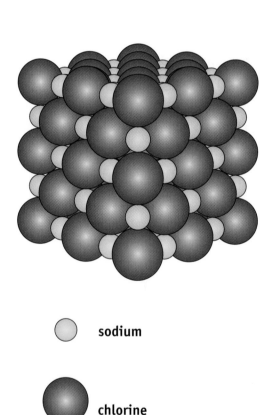

◯ sodium

⬤ chlorine

▲ The arrangement of sodium and chlorine atoms shows why salt grains are like cubes.

Describing Compounds

When writing about elements and compounds, scientists often use a shortcut. They use chemical symbols for elements and chemical formulas (fôr'myoo ləz) for compounds. A **chemical formula** is a group of symbols that shows the kinds and number of atoms in a single unit of a compound. For many compounds, but not all, a single unit is called a molecule (mäl'i kyool).

The drawings show models and formulas for two compounds, water and sugar. Look at the formula for a molecule of water. The number 2 written after the H tells you how many hydrogen atoms are in one molecule of water. When only one atom of an element is present, no number is written after its symbol.

Now look at the formula for the sugar fructose. What can you learn about this molecule from its formula? ■

Using Math

Look at the formula for fructose. How many atoms make up a molecule of fructose?

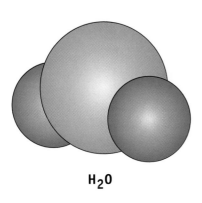

H_2O

▲ A water molecule is made up of two hydrogen atoms and one oxygen atom.

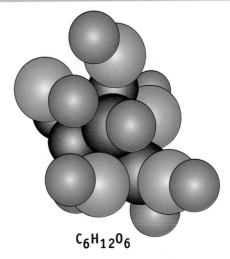

$C_6H_{12}O_6$

▲ This is a molecule of fructose, a type of sugar found in many fruits.

--- INVESTIGATION 1 WRAP-UP ---

REVIEW

1. Name the three states of matter.

2. Give the chemical symbols for three elements.

CRITICAL THINKING

3. Compare the results if you divided iron and water each into the smallest substance possible.

4. Scientists think that matter is made of invisible particles. What evidence supports this theory? What weaknesses, if any, do you see with this theory?

HOW CAN MATTER CHANGE STATE?

In many places you can swim in a lake in the summer and skate on it in the winter. It's possible to swim and skate on the same lake because matter changes state. In this investigation you'll learn about changes of state.

Activity

From State to State

What causes ice to change from a solid to a liquid? This activity will help you find out.

- -

Procedure

Hold a small piece of ice in your hand. Observe how the ice makes your hand feel and what happens to the ice. Record your observations in your *Science Notebook*. Now place one piece of ice on a dish in a sunny spot. Place a second piece of ice on a dish in a shady spot. Observe both dishes every 3 minutes for 15 minutes. Record your observations.

Analyze and Conclude

Compare the changes you observed in the ice in the two dishes. Hypothesize about the relationship between the way the ice made your hand feel and what happened to the ice in the dishes.

Observations of Ice		
Time (in minutes)	In Sun	In Shade
3		
6		

B36

Activity

Liquid From Thin Air

Clouds are made up of tiny drops of liquid water. What kind of change makes these drops appear? You'll have a clue by doing this activity.

Procedure

1. Wipe the outside of a can with a paper towel to make sure it's perfectly dry.

2. Place several ice cubes in the can. Carefully add water until the can is full. Gently mix the water with food coloring. If any water spills on or flows over the side of the can, wipe it dry right away.

Step 2

3. Allow the can of ice water to sit undisturbed. **Observe** it until you see drops of liquid forming on the sides of the container. **Observe** the color of the liquid. Identify this liquid and **record** your observations in your *Science Notebook.*

Analyze and Conclude

1. What is the reason for adding color to the water in the can?

2. What is the liquid that formed on the can? **Hypothesize** where it came from. **Compare** your hypothesis with those of other group members.

3. **Describe** any changes of state that you observed during this activity.

B37

Cool It

Reading Focus How can certain compounds help keep the air in a refrigerator cold?

A refrigerator helps to keep food from spoiling by keeping it cold. Heat always flows from warmer to colder matter. In a refrigerator, heat flows from the food it contains into the cold air around it. The air is kept cold with the help of compounds known as HFCs.

HFCs can exist as either a gas or a liquid and can easily be changed from one state to another. Look at the drawing to see how a refrigerator works to keep food cold.

After you've seen how the refrigerator works, grab something cold and chill out. Just don't leave the door open too long!

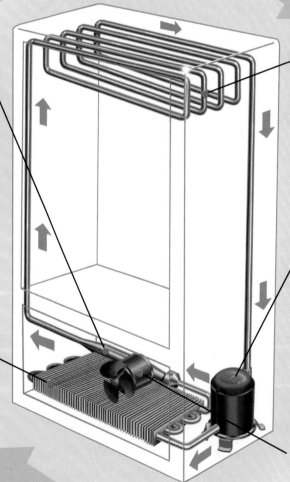

RECEIVER AND VALVE The receiver is a small storage tank. The receiver valve controls the flow of liquid HFC as it leaves the receiver and moves to the evaporator.

EVAPORATOR The evaporator is a section of tubing in the freezer section of the refrigerator. Here heat is absorbed by the liquid HFC as it evaporates, changing from a liquid to a gas.

COMPRESSOR The compressor is an electric pump that forces the HFC gas into the condenser. The HFC becomes hot in this process.

CONDENSER In the condenser, the HFC gas releases heat as it condenses, changing back to a liquid. The liquid HFC then moves into the receiver.

FAN The fan blows heat released by the HFC gas out the back of the refrigerator.

Causing Change

Reading Focus How can the gain or loss of heat energy change matter?

Are you someone who is always "on the go"? Such people are described as being full of energy. On the other hand, when you're sick, you often feel as if you have no energy at all. Although we often use the word *energy*, it's hard to explain exactly what energy is.

What Is Energy?

Energy is defined in several different ways. One definition of **energy** is "the ability to cause change." Change often involves movement. It takes energy to change motion. For example, to make your bike start to move, you push on the pedals. You use energy to move the bike (and yourself) from place to place.

Energy is also needed to change how fast something is moving. Suppose you want to make your bike go faster. You have to use more energy to pedal harder. You even have to use energy to make the bike slow down and stop.

▼ **The riders transfer energy from their bodies to their bikes.**

Energy and Change of State

What does energy have to do with matter? Recall that the particles of matter are constantly moving. If the motion of the particles is changed, a change of state can occur.

You know that matter can change state. A frozen juice bar can change from a solid to a liquid. But you can make more juice bars by putting liquid juice in a freezer.

You have probably seen a puddle of water seem to "dry up" and disappear on a warm day. What actually happens is that the water evaporates (ē vap′ə rāts). **Evaporation** is the change of state from a liquid to a gas.

Gaining Energy

All changes of state involve heat energy. As you continue reading, look at the drawings to see how heat energy affects the motion of particles.

❶ When heat is added to a solid, such as ice, the particles in the solid take in heat energy. As the particles absorb the heat energy, they begin moving faster.

❷ As the particles in the solid gain energy, they move farther apart. If they gain enough energy, the particles move far enough apart so that they can slide past each other. The matter begins to melt. **Melting** is the change of state from a solid to a liquid.

❸ If heating continues after all the solid has melted, the particles move still faster and farther apart. Some of the liquid begins to evaporate. It changes to a gas called water vapor, causing bubbles to form in the liquid. The formation of bubbles shows that the liquid has begun to boil. **Boiling** is the rapid change of state from a liquid to a gas.

❹ As long as heat is added to the liquid, it will continue to boil. Bubbles of water vapor will keep forming and escaping into the air until all the liquid changes to a gas.

Losing Energy

Suppose you hold a piece of ice in your hand, as is done in the activity on page B36. The ice makes your hand feel cold. What do you think happens to make your hand feel colder? Do you think that "cold" leaves the ice and then enters your hand? Wrong!

Your hand feels cold because heat leaves your hand and is taken in by the ice. Heat energy always moves from warmer to cooler matter. So matter cools down by losing heat—not by gaining "cold."

As you have just learned, when heat is added to matter, the particles

INVESTIGATE FURTHER!

RESEARCH

Research an early scientific theory of heat called the caloric theory. Write a report about the strengths and weaknesses of this theory. Then compare the caloric theory with the model of heat discussed in this lesson.

that make up the matter speed up. What do you suppose happens if heat is taken away from matter? Right— the particles that make up the matter slow down.

At what temperature does water boil? If you need help, see p. H14.

The frost (*left*), fog (*center*), and moisture on a windowpane (*right*) are all examples of condensation.

Let's take another look at water as it changes state—this time in reverse order, starting with water vapor. Suppose heat energy is taken away from water vapor. Then the particles that make up the gas begin to slow down and move closer together. If the particles lose enough energy, the gas changes to a liquid. **Condensation** (kän dən sā′shən) is the change of state from a gas to a liquid. In the activity on page B37, water vapor, an invisible gas in the air, condenses on the sides of a can.

Once condensation occurs, suppose that more energy is taken away from the liquid. Then the particles in the liquid slow down even more. If the particles in the liquid lose enough energy, the liquid begins to freeze. **Freezing** is the change of state from a liquid to a solid. ∎

INVESTIGATION 2 WRAP-UP

REVIEW

1. What kind of energy is involved when matter changes state?

2. What change of state occurs when boiling takes place?

CRITICAL THINKING

3. Recall what you know about changes of state. Then explain which properties of HFCs help keep the air in a refrigerator cold.

4. Compare the behavior of particles of matter during boiling and during condensation.

REFLECT & EVALUATE

Word Power

Write the letter of the term that best matches the definition.
Not all terms will be used.

a. atom
b. compound
c. energy
d. gas
e. liquid
f. melting
g. solid
h. substance

1. Matter that has a definite volume and a definite shape
2. The smallest part of an element that has the properties of that element
3. The change of state from a solid to a liquid
4. Matter that has no definite volume or shape
5. The ability to cause change
6. A kind of matter made up of two or more elements that are joined together

Check What You Know

Write the term in each pair that best completes each sentence.

1. Material made up of only one kind of matter is (an element, a compound).
2. The change of state from a liquid to a solid is called (boiling, freezing).
3. Particles in a liquid move faster than those in a (solid, gas).
4. The chemical symbol I stands for (iodine, iron).

Problem Solving

1. Common table sugar is called sucrose. A molecule of sucrose has the chemical formula $C_{12}H_{22}O_{11}$. What does the chemical formula tell you about a molecule of sucrose?

2. Explain why frost forms on the inside of a window rather than on the outside.

Copy this drawing of the water molecule and label each atom. Then describe the makeup of a water molecule and write its chemical formula.

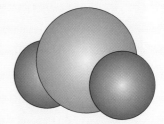

CHAPTER 3

CAUSING CHANGES IN MATTER

Imagine that you have a sore throat and can't swallow your vitamin tablet. How would you solve this problem? You could grind the tablet into a powder and dissolve the powder in fruit juice. In this chapter you'll think about other ways that matter, such as a vitamin tablet, can change.

PEOPLE USING SCIENCE

Research Pharmacist Dr. Beatrice Allis is a research pharmacist (fär′mə sist). She works for a company that makes vitamins. Here is what she told us.

Question: How do you make the liquid vitamins that are given to babies? Do you grind a vitamin tablet and add water?

Dr. Allis: It's not that simple. You need to be sure that the solution is not too strong for a baby. It also wouldn't taste very good. A flavoring is always added to the liquid.

Question: What does it take to be a research pharmacist?

Dr. Allis: You need to be curious and want to help people. We are always looking for ways to make changes for the better.

As you work through the investigations in this chapter, you'll make some changes yourself!

Coming Up

INVESTIGATION 1

WHAT ARE PHYSICAL CHANGES?
. . . . B46

INVESTIGATION 2

WHAT ARE CHEMICAL CHANGES?
. . . . B54

◄ Dr. Beatrice Allis, research pharmacist

INVESTIGATION 1

WHAT ARE PHYSICAL CHANGES?

Does a change in temperature, size, or shape of a material change the kind of matter it is made of? Does mixing materials together change them? In Investigation 1 you'll find out how matter can be changed without changing the kind of matter it is.

Activity

Same Stuff

Find out if changing the size, position, or shape of matter changes the kind of matter.

Procedure

Place a paper clip on one pan of a balance. Measure and record its mass in your *Science Notebook*. Work with your group to change the paper clip. Include turning it 90 degrees, flipping it over, and pushing it to a new position. After each change, measure and record the mass. Place a piece of chalk on a paper towel. Measure and record their total mass. Remove the objects. Wrap the chalk in the towel. Use a small rock to grind the chalk into powder. Measure and record the mass of the towel and the ground-up chalk.

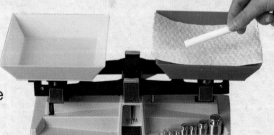

Analyze and Conclude

Did any of the changes affect the paper clip's mass? Did crushing the chalk affect the chalk's mass?

B46

Activity

All Mixed Up

Does mixing different kinds of matter cause a physical change? Find out!

- -

MATERIALS

- goggles
- marbles, paper clips, buttons
- 3 small plastic jars, labeled *A, B,* and *C,* with lids
- plastic spoon
- sand
- copper pellets
- sawdust
- strainer
- tweezers
- water
- *Science Notebook*

SAFETY ///////

Wear goggles during this activity. Clean up spills immediately.

Procedure

1. In your *Science Notebook,* make a chart like this.

Jar	Items Mixed Together	Appearance of Mixture	How Items Were Separated
A			
B			

See **SCIENCE** and **MATH TOOLBOX** page H10 if you need to review **Making a Chart to Organize Data.**

2. Place some marbles, paper clips, and buttons in jar *A.* Add a spoonful of sand and a spoonful of copper pellets to jar *B.* Add a spoonful of sand and a spoonful of sawdust to jar *C.* Cover each jar with a lid.

3. Shake each jar. Observe each jar and complete the second and third columns of your chart.

4. With your group, hypothesize ways to use materials from the list to separate each mixture into its different parts. Test your ideas and record in your chart the methods you used.

Analyze and Conclude

1. How did the size of the materials in each mixture affect the way you separated each mixture?

2. Infer if mixing different kinds of matter changes materials. How can you check your inferences?

Step 2

B47

A Change for the Better?

Reading Focus If matter changes but its properties do not, what can you infer about that change?

We live in a world of change. Seasons change as the months pass. People change as they grow older. Even rocks are changed by the action of water, wind, and ice—a slow change we're not likely to notice.

A Change in Size and Shape

If you break a stick, you end up with two pieces instead of one.

Breaking a stick is a physical change. A **physical change** is a change in the size, shape, or state of matter with no new matter being formed.

No new matter is formed when you break a stick. Each piece of the stick looks, feels, and acts like wood, and is, in fact, still wood.

Grinding a piece of chalk, as happens in the activity on page B46, causes a physical change. The ground-up chalk is still chalk. It still has all the properties of chalk.

Temperature and Change

A change in temperature can cause a physical change in matter. You may already know that a change in temperature can change the speed at which a liquid flows. A liquid flows faster when it is warmed and slower when it is cooled.

Changes in temperature can also cause the size, or volume, of matter to change. Recall that volume is the amount of space that matter takes up.

◀ How are the two pieces of wood like the stick they came from? How are they different?

▲ When heated, the metal cap expands more than the glass jar. How does this help you remove the cap from the jar?

Most matter expands, or increases in volume, when it's heated. When heat is taken away, most matter contracts, or decreases in volume. But water expands as it freezes and contracts as it melts.

A Change in State

Temperature change can also cause another kind of change—a change in state. You know that matter can exist as a solid, liquid, or gas. And you know that matter can change from one state to another. The melting of ice is an example of a change in state.

A change in state is a physical change, although it may be hard to understand why. After all, ice doesn't look like water, or feel like water, or act like water.

The reason a change in state is a physical change is that the kind of matter involved doesn't change. Ice and liquid water are both water. Even when water evaporates and changes to an invisible gas, it's *still* water. ■

Internet Field Trip

Visit **www.eduplace.com** to learn more about how matter can change from one state to another.

◀ You know that melting is a physical change, because liquid ice cream tastes just the same as the solid kind.

B49

Magnificent Mixtures

Reading Focus What substances do you get when you separate a mixture of substances?

Look at all the different vegetables shown above and to the right. Suppose you cut up these vegetables, put the pieces in a big bowl, and jumbled them all together. What would you have? A cook would call the vegetables a salad. A scientist would call them a mixture.

What's a Mixture?

A **mixture** is matter made up of two or more different substances. (Recall that a substance is an element or a compound.) When you mix two or more substances together, you produce a physical change. For example, a salad is different from each of the vegetables in it.

However, mixing substances together doesn't change the physical properties of the substances. A tomato is still a tomato, and a cucumber is still a cucumber, even when

Some mixtures, like this salad, can be separated by picking out the parts. ▶

they're mixed together. If you wish, you can separate a mixture into its individual substances. With a salad, that's easy. You just pick out the different vegetables. The activity on page B47 shows that some mixtures are harder to separate than others. That's because of the sizes of the particles. The smaller the particles in a mixture are, the more difficult it is to separate them.

Another Kind of Mixture

Have you ever added sugar to a liquid and watched the sugar "disappear"? If you taste the liquid, you know the sugar didn't really disappear. It just dissolved.

▲ Most rocks are mixtures of substances called **minerals** (min′ər əlz).

The mixture of sugar and water is one example of a solution. A **solution** is a mixture in which particles of different substances are mixed evenly throughout. One of the most common solutions in nature is sea water. Sea water is a mixture of water and several different salts. ■

Science in Literature

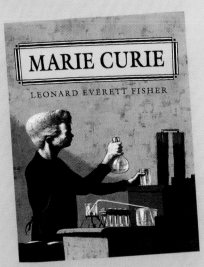

Marie Curie
by Leonard Everett Fisher
Macmillan, 1994

CURIE SEEKS A CURE

"It was the first time anyone had received the Nobel Prize twice, and for two different sciences—first physics, then chemistry. Marie's only wish was to see her work—and Pierre's—used to improve the human condition, especially to cure cancer."

These words are taken from *Marie Curie* by Leonard Everett Fisher. The book tells of Marie Curie's many years of hard work and sacrifice. Read this book to find out the two new elements she discovered and to learn how her work has helped people.

A Valuable Mixture

Reading Focus How do changes of state help to separate crude oil into many products?

SCIENCE TECHNOLOGY & SOCIETY

You may know that oil from the ground is used to make many kinds of fuels. But did you know that oil is also used in making hundreds of products, including plastics, fabrics, and the asphalt (as'fôlt) used on roads and driveways?

It's Too Crude

The material that comes out of an oil well is a dark liquid called crude oil, or petroleum (pə trō'lē əm). Crude oil is a mixture of many substances called hydrocarbons (hī drō kär'bənz). The name comes from the elements *hydrogen* and *carbon*, which make up hydrocarbons.

Like iron ore, crude oil is not useful as it comes from the ground. It must be refined, or separated into its useful parts. The separating of the mixture is done in tall structures many stories high. These structures are called fractionating (frak'shən āt iŋ) towers. Refer to the diagram on page B53 as you read about how crude oil is refined.

Changing the State of Crude

Each of the hydrocarbons in crude oil changes state at a different temperature. Chemists use these differences to separate the mixture of hydrocarbons.

The first step in separating crude oil is to heat it in a furnace to a temperature of 400°C (750°F). At this high temperature, the hydrocarbons are in the gas state. This mixture of gases passes from the furnace into the fractionating tower, where the mixture cools.

Technology Link
CD-ROM

INVESTIGATE FURTHER!

Use the **Best of the Net— Science CD-ROM**, Physical Sciences, *Energy Quest: The Energy Story* site (Chapter 5) to find out more about crude oil and how this mixture is split into different products.

Near the bottom of the tower, the hydrocarbons made up of the largest molecules change back into a liquid. The remaining gases cool as they rise in the tower. All but the fuel gases change back into liquids at different heights, depending on the sizes of their molecules.

These liquids leave the fractionating tower through pipes. Then the liquids and gases are collected in huge tanks. ■

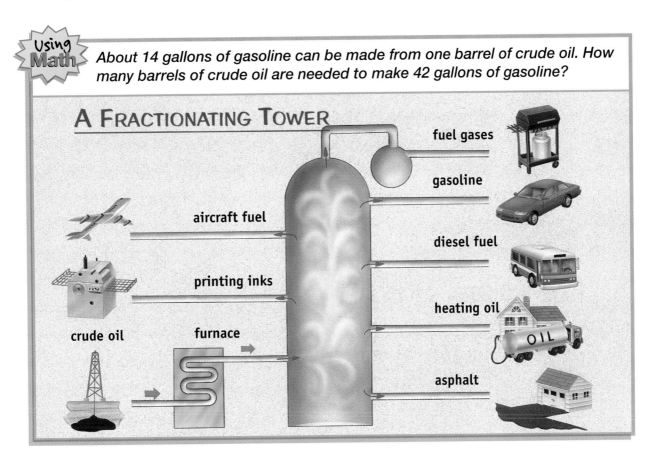

Using Math

About 14 gallons of gasoline can be made from one barrel of crude oil. How many barrels of crude oil are needed to make 42 gallons of gasoline?

A FRACTIONATING TOWER

fuel gases

gasoline

aircraft fuel

diesel fuel

printing inks

heating oil

crude oil   furnace

asphalt

INVESTIGATION 1 WRAP-UP

THINK IT
WRITE IT

REVIEW

1. Is a change of state a physical change or a chemical change?

2. Give one example of a mixture.

CRITICAL THINKING

3. When sugar dissolves in water, the sugar disappears. Why is this a physical change? Give examples of three other physical changes.

4. Suppose each substance in a liquid mixture changes to a solid at a different temperature. How could you use this information to separate the mixture?

INVESTIGATION 2

WHAT ARE CHEMICAL CHANGES?

You've seen that a sample of matter can change without changing the kind of matter it's made up of. But matter can change in other ways, too. In Investigation 2 you'll explore how one kind of matter can be changed into another kind of matter.

Activity

Different Stuff

Is a rusty nail the same as a shiny new nail? Find out how one kind of matter can be changed into another kind of matter.

- -

Procedure

1. Use a plastic spoon to add a spoonful of baking soda to a narrow jar. Carefully add vinegar to the jar until it is about one-quarter full. **Observe** the contents of the jar. **Record** your observations in your *Science Notebook*.

Math Hint
To estimate the one-quarter level of the jar, measure the height of the jar. Round to the nearest whole number. Divide by 4.

MATERIALS
- goggles
- plastic spoon
- baking soda
- 2 narrow plastic jars
- vinegar
- liquid *A*
- liquid *B*
- timer
- small plastic dish
- water
- steel wool
- 2 large wide-mouth plastic jars
- paper towel
- *Science Notebook*

SAFETY //////
Wear goggles during this activity. Clean up spills immediately. Be careful when handling steel wool.

B54

2. Observe liquid *A* and liquid *B*. Carefully pour both liquids into a clean narrow jar. Observe the mixture for 5 minutes. Record your observations.

3. Fill a small dish with water. Place one piece of steel wool next to the dish of water. Place a wide-mouth jar, mouth down, over the dish of water and over the piece of steel wool that is near it, as shown.

4. Place a second jar mouth down over a second piece of steel wool.

Step 2

Step 3

Step 4

5. Leave the jars undisturbed overnight. The next day, observe the two pieces of steel wool and record your observations.

Analyze and Conclude

1. How are the changes you observed in steps 1, 2, and 5 alike?

2. Make an **inference** about what mixed with the steel wool to cause it to change. Explain why you think as you do.

3. How are the changes that occur in this activity like the changes that occur in the activities on pages B46 and B47? How are they different?

INVESTIGATE FURTHER!

EXPERIMENT

Repeat the activity, but this time, coat one piece of steel wool with vegetable oil. Place this piece of steel wool under the large jar along with the dish of water (step 3). Compare the results of this activity with those of the original activity. Explain any differences in these results.

Changed for Good

Reading Focus How does a chemical change differ from a physical change?

Many physical changes can be undone. If you change the shape of a piece of clay, you can change it back. If liquid water freezes, the ice can be melted to get the liquid back.

Some physical changes, such as ripping up paper, can't really be "undone." However, you always have the same *kind* of matter before and after the change.

Something New

Many changes in matter are changes that can't be undone. For example, you can't turn a pile of ashes back into a log. Why? Because ashes are a different kind of matter than the wood they came from. When it's burned, a log changes into other kinds of matter. Any change in matter that results in one or more different kinds of matter forming is called a **chemical change**.

Recall that the physical properties of matter can be used to describe matter. These properties can be used to describe what matter looks like, smells like, and feels like. The physical properties of a material change when a physical change takes place. For example, sawdust doesn't look or feel much like a piece of wood.

Matter can also be described by its chemical properties. The **chemical properties** of matter describe how

The destruction of this building involves both chemical and physical changes. ▼

▲ The rusting of iron is a familiar example of a chemical change. You know it's a chemical change because iron and rust have different physical and chemical properties.

that matter reacts with other matter. The chemical properties of two liquids when they are mixed together can be observed in the activity on pages B54 and B55.

Slow Change

Look at the cars in the two pictures on this page. It's hard to believe that the car on the right once

looked like the one on the left. What happened to it? What kind of change in matter do you think this is?

In the activity on pages B54 and B55, damp iron combines with some substance in air to produce a new substance—rust. The scientific name for rust is *iron oxide*. From the name of this compound, can you guess what substance in the air combines with iron to form rust?

The combining of iron and oxygen to form rust is a chemical reaction (rē ak'shən). A **chemical reaction** is the process in which one or more substances are changed into one or more different substances.

Rapid Change

Some chemical changes, like the rusting of metal, take place slowly.

▲ The burning of a fuel, such as wood, is similar to the rusting of iron. When a fuel burns, it combines very rapidly with oxygen in the air.

Others take place very rapidly and can be violent and dangerous. The exploding of dynamite or the burning of a fuel, such as wood, are examples of such changes.

You Can't Get Rid of Matter

Think of all the different ways that matter can be changed. You can grind a solid into powder. You can mix several different kinds of matter together and then unmix them. You can make one kind of matter seem to disappear by dissolving it in another kind of matter. You can evaporate matter. You can burn it. But there's one thing you can't do to matter—you can't destroy it. The total amount of matter that exists doesn't change. ■

UNIT PROJECT LINK

Ask your teacher for some disappearing ink. For each Matter Mystery you displayed, write the answer on a card in this ink. (The ink will become invisible when it dries.) Invite visitors to answer your Matter Mysteries. When everyone is ready, ask your teacher to make the answers on the cards visible.

Technology Link
For more help with your Unit Project, go to www.eduplace.com.

Get the Picture?

Reading Focus What are the chemical changes that occur, in order, when you take a photograph?

How does the film in a camera work? Many chemical changes are needed to transform a roll of film in a camera to a handful of photographs. The film for taking black-and-white photographs is coated with a thin layer that contains two compounds—silver chloride (klôr′īd) and silver bromide (brō′mīd). These compounds change when light strikes them.

The following paragraphs explain the main steps in making a photograph. Notice the numbers in the red circles. As you read, look at the picture on the next page that has the matching number.

Taking the Picture

Think of some subject you want to take a picture of. Some parts of the subject will be darker than others. For example, shadows will be darker than brightly lighted areas. Black objects will be darker than white ones. So your camera receives different amounts of light from these bright and dark areas.

❶ When you click your camera, light from the subject passes through the camera lens and strikes the film. The light causes the silver compounds on the film to change. This change can't be seen until the film is developed.

The parts of the film that receive bright light turn very dark. The parts of the film that receive only weak light turn gray. The parts that receive no light remain unchanged.

The Film and Photo

❷ The film is developed by treating it with a solution. The picture, or image, that forms on the developed film is a "reverse" picture, called a negative (neg′ə tiv). Light parts are dark and dark parts are light on the negative.

B59

3 The negative is placed on photographic paper. Like the film, this paper also contains a coating of silver compounds. When light strikes the paper, a black-and-white image of your subject is produced.

4 The paper is then developed into a black-and-white photograph that shows the subject you photographed. As you can see, it takes chemical changes to change film in a camera into a photograph. Get the picture? ■

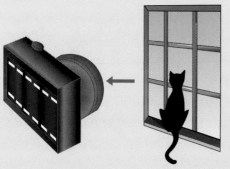

1 Light from the subject passes through the camera lens and strikes the film.

2 After being developed, the film is a negative. Light parts are dark, and dark parts are light.

3 To make a print, the negative is placed on a piece of photographic paper. Light is shined through the negative onto the paper.

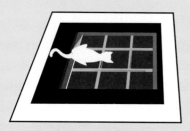

4 When the photographic paper is developed, a black-and-white print remains. The print looks exactly like the subject.

INVESTIGATION 2 WRAP-UP

REVIEW

1. Which produces a different kind of matter, a physical change or a chemical change?

2. Give one example of a chemical change.

CRITICAL THINKING

3. How is the burning of paper like the rusting of iron? How are the two changes different?

4. You sharpen a pencil. Then you throw the pencil shavings in the fireplace and burn them. Describe the different ways the wood changes.

REFLECT & EVALUATE

Word Power

Write the letter of the term that best matches the definition. *Not all terms will be used.*

1. The process in which one or more substances are changed into one or more different substances

2. A mixture in which particles of different substances are mixed evenly throughout

3. Any change in matter that results in one or more different kinds of matter forming

4. Matter made up of two or more different substances

5. A change in the size, shape, or state of matter with no new matter being formed

a. chemical change
b. chemical properties
c. chemical reaction
d. mixture
e. physical change
f. solution

Check What You Know

Write the term in each pair that best completes each sentence.

1. A change in state is a (physical change, chemical change).

2. Most matter (expands, contracts) when it is heated.

3. One example of a chemical change is (rusting iron, melting ice cream).

4. Matter cannot be (changed, destroyed).

Problem Solving

1. How is the melting of an ice cube similar to the grinding of chalk into a powder? How are the two changes different?

2. You have a mixture of sand and sugar. Suggest a method for separating this mixture into its parts.

3. A carpenter installs a cast-iron railing for your front steps. Why is it a good idea to paint the railing as soon as possible?

Study the photographs of an egg before and after being cooked. Write a paragraph that describes the physical and chemical changes that occurred.

Cause and Effect

When you read, it is important to figure out what happens and why it happens. What makes things happen is called the *cause*. What happens is called the *effect*.

Read the paragraphs. Then complete the exercises that follow.

> **Use these hints to determine cause and effect.**
>
> • Look for signal words: *because, and so, as a result*
>
> • As you read, ask yourself why something is happening.

What Is Energy?

Energy is defined in several different ways. One definition of **energy** is "the ability to cause change." Change often involves movement. It takes energy to change motion. For example, to make your bike start to move, you push on the pedals. You use energy to move the bike (and yourself) from place to place.

Energy is also needed to change how fast something is moving. Suppose you want to make your bike go faster. You have to use more energy to pedal harder. You even have to use energy to make the bike slow down and stop.

Copy each statement. Write *C* in the blank after each cause. Write *E* in the blank after each effect.

1. To make your bike move ——, you push on the pedals ——.

2. You use energy —— to move the bike from place to place ——.

3. Suppose you want to make your bike go faster ——. You have to use more energy to pedal harder ——.

4. You even have to use energy —— to make the bike stop ——.

Using Math Volume

Volume is the amount of space something takes up. You can measure the volume of both liquids and solids.

You can measure the volume of liquids by using liters (L) and milliliters (mL).

$1L = 1,000$ mL

1 liter

Use these containers to answer the questions that follow.

A B C D E

1. Which container has about 750 mL of water in it?

2. What fraction tells how much water is in container *C*?

You can measure the volume of solids by using cubic units.

Volume = length $\times$ width $\times$ height

$3 \times 3 \times 3 = 27$

The volume of the cube is 27 cubic centimeters (cm³).

3 cm
3 cm
3 cm

Find the volume of each in cubic centimeters.

3.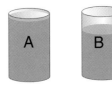

4 cm
6 cm
4 cm

4.

1 m
1 m
1 m

5.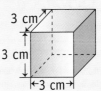

10 cm
5 cm
5 cm

6. These containers hold the same amount of liquid. Explain.

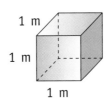

3 cm
3 cm
4 cm

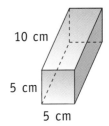

3 cm
2 cm
6 cm

B63

WRAP-UP!

**UNIT B**

On your own, use scientific methods to investigate a question about the properties of matter.

THINK LIKE A SCIENTIST

Ask a Question

Pose a question about the properties of matter that you would like to investigate. For example, ask, "How does the temperature of a liquid affect how fast the liquid flows?"

Make a Hypothesis

Suggest a hypothesis that is a possible answer to the question. One hypothesis is that raising the temperature of a liquid will cause the liquid to flow more rapidly.

Plan and Do a Test

Plan a controlled experiment to find the effect of temperature on how fast a liquid flows. You could start with goggles, two clear plastic cups, a timer with a second hand, and a plastic bottle of cold liquid. Develop a procedure that uses these materials to test the hypothesis. With permission, carry out your experiment. Follow the safety guidelines on pages S14–S15.

Record and Analyze

Observe carefully and record your data accurately. Make repeated observations.

Draw Conclusions

Look for evidence to support the hypothesis or to show that it is false. Draw conclusions about the hypothesis. Repeat the experiment to verify the results.

WRITING IN SCIENCE
Research Report

Research information about new materials that are being developed by chemists. Find out how the materials will be used. Follow these guidelines to write your research report.

• State the topic you are researching.

• Summarize several articles on that topic.

• Write a statement that sums up your findings.

Classifying Living Things

Theme: Systems

THINK LIKE A SCIENTIST
SCHOOL'S OUT C2

CHAPTER 1

All Kinds of Living Things C4

Investigation 1   How Can Living Things Be Classified? . . .C6
Investigation 2   How Do Vertebrates Differ? C16
Investigation 3   How Do the Groups of
Invertebrates Differ? C24
Investigation 4   How Are Plants Classified? C32

CHAPTER 2

The Survival of Living Things C40

Investigation 1   What Are the Basic Needs of
Living Things? C42
Investigation 2   How Do Living Things Meet
Their Needs? .C50

Using Reading Skills C62
Using Math Skills C63
Unit Wrap-up! C64

THINK LIKE A SCIENTIST

SCHOOL'S OUT

Fish, such as this school of brightly colored fairy basslets, are just one of the many kinds of living things in the world. Scientists who study living things observe their traits, or characteristics. These traits are used by scientists to classify living things. And by classifying living things, scientists can study them more easily and can learn how living things meet their basic needs.

THINK LIKE A SCIENTIST

Questioning In this unit you'll study fish and many other living things. You'll investigate questions such as these.

- How Can Living Things Be Classified?
- How Do Living Things Meet Their Needs?

Observing, Testing, Hypothesizing In the Activity "Animals Are Different," you'll make observations about the traits of three different animals. You'll also infer how body parts help each animal survive.

Researching In the Resource "Variety of Life on Earth," you'll gather more information about how animals and other living things are classified.

Drawing Conclusions After you've completed your investigations, you'll draw conclusions about what you've learned—and get new ideas.

ALL KINDS OF LIVING THINGS

What's your favorite plant or animal? Are there other plants or animals that are similar to it? In this chapter you'll learn about many kinds of living things. As you explore, think about ways that living things are similar and different.

PEOPLE USING SCIENCE

Field Biologist You may have seen a macaw (mə kô′) at the zoo, a pet store, or in someone's home. These large parrots live in the tropical rain forests of South America. Macaws nest in trees more than 31 m (100 ft) off the ground. Eduardo Nycander is a field biologist. He studies wild macaws at a research station in the Amazon forest of Peru. He discovered that macaws have a hard time finding hollow tree trunks that can serve as suitable places to build nests.

Eduardo Nycander now works at providing macaws with plastic nests. The nests are hollow tubes about 35.6 cm (14 in.) wide and 2.4 m (8 ft) long. Nycander climbs high above the ground and straps the nests to the tree trunks. The birds love them! The nests look like hollow tree trunks. What would you ask Eduardo Nycander about his work?

Coming Up

INVESTIGATION **1**

HOW CAN LIVING THINGS BE CLASSIFIED?
.... C6

INVESTIGATION **2**

HOW DO VERTEBRATES DIFFER?
.... C16

INVESTIGATION **3**

HOW DO THE GROUPS OF INVERTEBRATES DIFFER?
.... C24

INVESTIGATION **4**

HOW ARE PLANTS CLASSIFIED?
.... C32

◀ Field biologist Eduardo Nycander checks on a macaw chick 31 m (100 ft) above the ground.

How Can Living Things Be Classified?

Suppose you made a list of all the living things that you could think of. How would you classify them to make it easy to study them? Find out in this investigation how scientists classify living things.

Activity

Animals Are Different

Which animal is a cat more like—a catfish or a dog? How would you decide? In this activity you'll make observations that could be used to classify animals.

Procedure

1. Your teacher will give your group three different animals to observe. As you observe the animals, look for ways that they are alike and ways that they are different.

MATERIALS
- hand lens
- 3 animals for observation
- *Science Notebook*

SAFETY //////
Do not touch the animals unless you have your teacher's permission.

Step 1

2. In your *Science Notebook*, **make a chart** like the one shown below. Add as many different traits, or characteristics, as you can think of. **Record** your observations under the column for each animal.

Traits	Animal 1	Animal 2	Animal 3
How It Moves			
Type of Body Covering			
Number of Legs/Description			
Number of Eyes			
Number of Ears			
Where It Might Live			

Step 4

3. **Record** the ways you think these living things are alike and the ways they are different.

4. You may want to use a hand lens to **observe** some animals more closely. **Record** any further observations you make. **Infer** where each animal might live and **record** your inference.

 See **SCIENCE** and **MATH TOOLBOX** *page H2 if you need to review Using a Hand Lens.*

Analyze and Conclude

1. Are there any traits that all the animals share? If so, what are they?

2. **Infer** how each animal's body parts help it survive.

3. **Infer** which of the animals might have a backbone. Give reasons for your inferences.

Variety of Life on Earth

Reading Focus Into what large groups can organisms be classified?

How many kinds of living things could there be on Earth—hundreds? thousands? The answer is millions! Millions of kinds of **organisms** (ôr′gə niz əmz), or living things, exist on Earth.

Living things can be found in oceans, forests, deserts, mountains, soil, air—almost everywhere on Earth. And incredibly, many scientists classify, or group, all organisms into just five large groups, called kingdoms.

Organisms placed in the same kingdom share certain traits, or characteristics. Scientists use the

different traits of living things to classify them. The number of cells, the basic units that make up all organisms, is just one trait used to classify living things. Other traits include life processes, such as how an organism gets food or reproduces. Study the table and the pictures on the next page to see the general traits shared by living things in each kingdom.

How many kinds of living things can you find in this picture? ▼

Kingdoms of Living Things

Kingdom	Examples	Traits
Animal	horse, dog, bird, fish, spider, worm, starfish, coral	• many-celled • most have structures for moving from place to place • feed on other organisms • reproduce by eggs or live birth
Plant	pine tree, cactus, tulip, tomato, ivy, maple tree	• many-celled • no structures for moving from place to place • make their own food • reproduce by seeds or spores
Fungus	yeast, slime mold, mushroom, mold	• many-celled; some one-celled • most don't have structures for moving from place to place • absorb food from other organisms
Protist	amoeba, paramecium, diatom, algae	• most one-celled; some many-celled • can make their own food or feed on other organisms • some have structures for moving from place to place
Moneran	bacteria	• very simple cells • some make their own food; some feed on other organisms • some have structures for moving from place to place

ANIMAL KINGDOM   The clownfish and the orangutan look very different from one another. But they are both members of the animal kingdom. Like most kinds of animals, they move from place to place, often in search of food.

▼ orangutan

▲ clownfish

PLANT KINGDOM   The largest members of the plant kingdom are trees. Trees, like other plants, use the Sun's energy to make food in their leaves. An oak tree can produce over a million leaves in a single year!

oak tree ▶

FUNGUS KINGDOM   You might think these mushrooms look like plants, but they're not plants. They belong to a different kingdom— the fungus kingdom. Unlike plants, mushrooms can't make their own food. Most mushrooms get their food from the dead plant material on which they grow.

mushroom ▶

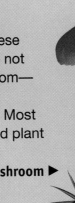

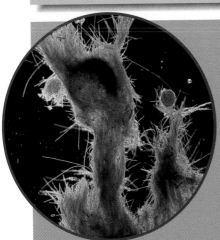

▲ paramecium

PROTIST KINGDOM   A paramecium is a member of the protist kingdom. Like most other protists, the paramecium is made up of one cell and so is micro- scopic. Some protists have structures for moving from place to place. The paramecium has hairlike parts that pull it through the water.

paramecium in pond water ▶

MONERAN KINGDOM   Bacteria belong to the moneran (mə-nir'ən) kingdom. Unlike other monerans, blue-green bacteria make their own food. All moner- ans are made up of one cell.

bacteria cells that form a chain ▶

▲ blue-green bacteria

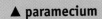

Internet Field Trip

Visit **www.eduplace.com** to learn more about how living things are classified.

Classifying— Past and Present

Reading Focus How has the way people classify living things changed since ancient times?

For over 3,000 years, scientists have looked for traits that would relate living things to one another. From about 350 B.C. to the mid-1900s, most scientists were content to classify organisms into just two groups—plants and animals.

But as science has advanced over the years, so have ideas about classifying organisms. The time line tells about a few of the people throughout history who have invented classification systems. Scientists continue to change classification systems as they learn more about living things.

Georges Cuvier classifies everything that can move from place to place on its own as a member of the animal kingdom.

1812

Aristotle, a scientist and teacher in ancient Greece, invents a system that places living things in two groups—plants and animals.

350 B.C.

1750s

Carolus Linnaeus, a Swedish scientist, develops a system for naming organisms that is still used today. He is known as the Father of Modern Classification.

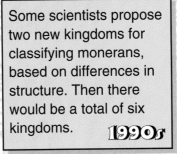

Some scientists propose two new kingdoms for classifying monerans, based on differences in structure. Then there would be a total of six kingdoms. **1990s**

Leon Roddy, an African American scientist, classifies more than 6,000 spiders and becomes a world expert on this group of animals. **1960s**

1988

Lynn Margulis, an American scientist, suggests a protoctist (prə tōk′tist) kingdom to replace the protist kingdom. This larger kingdom includes the protists as well as many-celled organisms that don't fit in the other four kingdoms. This system is not yet widely accepted.

1959

Robert Whittaker, an American professor of biology, introduces the five-kingdom classification system that is widely used today.

UNIT PROJECT LINK

For this Unit Project you will make a field guide to local plants or animals. With your group, choose the plants or animals to include. Find out information about each one. You might contact your state's Department of Natural Resources for help. Then put the information you gather in your field guide.

TechnologyLink

For more help with your Unit Project, go to **www.eduplace.com**.

Classification of Animals

Reading Focus Into what two groups are all animals classified, and how are the groups alike and different?

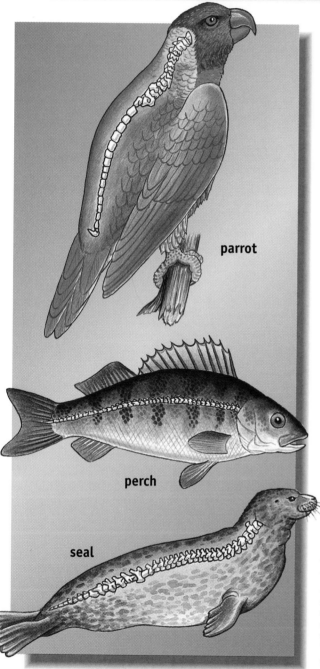

parrot

perch

seal

▲ **Examples of vertebrates**

Each organism in the animal kingdom moves on its own, is large enough to be seen without a microscope, gets its own food, and produces young. These few traits are common to all animals. The activity on pages C6 and C7 shows that different kinds of animals can have different traits. For this reason, scientists have further classified animals into smaller groups within the animal kingdom.

Who Has a Backbone?

Animals that have backbones make up one group. You can feel the knobs of your backbone down the center of your back. Each knob is part of a separate bone. Each bone that makes up the backbone is called a **vertebra**. Animals that have backbones are called **vertebrates** (vur'tə brits).

Vertebrates include many different kinds of animals. They can be found just about anywhere—in oceans, rivers, forests, mountains, and deserts. Horses, hippos, cats, birds, snakes, lizards, frogs, and fish are all vertebrates. All vertebrates have one thing in common—a backbone.

Life Without a Backbone

The members of many different animal groups don't have backbones. Animals that don't have backbones are called **invertebrates**. In fact, 97 percent of the animal kingdom is made up of invertebrates! They include some of the smallest animals, such as spiders, mites, and insects. Some invertebrates can be found in ponds, oceans, and other water environments where they can move about easily. Others have no trouble moving about on land or in the air.

Insects and some other invertebrates have exoskeletons (eks ō-skel'ə tənz). An **exoskeleton** is a hard outer covering that protects an animal's body and gives it support.

The animals within each of the major groups of the animal kingdom have many different traits. These major animal groups, then, are classified into even smaller groups. These groups are based on traits that the animals within the groups share. ■

Examples of invertebrates ▼

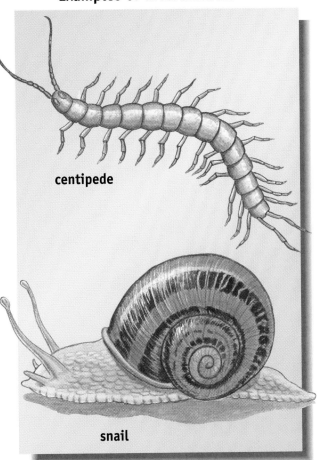

centipede

snail

INVESTIGATION 1 WRAP-UP

REVIEW

1. Name three kingdoms of living things. Name one organism that belongs to each kingdom.

2. Which group makes up most of the animal kingdom, vertebrates or invertebrates?

CRITICAL THINKING

3. An organism has no structures for moving from place to place. It makes its own food, and it reproduces by seeds. In what kingdom would you place this organism? Explain your answer.

4. As you pet a dog, you feel hard knobs along its back. What are these knobs? Based on this feature, into what group of animals would you classify the dog? Explain your answer.

INVESTIGATION 2

HOW DO VERTEBRATES DIFFER?

A backbone, two eyes, and one mouth are some traits shared by a snake, a cat, and a human. But you probably can name many more ways in which snakes, cats, and people are different. In Investigation 2 you'll explore ways that vertebrates differ.

Activity

Cold Fish

How is the way a fish breathes different from the way you breathe? Find out what change might make a fish breathe faster or slower.

Procedure

1. In your *Science Notebook*, **make a chart** like the one shown.

	Water Temperature	Breathing Rate
First reading		
Two minutes after ice cubes were added		

2. Your teacher will give your group a plastic jar with a goldfish in it. Use a thermometer to **measure** the temperature of the water. **Record** the temperature in your chart.

3. **Observe** two flaps behind the fish's eyes. Under the flaps are **gills**, which help the fish "breathe." The flaps open and close once with each breath. **Count** and **record** the number of breaths the fish takes in one minute. Repeat your counting several times. Then find the average of your results.

See **SCIENCE** and **MATH TOOLBOX** page H5 if you need to review **Finding an Average**.

Step 5

4. **Predict** how the number of times the flaps open and close in one minute will change if ice cubes are added to the water. **Record** your prediction. Gently place two or three ice cubes in the water in the jar.

5. Wait two minutes. Then **measure** the temperature of the water again. **Count** the number of times the flaps open and close in one minute. **Record** your observations. Repeat your counting several times and find the average. Remove the ice.

Analyze and Conclude

1. How does the temperature of the water affect how the fish breathes? **Compare** your results with your prediction.

2. Think about what happens when you go outside in very cold weather. Does your breathing rate change when you go from warm air into cold air? **Draw a conclusion** about how you are different from a fish, in terms of breathing.

Technology Link
CD-ROM

INVESTIGATE FURTHER!

Use the **Science Processor CD-ROM**, *Animals* (Investigation 2, Skin and Bones) to explore how the skeletons of fish, mammals, birds, reptiles, and amphibians are alike. Watch a video about how a backbone is useful. Learn about the body temperatures of different groups of animals.

Swim, Leap, and Slither

> **Reading Focus** What traits are used to classify a vertebrate as a fish, an amphibian, or a reptile?

Has anyone ever told you that you're one in a million? Actually, as a vertebrate, you're one in several thousand. Vertebrates can be sorted into smaller groups, classified by traits that they have in common. Fish, amphibians (am fib′ē ənz), and reptiles are three of these groups.

Fish Tales

Did you know that fish are the largest group of vertebrates? There are more than 30,000 different kinds of fish in all. They come in many sizes and shapes, from the tiny minnow to the great white shark.

Many vertebrates that live in water are classified as **fish**. Most fish have body temperatures that vary with the temperature of the environment.

Most fish also have fins that help them steer and balance in the water. The feathery parts on the side of a fish's head are called **gills**. Water flows over the gills and allows the fish to "breathe" underwater. Many fish are covered with scales. Scales, which are hard, help protect fish.

Fish are vertebrates that live in water. ▶

Slippery Amphibians

There are almost 4,000 varieties of frogs, toads, salamanders, and other amphibians. An **amphibian** is a vertebrate that usually lives in water after hatching from an egg, but as an adult can live on land. The body temperature of an amphibian varies with the temperature of its surroundings. On land, amphibians live in wet environments. Some amphibians have smooth, moist skin, which makes them look and feel slippery.

Amphibians hatch from jelly-coated eggs. Their young usually do not look anything like the parents. Young amphibians start life with gills and breathe like fish. They even have tails that help them swim.

As they get older, amphibians grow legs and lose their gills. Adult amphibians breathe air with lungs. Frogs and toads lose their tails as adults, but salamanders keep theirs.

Using Math *A wood frog develops from a tadpole in about 77 days. How many weeks is that?*

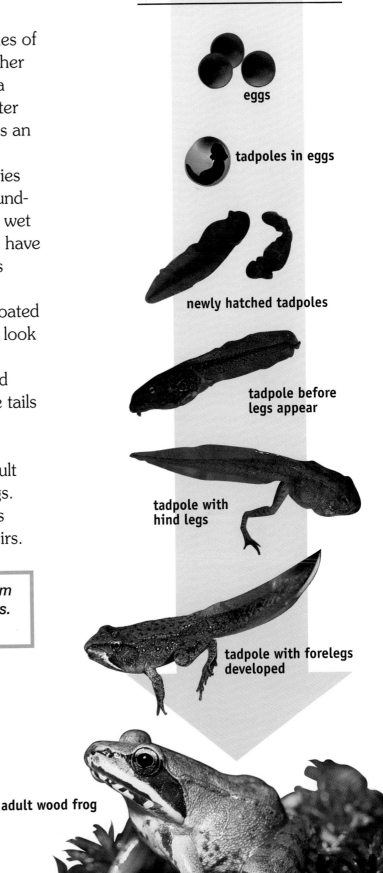

THE DEVELOPMENT OF A FROG

eggs

tadpoles in eggs

newly hatched tadpoles

tadpole before legs appear

tadpole with hind legs

tadpole with forelegs developed

adult wood frog

Variety Is the Spice of Reptile Life

Reptiles have some features that differ from those of amphibians and fish. A **reptile** is a vertebrate that has dry, scaly skin and lays eggs that have a leathery shell. All reptiles lay their eggs on land, and all breathe air. Like fish and amphibians, reptiles have body temperatures that vary with the temperature of the environment.

Reptiles include animals as large as the Nile crocodile, 5.5 m (18 ft) long. They also include animals as small as the bog turtle, 10 cm (4 in.) long. Reptiles live in hot, dry deserts and in warm, wet tropical rain forests.

These animals vary in other ways as well. They may move as quickly as a rattlesnake or as slowly as a tortoise. Snakes are reptiles that slither. Some turtles swim underwater. Reptiles may or may not have tails or even legs. Lizards and snakes are able to shed their skins, and chameleons can change colors!

Fish, amphibians, and reptiles have some very different features. But these vertebrates all have one thing in common—a backbone! ■

A crocodile is a reptile. ▼

▲ Jackson's chameleon

Fly, Dive, and Gallop

Reading Focus What traits are used to classify a vertebrate as a bird or a mammal?

Besides fish, amphibians, and reptiles, there are two other groups of vertebrates with some very different traits. These are the birds and the mammals.

To Fly Like a Bird

There are about 9,000 types of birds in the world. **Birds** are vertebrates that have wings and are covered with feathers. These vertebrates lay hard-shelled eggs, which hatch in their nests. Birds range in size from the very small hummingbird, no bigger than your finger, to the large ostrich, taller than an adult human.

A bird's skeleton is very light in weight. Its bones are hollow. Having hollow bones helps to make the bird light enough to fly through the air. The fastest of all birds is the white-throated spinetail swift. This little bird can fly over 160 km/h (100 mph)!

◄ A bird's hollow bone

No matter their size, their color, or where they live, all birds have feathers covering their bodies. No other group of animals has this feature.

A scarlet macaw ▼

▲ A close-up view of a macaw's feathers

C21

Using Math *A baby whale can drink 11 L (3 gal) of milk in less than five minutes. About how much milk is that in one minute?*

Our Group, the Mammals

Do you remember your first meal? It was milk, and it probably made you stop crying. Vertebrates that feed milk to their young and have hair or fur are called **mammals**. The young of most mammals grow inside the mother. When they have developed enough, the young are born live. But the young of the duckbill platypus, also a mammal, are not born live. Instead, they hatch from eggs.

You may not have realized that mammals include a wide range of animals. Apes, lions, hippos, dogs, elephants, kangaroos, squirrels, cats, pigs, bats, horses, rabbits, and even whales are all mammals. They're mammals because they all have hair or fur and feed milk to their young.

◀ A squirrel is a mammal that can live in a city.

Most mammals have furry coats. Hair or fur traps a layer of air near the body, which helps the mammal stay warm. Humans don't have as much hair as other mammals. So wearing clothes helps people stay warm.

There are many different kinds of mammals in the world around you. The next time you watch a squirrel scramble up a tree or find a raccoon in your trash, remember that they're mammals, just as you are! ■

▲ The timber wolf pup will get a thicker coat of fur as it grows.

INVESTIGATION 2 WRAP-UP

REVIEW

1. What are the five groups of vertebrates? Name one animal that belongs to each group.

2. Give the traits of any two groups of vertebrates.

CRITICAL THINKING

3. Animal *A*, at a zoo where you work, comes from a rain forest. Animal *B* comes from a desert. Both lay eggs that do not have hard shells. Their body temperature varies with the temperature of the environment. To what vertebrate section of the zoo should you assign each animal?

4. Compare a salmon, a penguin, and a whale.

HOW DO THE GROUPS OF INVERTEBRATES DIFFER?

You learned that many animals don't have a backbone supporting their body. How are these animals without backbones grouped? Find out in this investigation.

Activity

Worming Their Way Home

Earthworms have no backbone and no eyes. How do you think these animals find their way around? How do they know when they are in their "home" environment? After doing this activity, you'll know how.

MATERIALS

- goggles
- cardboard box
- dry soil
- damp soil
- sand
- dry leaves or shredded newspaper
- hand lens
- earthworm
- timer
- *Science Notebook*

SAFETY

Wear goggles. Wash your hands when you have finished.

Procedure

1. Mark off four sections inside a cardboard box. Label the sections 1 through 4, as shown.

2. Place each material in a different section of the box, as shown in the diagram.

3. Remove the earthworm from its container and gently place it in section 1 of the box. With your group, **predict** which numbered section the worm will move toward. **Record** your prediction in your *Science Notebook*.

	Step 1
1 newspaper	2 dry soil
3 damp soil	4 sand

Step 4

4. Using a hand lens, observe the location of the worm each minute for ten minutes. Also observe how it uses its body parts to move. Record your observations. When you finish observing the worm, gently place it back in its container.

See SCIENCE and MATH TOOLBOX page H2 if you need to review *Using a Hand Lens*.

Analyze and Conclude

1. Into which sections did the worm move during the ten minutes? Which materials are in those sections? Where did the worm spend the most time? the least time?

2. Describe how the worm used its body parts to move.

3. Compare your results with your predictions. Infer the kind of environment earthworms like best.

INVESTIGATE FURTHER!

RESEARCH

Some people are using earthworms to recycle trash. Find out how worms are able to turn trash like paper into a useful material called compost.

Lifesaving Leeches

Reading Focus How were leeches once used, and how are they used today?

It may be brown, black, or covered with colored spots and stripes. It has 32 body segments and can grow as long as 45 cm (18 in.). What is it? It's an invertebrate called a leech. It feeds on the blood of other animals.

Doctors of the 1800s often used leeches to treat sick people. They believed that removing blood from a patient would help cure the patient's disease.

Today leeches have a different kind of role. Scientists have found that chemicals in the saliva of a leech can prevent blood clots. Blood clots can cause a heart attack or a stroke. Scientists hope that the use of leeches will help prevent these life-threatening events.

Scientists have also found that damaged nerves in a leech can re-grow. By studying leeches, scientists may increase their understanding of nerves in humans.

In the past, people used leeches to cure almost any illness. ▼

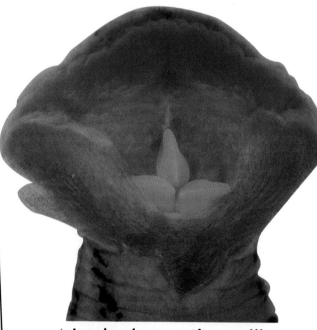

▲ Leeches have suction-cuplike mouths. They use their pointed teeth to attach themselves to another animal. Then they feed on its blood.

Nothing Much in Common

Reading Focus What are the traits of some groups of invertebrates?

Some tumble along the ocean floor. Others glide through the water. Some burrow into the soil. Others fly through the air. The groups of animals without backbones are very different from one another. From spikes and soft bodies to claws and hard shells, you'll see how different some of these groups are.

Sponges

In the ocean you might mistake some animals for plants. Sponges are one group of invertebrates that look like plants. That's because they stay fixed in one place—on a rock, for example. Sponges are animals that have bodies full of holes and skeletons made of spiky fibers.

If a sponge can't move around, how does it catch a meal? Water flows through the holes of a sponge. Small pieces of food in the moving water become trapped in the sponge.

These animals, called sponges, ▶
look like plants. The holes in
a sponge (*inset*) trap food
for the animal.

C27

Corals, Hydras, and Jellyfish

Corals may also look like plants, but they belong to another group of invertebrates. The animals in this group have soft, tubelike bodies with a single opening surrounded by armlike parts called tentacles. At night, corals feed by catching tiny animals in their tentacles.

Sea anemones (ə nem'ə nēz) and hydras also belong to this group. Sea anemones have tentacles that may look like the petals of a flower. But unlike flowers, sea anemones can move from place to place, gliding or tumbling along the ocean floor. Hydras are much smaller animals, with lengths of about 1 cm (0.4 in.). Like the larger animals in their group, hydras use their tentacles to trap food.

Jellyfish are part of the group that includes corals, sea anemones, and

▲ **Featherworm, a segmented worm that lives in the ocean**

hydras. If you've ever gone to the seashore, you may have seen jellyfish floating in the water or washed up on the sand. As a jellyfish drifts through the ocean, it catches shrimp, fish, and other animals in its tentacles.

Worms of Different Shapes

Worms are tube-shaped invertebrates. They can be found in both land and water environments. Worms are classified into groups by their body designs.

Although they may not look as if they belong, corals are members of the animal kingdom. ▼

Jellyfish shoot tiny poison darts from their tentacles to paralyze or kill their prey. ▼

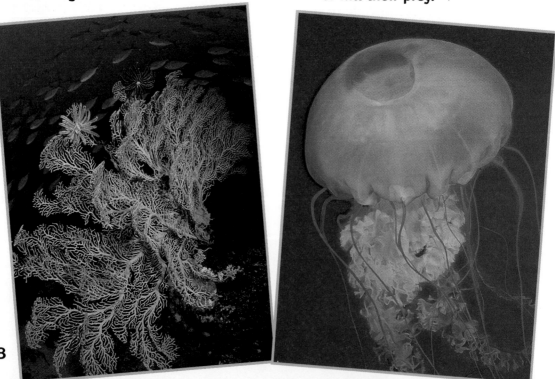

▲ Flatworm

▲ Roundworms

Flatworms are a group of worms that have heads and tails, and flattened bodies. A tapeworm is a flatworm that can live inside the body of other animals—even humans!

Roundworms are another group of worms. As you might guess, these worms have rounded bodies. They live in damp places and can also live inside humans and other animals. Both flatworms and roundworms can make people and other animals sick.

Another worm group, called the segmented worms, includes leeches and earthworms. The observation of the earthworm in the activity on pages C24 and C25 shows that an earthworm's body is divided into segments, or sections. All earthworms and other worms in this group have bodies made up of segments.

The earthworm activity also shows that the earthworm prefers burrowing through moist soil. In such a dark, damp environment, the earthworm can move easily and can keep from drying out.

Starfish and Sea Urchins

A starfish is an odd-looking underwater animal. It belongs to a group of invertebrates that have many tiny tube feet. Animals in this group have body parts arranged around a central area. The starfish shown has five arms and no head! It's hard spiny covering helps to give the animal protection.

The sea urchin belongs to the same group as the starfish. A sea urchin's body is covered with long spines. Like a starfish, it moves around on tiny tube feet.

Using Math *A starfish, such as the one shown here, can move over the sea floor at a rate of 10 cm (4 in.) per second. How far is that in one minute?*

Shells Outside or Inside

The mollusks make up another group of invertebrates. A mollusk has a soft body, a hard shell, a rough tongue, and a muscular foot. A snail is a mollusk with a single hard shell protecting its soft body. A clam has two shells joined together by a hinge.

Squids and octopuses also belong to this group. But their hard shells are small and *inside* their bodies.

Lobsters to Butterflies

Arthropods are a group of invertebrates with jointed legs and hard exoskeletons that protect the animals. There are nearly 1 million known kinds of arthropods!

As an arthropod grows, it **molts**, or sheds its old exoskeleton. Then the animal grows a new, larger exoskeleton that allows its body to continue growing. A lobster is an arthropod with a thick exoskeleton.

Insects make up the largest subgroup in the arthropod group and include the only invertebrates that can fly. Insects, such as ladybugs, have bodies divided into three parts, and six legs arranged in three pairs. Most insects have two pairs of wings.

Like other arthropods, spiders have jointed legs. But spiders are *not* insects. Spiders have eight legs—two more legs than insects. They also have jaws and fangs!

◀ **An octopus is a mollusk.**

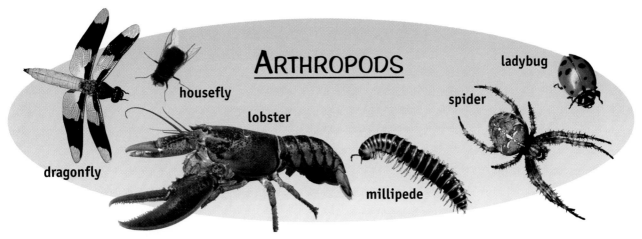

ARTHROPODS

dragonfly

housefly

lobster

millipede

spider

ladybug

Centipedes and millipedes are also arthropods. But they are not insects either. Centipedes can have up to 175 pairs of legs. They can use their many legs to run from enemies.

Millipedes can have up to 240 pairs of legs! But unlike centipedes, they don't use their legs to run from enemies. Instead, millipedes roll up their bodies when they sense danger approaching.

As you can now see, some of the groups of invertebrates are very different indeed. A sponge is very different from an arthropod. And a worm is very different from a jellyfish. But there is one way in which they are all alike—they have no backbone. ■

▲ **Arthropods can look very different from each other.**

UNIT PROJECT LINK

Make a drawing (or use a camera to take photos) of plants or animals for your field guide. Think about ways you can classify the plants or animals. How might you organize the descriptions and pictures in your guide?

Technology Link

For more help with your Unit Project, go to **www.eduplace.com**.

INVESTIGATION 3 WRAP-UP

REVIEW

1. What are eight of the groups of invertebrates? Name one animal that belongs to each group.

2. Give the traits of two groups of invertebrates.

CRITICAL THINKING

3. How could you use a mirror on this page to show that a spider has symmetry—that one half matches the other?

4. Normally, clotting stops bleeding. Suppose you have cut your finger badly. Might leeches play a role in helping stop the bleeding? Explain your answer.

INVESTIGATION 4

HOW ARE PLANTS CLASSIFIED?

From an airplane high in the sky, a forest looks like just a sea of green. But up close, you can see that the forest is made up of many different plants. How are all these different plants classified?

Activity
Looking at Leaves

What traits can you use to classify plants? In this activity you'll classify plants according to their leaves.

Procedure

1. With your teacher's permission, go outdoors with a partner to **observe** the variety of plants.

2. Look at the trees, shrubs, flowering plants, and nonflowering plants. Choose five very different plants to examine closely. **Observe** the whole plant.

3. On a separate sheet of paper, draw each plant and one of its leaves. Place the drawings for each plant in a separate plastic bag. Label the bags 1–5.

4. Carefully remove a small sample of leaves from each plant. Place each sample in the bag with its drawings. Seal each bag. Take your samples back to class.

5. **Observe** the leaves on the plants you chose. Are the leaves needlelike or are they broad leaves that drop in autumn? Are their veins branched or do they run side by side down the length of the leaf? In your *Science Notebook*, make a chart like the one shown. **Record** your observations in the chart. Write each plant's name if you know it.

INVESTIGATE FURTHER!

RESEARCH

Use field guides to plants that are written for your region of the country. Try to identify the names of the plants you classified in the activity.

Classifying Leaves		
Bag	Leaf Characteristics	Group Name
1		

 See **SCIENCE** and **MATH TOOLBOX** *page H10 if you need to review **Making a Chart to Organize Data**.*

Analyze and Conclude

1. Look at the information in the "Leaf Characteristics and Classification" table. Use the table to **classify** each plant you chose as one of the major plant groups. **Record** your classification in your chart.

2. **Compare** your conclusions with those of other groups. **Discuss** any differences in the way the plants were classified.

3. Which plant group is most common? Are there any plant groups you did not find examples of? If so, **infer** why.

Step 5

Plants to the Rescue

Reading Focus What are some ways that plants can be useful in the field of medicine?

SCIENCE
TECHNOLOGY
& SOCIETY

Who usually answers a call for help? It might be a fire department or police department. It might be a paramedic or lifeguard. Would you ever expect it to be a plant?

You probably already know some ways that plants are used to help people. For example, plants are used to make clothing and shelter. And without plants, there would be no food. But did you know that plants are the source of most medicine?

Today, scientists search the world over for more plants used as medicine. The discovery of new medicines from plants is a costly business. But the business of healing is very important.

PLANTS USED FOR HEALING

GINKGO The leaves of the ginkgo tree are thought to help in treating Alzheimer's (älts'hī mərz) disease. This disease affects the way brain cells function. Ginkgo leaves are also believed to help relieve hearing loss, headaches, and asthma.

GINGER The root of this plant was used as long ago as the 16th century to settle upset stomachs. It has also been used for colds and flu.

PACIFIC YEW In the 1960s, scientists found a cancer-killing drug in the bark of the Pacific yew tree.

CHILIES Scientists have found that these peppers send signals to the brain to kill pain. Today a cream made from chilies is used to "rub out" pain.

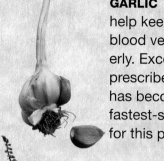

GARLIC Garlic is used to help keep the heart and the blood vessels working properly. Except for medicines prescribed by doctors, garlic has become one of Europe's fastest-selling "medicines" for this purpose.

FOXGLOVE The medicine digitalis, from the foxglove plant, is used to stimulate the heart.

All Kinds of Plants

Reading Focus What traits are used to classify the members of the plant kingdom?

All plants are members of the plant kingdom. The family tree of the plant kingdom on this page shows that all plants are related. But in the activity on pages C32 and C33, different types of plants are shown to have different traits. Scientists use such differences to classify plants. For example, they divide the plant kingdom into two major groups: nonseed plants and seed plants. **Nonseed plants** do not reproduce with seeds. This group includes mosses and ferns. **Seed plants** do reproduce with seeds. This group includes plants that have flowers or cones.

Mosses and Liverworts

If you walk through a forest, you may notice a spongy carpet underfoot. This carpet is formed of mosses. **Mosses** are small nonseed plants that lack true roots, stems, and leaves.

Like other nonseed plants, mosses can reproduce by means of spores. Spores are one-celled structures that grow into new plants. Mosses also have male and female parts used in reproducing.

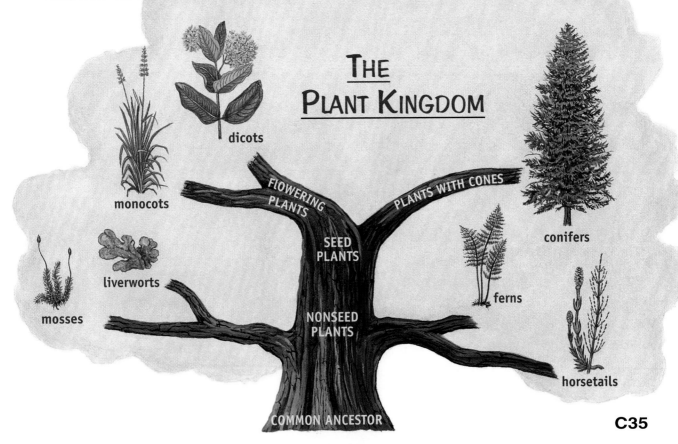

dicots

monocots

liverworts

mosses

THE PLANT KINGDOM

FLOWERING PLANTS

PLANTS WITH CONES

SEED PLANTS

conifers

ferns

NONSEED PLANTS

horsetails

COMMON ANCESTOR

C35

▲ Mosses produce spores at the tips of tall leafless stalks.

▲ The liverwort *Marchantia* produces spores on stalks with umbrella-shaped tops.

Mosses don't have special structures for carrying water. Because mosses lack such structures, water must move from cell to cell throughout the plant. This explains why mosses are small plants that are found growing only in moist places.

Liverworts are nonseed plants that lack true roots, stems, and leaves. Liverworts grow in moist places, such as along the banks of streams.

Ferns and Horsetails

Ferns are spore-forming plants that have roots, stems, and leaves. Before the dinosaurs lived, giant ferns covered much of Earth. Today, there are still many kinds of ferns. But they are not so common. They grow in very moist places that are not too hot or cold.

Like mosses, ferns reproduce by spores. They also have male and female parts used in reproducing.

Unlike mosses, ferns have special tubes that carry water from the roots to other parts of the plant. The roots of ferns anchor the plant in soil and carry water to scaly underground stems.

The most obvious parts of ferns are their leaves, called fronds. Some fern fronds appear to be made of many smaller leaves attached to a central stem. Actually, all of these smaller leaflike parts form one large fern frond. Spore cases are often produced on the undersides of the fronds. Spore cases contain spores.

Horsetails look more like paintbrushes than the tails of horses. About 30 species of horsetails live in marshes and swamps around the world. Like ferns, horsetails reproduce by spores and have underground stems.

Horsetails, nonseed plants ▶

Each spot on the underside of a fern frond is a cluster of spore cases. ▶

Using Math

Suppose this ponderosa pine cone has 76 scales. Each pine cone can release 2 seeds per scale. About how many seeds could be released from this cone?

Conifers

Many plants, such as firs, produce seeds in cones. Cone-bearing plants are called **conifers** (kän′ə fərz). Like ferns, conifers have roots, stems, and leaves. However, conifers differ from ferns in the way they reproduce. Conifers reproduce by forming seeds. The seeds are located between the scales of protective cones.

Conifers may be small shrubs or tall trees. Huge forests of conifers cover much of the northern part of the world. Unlike other kinds of trees, most conifers keep their leaves in autumn. Many conifers, such as pines, spruces, and firs, have needlelike leaves. Others, such as cedar trees, have leaves that look like overlapping scales.

Science in Literature

LEAF TALK

Eyewitness Living Earth
by Miranda Smith
DK Publishing, 1996

"Leaves are so varied that botanists had to invent a whole new language to describe their shapes. . . . A plant living on the gloomy floor of a rain forest may need large leaves to catch enough sunlight. However, a plant growing on a mountaintop has plenty of light, but is battered by winds, and needs small, strong leaves to survive."

These words come from *Eyewitness Living Earth* by Miranda Smith. This book will amaze you with facts about all kinds of living things.

▲ The leaf of a hosta plant, a monocot, has parallel veins.

▲ The leaf of a cyclamen plant, a dicot, has netted veins.

Flowering Plants

Most of the plants familiar to you are flowering plants. Flowering plants are plants that have roots, stems, and leaves. These plants reproduce by seeds formed in flowers. As the seeds are formed, a fruit develops to cover and protect them.

A flowering plant may be classified as a monocot (män′ō kät) or as a dicot (dī′ kät). A **monocot** is a flowering plant that produces seeds that are in one piece. The seed stores food for the developing plant. Corn plants are examples of monocots. Each kernel is a seed. A **dicot** is a flowering plant that produces seeds that have two sections. A lima bean plant is an example of a dicot.

One way to tell if a plant is a monocot or a dicot is to look at its leaves. The leaf of a mature monocot has veins that are parallel (par′ə lel). Parallel veins run side by side down the length of the leaf. The leaf of a mature dicot has netted veins. Netted veins form a branching pattern. You can see the two kinds of vein patterns in the pictures on this page.

Flowering plants are important. If you eat an orange or a carrot, you've eaten part of a flowering plant. On a summer day, you might cool off in the shade of a flowering plant, such as a maple tree. You might sit on a chair made of cherry wood. When you're sick, you might even take medicine made from flowering plants! ■

INVESTIGATION 4 WRAP-UP

THINK IT WRITE IT

REVIEW

1. What are the two main groups of plants?

2. Name the two main groups of seed plants. Give one example from each group.

CRITICAL THINKING

3. How are monocots and dicots alike and different?

4. In late autumn, you find a shrub that has no flowers. Its leaves are needlelike and green. How would you classify this plant? Explain your answer.

C38

REFLECT & EVALUATE

Word Power

Write the letter of the term that best matches the definition. *Not all terms will be used.*

1. Vertebrates that have hair or fur and feed milk to their young
2. Seed plants that reproduce with cones
3. Feathery parts on the side of a fish's head
4. Each bone that makes up the backbone
5. Plants that have flowers or cones
6. Hard outer covering that protects an animal's body and gives it support

a. conifers
b. exoskeleton
c. gills
d. vertebra
e. mammals
f. mosses
g. seed plants
h. invertebrates

Check What You Know

Write the term in each pair that best completes each sentence.

1. Nonseed plants that look like paint-brushes are (dicots, horsetails).
2. Vertebrates are animals that have (backbones, exoskeletons).
3. An animal that lives in water after hatching but can live on land as an adult is (a mammal, an amphibian).
4. The leaves of dicots are (netted, parallel).

Problem Solving

1. Suppose you have discovered a new plant. How could the plant's leaves help you classify the plant as a fern, conifer, or flowering plant?

2. The body temperature of amphibians and reptiles varies with the temperature of their environment. How could this trait be a disadvantage for these animals?

BUILD YOUR PORTFOLIO

Look at the photograph to classify this organism. Write a paragraph or draw a diagram to explain your classification.

CHAPTER 2

THE SURVIVAL OF LIVING THINGS

How smart are the cats and dogs you know? They, like all other animals, have the ability to learn. They can learn behaviors that help them meet their needs for survival. All living things have those needs. And they have ways to meet those needs.

PEOPLE USING SCIENCE

Dog Trainer Ellen Torop at Canine Companions for Independence trains dogs to help disabled people. She can teach these "helping dogs" to follow about 60 commands. Thousands of disabled people depend on these well-trained animals. The helping dogs carry out simple, but important, tasks, such as turning lights on and off. They can push elevator buttons and carry items for disabled persons. Some dogs have even learned to push and pull wheelchairs.

Some of the animals are trained as "hearing dogs." They work with people who have hearing problems. Hearing dogs have learned how to alert their owners to important sounds, such as ringing telephones, smoke alarms, and doorbells.

In this chapter you'll find out more about all kinds of animals and about some of the things they learn to do.

INVESTIGATION 1

WHAT ARE THE BASIC NEEDS OF LIVING THINGS?
. . . .**C42**

INVESTIGATION 2

HOW DO LIVING THINGS MEET THEIR NEEDS?
. . . .**C50**

◀ Dog trainer Ellen Torop's student learns to take a telephone to a disabled person.

INVESTIGATION 1

WHAT ARE THE BASIC NEEDS OF LIVING THINGS?

Have you ever seen a duck put its head and neck underwater? The duck is looking for food. Food is one thing that all animals need. Find out in Investigation 1 about some other needs animals have in common.

Activity

MATERIALS

• *Science Notebook*

Needs in Common

Scientists are trained to make careful observations. In this activity, see what you can find out about the needs of animals through careful observation.

- - - - - - - - - - - -

Procedure

1. In your *Science Notebook*, **make a chart** like the one shown. **Identify** the animals pictured on pages C42 and C43. In your chart, **record** the names of the animals.

Animal	Need

See **SCIENCE** and **MATH TOOLBOX** page H10 if you need to review **Making a Chart to Organize Data**.

C42

2. **Infer** what need each animal is trying to meet. Then **record** your inference in your chart.

Analyze and Conclude

1. How many different needs did you identify? Do some needs seem more important than others? Explain your answer.

2. Do all animals seem to share the same basic needs? **Predict** how the other basic needs of each animal shown might be met.

3. **Compare** your predictions with those of other group members. Explain each prediction you made.

The ABCs of Survival

Reading Focus What basic needs of living things can the environment provide?

If you had to take care of a pet dog, cat, and bird, how would you remember what each one needs? It wouldn't be very difficult. All three animals share a basic need for food and water.

Animals in the wild need food and water, too. What other basic needs do animals share? The activity found on pages C42 and C43 shows how some animals' needs are being met. Besides food and water, animals also need shelter to survive.

All animals need a suitable environment (en vī'rən mənt). An animal's **environment** is everything, both living and nonliving, that surrounds and affects the animal. To survive in its environment, an animal needs to keep

A hippopotamus spends much of its time in water. What does a hippopotamus eat? ▼

C44

▲ The food of a killer whale includes penguins, walruses, and fish such as salmon, cod, and herring.

▲ A leopard takes its meal high up into a tree, where other animals cannot easily get at its food.

its body temperature within a certain range. This range varies, depending on the type of animal. In an environment that is suitable for an animal, that animal can meet all of its basic needs.

First, Some Food

All animals need food to grow, stay healthy, and survive. A mole dies after only a few hours without food! Other animals can wait an entire day for their next meal. Some animals, like snakes, can go for weeks without a meal.

Different animals eat different kinds of food. In the spring and summer, a rabbit feasts on plants such as dandelions and chickweed. But in the winter it settles for bark, roots, and dry leaves. A hippopotamus wanders out of the water to

enjoy a meal of grass. A killer whale fills its stomach with fish, squid, sea birds, and even seals. Look at the photo caption to find out more about the foods a killer whale eats. A leopard hunts and kills other animals and then eats them while high up in the trees.

▼ A mole eats mainly worms and insects.

Some Water, Please

Plants and animals need more than just food to survive. They also need water. Many animals drink water every day from water holes, ponds, lakes, rivers, and streams. A budgerigar (buj'ər i gär), an Australian parakeet, can go a long time without taking a drink. But when it's time for that drink, the bird will probably flock together with tens of thousands of other budgerigars at one water hole.

A few animals hardly ever, or even never, drink! A kangaroo rat rarely drinks. It gets its water from the seeds and cactus pulp that it eats. An Australian koala never needs to drink. It gets the water it needs by eating eucalyptus (yo͞o kə lip'təs) leaves.

Using Math *This koala is eating leaves. A koala eats about 1 kg (2.2 lb) of leaves each day. Estimate how much it eats in one year.*

▲ **A flock of budgerigars visit a water hole to drink.**

▲ **Plants, such as these mangroves, need water to survive.**

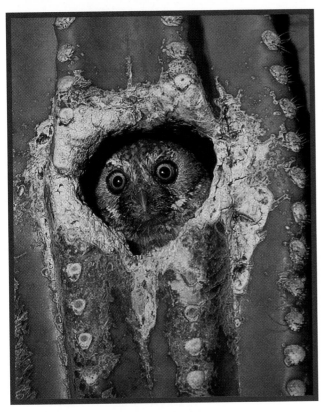

▲ **An elf owl finds a home in a cactus.**

example, many reptiles will lie in the sun if their body temperature is too cold. They will find shade if their body temperature is too hot. The body temperature of other animals stays within a certain range even while the temperature of the surroundings changes. Whether the air is hot or cold, your normal body temperature remains about 37°C (98.6°F).

As you can see, proper temperature, food, water, and shelter are some of the ABCs of survival for animals. Like animals, plants also need proper temperature, water, and shelter, or protection. But plants make their *own* food for growth. To do that, a plant needs energy from sunlight. For living things to survive and stay healthy, their needs must be met. ■

Home Sweet Home

Animals need shelter for protection from enemies and harsh weather. For example, the nest in which a baby bird hatches provides shelter for the bird. Young elf owls are kept safe in an old woodpecker hole in a cactus. A mouse can find shelter in a hole in the ground. Animals with hard coverings, such as turtles, carry their shelter with them.

Not Too Cold, Not Too Hot

An animal needs to live where its body temperature can be kept within a certain range. The body temperature of some animals changes with the temperature of the surroundings. For

UNIT PROJECT LINK

Think about each of the plants or animals you have decided to include in your field guide. What special parts do the plants or animals have to help them survive? What behaviors help them survive? Think of interesting ways to add these important facts to your field guide descriptions.

TechnologyLink
For more help with your Unit Project, go to **www.eduplace.com**.

weaverbird

The African Savanna

Reading Focus How does the environment of the animals of the savanna provide what they need to survive?

wildebeest

gazelle

wart hog

Wildebeests (wil'də bēsts) munch on grasses. Some drink from a water hole. Female lions hunting together catch a fast gazelle (gə zel'). A group of mongooses perch on a large termite mound made out of soil. These are some animals of the African savanna (sə van'ə). Like other animals, they need food, water, and shelter.

A **savanna** is a grassland found in tropical climates. It's a wide-open area that is covered with grasses but has only a few trees and bushes. Savannas cover almost one half of Africa. They are also found in India, South America, and Australia.

Food and Water in the Savanna

Like animals everywhere, animals of the African savanna need food. Zebras, wildebeests, and gazelles eat different parts of the grasses. The zebras feed on the tops of the grasses. Then wildebeests move into the area and feed on the middle parts. Later, gazelles chomp on the remaining bottom parts.

Giraffes eat the leaves of acacia (ə kā'shə) and baobab (bā'ō bab) trees. Secretary birds eat animals such as snakes and insects. Crocodiles in the water attack and eat wildebeests and other large animals as the animals try to cross rivers.

Animals of the savanna also need water. Many of them drink from the

Using Math Estimate the fraction of Earth's land mass that is covered by savannas.

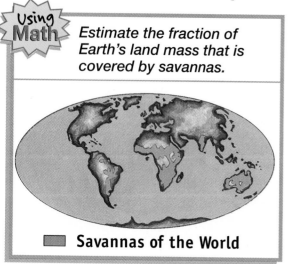

▢ **Savannas of the World**

acacia tree

giraffe

zebra

rock hyrax

secretary bird

mongoose

same water hole. Some drink there once a day. Others only go there once in a while. Animals may also drink water from nearby rivers.

Savanna Shelters

Animals of the savanna need shelter, too. Rock hyraxes (hī′rak sez) live in holes in small hills of rocks called *kopjes* (käp′ēz). A wart hog's shelter is a large hole in an old termite mound.

Weaverbirds make nests of woven grasses that hang from tree branches. The opening to such nests is on the bottom. This design makes it more difficult for enemies to reach the birds inside.

Animals of all the world's savannas share the same basic needs. And although the animals all need the same things to survive, they must meet these needs in different ways. ■

INVESTIGATION 1 WRAP-UP

REVIEW

1. Baby birds have just hatched in a nest outside your window. Name three basic needs of the young birds.

2. How does a plant get the food it needs?

CRITICAL THINKING

3. How would a drought, or dry period, on the savanna affect a zebra's ability to meet its needs?

4. Think about the roles of animals of the savanna. Identify the animals that are meat eaters and those that are plant eaters.

HOW DO LIVING THINGS MEET THEIR NEEDS?

What do teeth have in common with a bird's beak? Both kinds of body parts are used by animals to get food. In Investigation 2 you'll discover how the body parts and behaviors of living things help them meet their basic needs.

Activity

Feather Feats

A body covering is one of the body parts that help an animal meet its needs. A bird is covered with two types of feathers. Find out the purpose that each type serves!

Procedure

1. **Observe** a tail feather or wing feather under a hand lens. In your *Science Notebook*, **make a drawing** of what you see.

 See SCIENCE and MATH TOOLBOX page H2 if you need to review *Using a Hand Lens.*

Tail feather ▼

barbs

central shaft

2. Work with group members to **identify** the central shaft and the barbs on your feather. Use the picture on page C50 for help. Gently pull some of the barbs apart. **Record** your observations.

3. Pull the feather through your fingers as shown. **Observe** and **record** what happens.

4. Repeat steps 1 and 3, but this time examine a down feather.

5. Wave the tail or wing feather through the air. Then do the same with the down feather. **Observe** how the two types of feathers push the air around them. **Record** your observations.

Analyze and Conclude

1. **Compare** the two types of feathers. In what ways are they alike? What differences did you observe?

2. **Infer** which type of feather would help a bird fly. **Infer** which type of feather would help a bird keep warm. Discuss your inferences with other members of your group. Explain your thinking.

▲ **Down feather**

INVESTIGATE FURTHER!

EXPERIMENT

Make a plan to find out about body coverings other than feathers. With your teacher's help, collect samples of different body coverings. Then use a microscope to examine them. Make a drawing of each type of body covering. List questions about what you observe under the microscope.

Activity

Tap, Tap, Tap

In this activity you'll test whether you can change the behavior of goldfish as they learn that food is on the way.

Procedure

1. In your *Science Notebook*, **make a chart** like the one shown. With your group, **observe** how goldfish move in their tank. In your chart, **record** the movement you observe.

Day	Conditions	Observations
1	Without tapping or food (step 1)	
	With tapping but no food (step 3)	
1–10	With tapping and with food (step 5)	Day 1 _____ Day 2 _____ Day 3 _____ Day 4 _____ Day 5 _____
10	With tapping but no food, at the end of two weeks (step 6)	

See **SCIENCE** and **MATH TOOLBOX** page H10 if you need to review **Making a Chart to Organize Data**.

2. **Talk with your group** and **predict** how the behavior of the goldfish might change if you try to attract them by making a sound. **Record** your prediction.

Step 1

3. **Test your prediction.** Use a pencil to tap gently ten times on one wall of the fish tank. **Record** what you observe. Look for any changes in the behavior of the fish.

4. Sprinkle some fish food on the surface of the water at one end of the fish tank. At the same time, have another student tap the wall of the fish tank near where the food is sprinkled. **Record** the behavior of the fish.

5. Repeat step 4 each school day for two weeks. **Record** what you observe.

Step 4

Math Hint *"Each school day for two weeks"* *means you will do this 10 times.*

6. At the end of two weeks, tap on the wall of the fish tank ten times, but do *not* put any food in the water. **Observe** and **record** the behavior of the goldfish.

Analyze and Conclude

1. With your group, **compare** what you observed during step 3 with what you observed in step 6. How did the behavior of the goldfish change?

2. **Hypothesize** about how a sense of hearing might help fish survive. **Compare** your hypothesis with hypotheses of other group members. Explain why you came up with the hypothesis you did.

UNIT PROJECT LINK

Create a plan to publish your field guide to local plants or animals. Think of different ways to present your facts, such as in a booklet, in a bulletin-board display, or on audiotape.

 Technology Link

For more help with your Unit Project, go to **www.eduplace.com**.

The Survival Game

Reading Focus How do body parts and behaviors help living things survive?

Have you ever wondered how penguins, birds that can't fly, use their wings? Animals have different parts, or adaptations (ad əp tā'shənz), that help them meet their needs. **Adaptations** are body parts or behaviors of living things that help them survive in a certain environment.

Wings, Trunks, and Teeth

What are some body parts that help an animal get food? A penguin's strong wings are terrific for paddling underwater. A penguin can chase after fish and squid at speeds up to 32 km/h (20 mph).

An alligator snapping turtle swims with its mouth open. At the end of its tongue is a pink flap that looks like a worm. When a fish swimming by tries to eat the "worm," the turtle eats the fish.

Animals also have parts that are adaptations for getting water. An elephant can use its tusks for drilling to underground water. Then it uses its trunk to lift the water to its mouth. Dogs use their long tongues to scoop up water into their mouths.

Animals get some water from their food. A vampire bat's food is the blood of another animal. The blood

▲ An alligator snapping turtle waits underwater for food.

▲ An elephant can use its tusks and trunk to get water.

▲ The ears of a fennec, a kind of fox, help keep the animal cool.

▲ An armadillo's covering is its shelter.

contains water. To get the blood, the bat sticks its sharp teeth into the skin of its prey.

Claws, Feathers, and Ears

Some animals have parts that serve as shelters or help them make shelters. Snails and armadillos have hard outer coverings. Pocket gophers have large front teeth, sharp claws, and flexible bodies. These adaptations help the gophers dig tunnels that shelter them.

Animals have parts that help provide a proper temperature for them. The fluffy down feathers used in the activity on pages C50 and C51 help keep a bird warm. The large ears of an animal such as an elephant or a fennec help keep it cool. Blood passing through the animal's ears gives off heat, cooling the entire animal.

Behaviors for Survival

Suppose you go to a park and see a dog and its owner playing with a ball.

When you walk over to pet the dog, the owner tells the dog to sit. The dog sits. Then the owner tells the dog to lie down. But just as the dog is beginning to lie down, a squirrel scampers past. The dog leaps up and runs after the squirrel. You have just observed some interesting **behaviors**, or ways living things act or respond to their environment.

Technology Link
CD-ROM

INVESTIGATE FURTHER!

Use the **Science Processor CD-ROM**, *Animals* (Investigation 1, Feed Me!) to discover how different animals use their body structures to get food. Watch a video about how mammals use their bodies to meet their needs.

▲ A mother crocodile cradles baby crocodiles in her mouth.

Animals sometimes respond in ways that are instinctive. **Instinctive behaviors** are behaviors that living things inherit from their parents. Other behaviors, called **learned behaviors**, develop after birth. When the dog in the park sits on command, it is performing a learned behavior. The owner taught the dog to sit when told. But the dog's owner didn't teach it to chase squirrels! Running after a squirrel is an instinctive behavior of dogs.

Internet Field Trip

Visit **www.eduplace.com** to learn more about animal behavior.

Chasing and Cradling

Both kinds of behavior—learned and instinctive—help animals survive. A young wolf is born with deer-chasing behavior but must learn how to catch the deer for food. As a pup, a wolf learns this behavior by chasing and jumping on other wolf pups and its parents. It also learns by watching other wolves catch deer.

Animals have behaviors that help them protect themselves or their young. When there is danger, a mother crocodile instinctively keeps her young safe by cradling them in her mouth and throat. When the danger is past, the crocodile spits out her young!

Unlike a crocodile, a newborn rattlesnake doesn't need help from a parent. It can defend itself. A young rattlesnake instinctively coils and strikes at danger, just as its parent does.

Spinning and Shivering

Different kinds of animals have different behaviors for getting food. Some spiders have the instinctive

◄ Wolf pups pounce on and playfully bite each other.

◀ **A spider spins a web that catches prey.**

move to cooler shady places. Birds and many other animals shiver when they're cold. This behavior warms up their bodies. ■

behavior of spinning a silk web that catches prey. When an unlucky bee gets stuck in a spider's web, the spider bites the bee to paralyze it. The spider then wraps the bee in silk, preventing the bee from escaping.

Animals also have behaviors for keeping their temperatures within a certain range. Turtles and lizards bask in the sun to warm up. When their body temperatures get too high, they

Basking in the sun helps warm a lizard. ▶

Science in Literature

Snakes and Other Reptiles
by Mary Elting
Illustrated by Christopher Santoro
Simon & Schuster, 1987

BEWARE OF SNAKES!

"When an animal—perhaps a wild pig—comes to the stream for a drink, the snake moves suddenly. It grabs the pig's leg in its mouth. Then with swift looping motions it wraps itself in coils around the animal's body. The pig cannot move. Little by little the snake squeezes its coils tighter and tighter till the pig cannot breathe and in a short while is dead."

This description of an anaconda is from the book *Snakes and Other Reptiles* by Mary Elting. Read this book for more exciting tales of reptile survival.

Is It Ever Too Late?

Reading Focus What can happen if the needs of living things are not met?

A species, or group of living things that produce living things of the same kind, has many members. Some members may die out because their needs can't be met. Other members have characteristics that help them to survive. If the needs of *all* members of a species can't be met, that species becomes **extinct** (ek stiŋkt'), or dies out.

Organisms are produced, grow and mature, produce young, and then eventually die. But as long as an organism has produced young, its species will continue to exist.

To survive, an organism must be able to meet its needs in the environment where it lives. But environments differ. A polar bear cannot survive in a desert. It would die from the heat. But camels, who can live in desert heat with little water, can survive there. A camel cannot survive in the Arctic. It would die from the cold. But polar bears have a layer of fat that helps them survive the cold.

When Environments Change

Naturally caused forest fires, earthquakes, and long periods of drought or rainfall may change an environment. Then living things in that environment may die.

But not all living things die because of natural forces. Sometimes people change environments. Then the needs of plants and animals in that environment may no longer be met. When trees are cut down, many animals lose both their food and their shelter. Oil spills can ruin water environments. For example, crabs soaked with oil die. Then the animals that rely on the crabs as food also die.

▲ **Florida's 1998 forest fires destroyed the environment of many living things.**

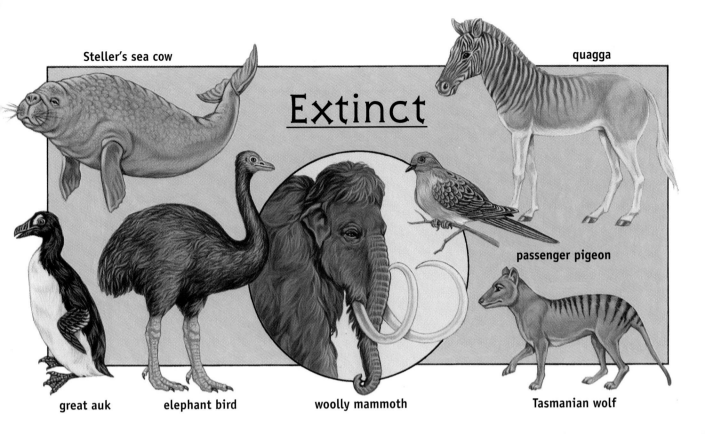

Steller's sea cow

quagga

Extinct

passenger pigeon

great auk   **elephant bird**   **woolly mammoth**   **Tasmanian wolf**

When It's Too Late

There are fewer than 50,000 Asian elephants left in the world. But because these animals do exist, it isn't too late for that species to survive. It is too late, however, for species that are already extinct. Some of these are shown on this page.

One species of extinct animal is the woolly mammoth. As you can see in the picture above, it looked very much like an elephant. Elephants exist today. But for 10,000 years, there have been no woolly mammoths.

Among extinct animals that lived before recorded history, dinosaurs are the most famous. Dinosaurs lived more than 50 million years ago. According to some scientists, today's birds are very similar to dinosaurs. Those scientists think that birds should be considered living dinosaurs. Dinosaurs were very

large reptiles. Even though there are no more dinosaurs, other reptiles, such as alligators and crocodiles, exist today.

When It's Not Too Late

Sometimes plants and animals become endangered, or scarce, because they are killed for use in products. Because snow leopards have been killed for their skins, these animals have become endangered. By law, endangered animals can no longer be hunted and killed.

On the island of Guam, brown snakes ate albatross young and their eggs until none were left on the island. On other islands in the Pacific, the albatross was hunted for its feathers. After a period of time, the species was declared extinct. Then a few remaining birds were discovered, so the albatross is not extinct after all.

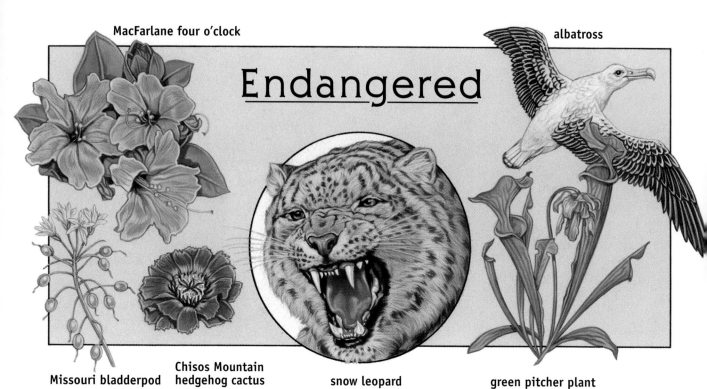

MacFarlane four o'clock

albatross

Endangered

Missouri bladderpod

Chisos Mountain
hedgehog cactus

snow leopard

green pitcher plant

As long as some individuals of a species exist, it's not too late to save the species. People can help endangered species recover. It's not too late, then, for the snow leopard. It's also not too late for the fewer than 50,000 Asian elephants left in the world. For the albatross, it was almost too late.

A change in environment, whether natural or caused by people, affects living things. Living things in the environment can become endangered or even extinct. For extinct species, it's too late. But it's never too late for people to rebuild environments. And it's never too late for people to protect environments. ■

INVESTIGATION 2 WRAP-UP

THINK IT
WRITE IT

REVIEW

1. What is instinctive behavior? Describe an example of it.

2. Name two animals. Describe one behavior that helps each animal meet a basic need.

**CRITICAL
THINKING**

3. Choose a circus animal. Describe one instinctive behavior and one learned behavior.

4. Think about the adaptations of animals that help them to survive. What traits might help some Asian elephants to survive?

REFLECT & EVALUATE

Word Power

Write the letter of the term that best completes each sentence. *Not all terms will be used.*

1. Behaviors that living things inherit are called —.
2. Everything, both living and nonliving, that surrounds and affects an animal is its —.
3. To die out is to become —.
4. Behaviors that develop after birth are —.
5. A grassland found in tropical climates is a —.

a. adaptations
b. environment
c. instinctive behaviors
d. learned behaviors
e. savanna
f. extinct

Check What You Know

Write the term in each pair that best completes each sentence.

1. The basic needs of animals include food, water, proper temperature, and (learned behaviors, shelter).
2. An example of an extinct animal is the (elephant, dinosaur).
3. Body parts or behaviors that help living things survive in a certain environment are called (adaptations, instinctive behaviors).
4. Endangered animals are animals that have become (extinct, scarce).

Problem Solving

1. Suppose you take an imaginary trip to an African savanna. You see many different kinds of animals. Identify some of the things the animals of the savanna use for food.

2. On a cold day you see a bird sitting with its feathers fluffed out. It's shivering. What need is the bird meeting? What adaptations does the bird have to help meet that need?

Study the photograph. Make a list of the armadillo's basic needs. Describe how the animal is meeting one of its basic needs.

Compare and Contrast

Making comparisons when you read helps you understand what a writer is saying. As you read, ask if two things or ideas are alike or different from each other.

Read the passages below. Then complete the exercises that follow.

Look for these signal words to help you compare and contrast.

- To show similar things: *like, the same as, in common*
- To show different things: *different from, by contrast*

Who Has a Backbone?

Animals that have backbones make up one group. You can feel the knobs of your backbone down the center of your back. Each knob is part of a separate bone. Each bone that makes up the backbone is called a **vertebra**. Animals that have backbones are called **vertebrates**.

Vertebrates include many different kinds of animals. Horses, hippos, cats, birds, snakes, lizards, frogs, and fish are all vertebrates. All vertebrates have one thing in common—a backbone.

Life Without a Backbone

The members of many different animal groups don't have backbones. Animals that don't have backbones are called **invertebrates**. In fact, 97 percent of the animal kingdom is made up of invertebrates! They include some of the smallest animals, such as spiders, mites, and insects. Some invertebrates can be found in ponds, oceans, and other water environments where they can move about easily. Others have no trouble moving about on land or in the air.

1. What two things are being compared?

2. What is the main difference between the two things that are being compared? Write the letter of the answer.

    a. Where they live   **c.** How big they are

    b. How they move   **d.** Whether they have a backbone

Using Math — Analyze Data

The average lengths in meters of various dolphins and whales are shown in this table.

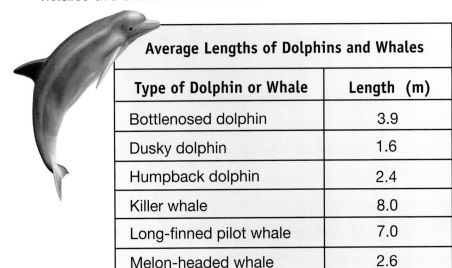

Average Lengths of Dolphins and Whales	
Type of Dolphin or Whale	**Length (m)**
Bottlenosed dolphin	3.9
Dusky dolphin	1.6
Humpback dolphin	2.4
Killer whale	8.0
Long-finned pilot whale	7.0
Melon-headed whale	2.6

Use the information in the table to complete the exercises that follow.

1. Which animal has the greatest length? the shortest length?

2. Which two types of animals, lined up nose to tail, would have a length of exactly 5 m?

3. Which animal is as long as five dusky dolphins lined up nose to tail?

4. About how many times longer is a killer whale than a bottlenosed dolphin?

5. The range of a set of data is found by subtracting the smallest number from the largest number in the set of data. What is the range of data in the table?

6. Estimate how many of your arm spans would equal the length of the killer whale.

WRAP-UP!

On your own, use scientific methods to investigate a question about living things.

THINK LIKE A SCIENTIST

Ask a Question

Pose a question about living things that you would like to investigate. For example, ask, "How can an animal's color help it survive?"

Make a Hypothesis

Suggest a hypothesis that is a possible answer to the question. One hypothesis is that an animal's color helps it blend into its environment so that predators cannot find it.

Plan and Do a Test

Plan a controlled experiment to find out if an animal's color helps it hide from predators. You could start with a large brown cloth, pipe cleaners in assorted colors (including brown), and a timer. Develop a procedure that uses these materials to test the hypothesis. With permission, carry out your experiment. Follow the safety guidelines on pages S14–S15.

Record and Analyze

Observe carefully and record your data accurately. Make repeated observations.

Draw Conclusions

Look for evidence to support the hypothesis or to show that it is false. Draw conclusions about the hypothesis. Repeat the experiment to verify the results.

WRITING IN SCIENCE
Summary

Write a summary of "The ABCs of Survival," pages C44-C47. Use these guidelines to write your summary.

- State the main ideas of the resource.
- Briefly list the main supporting details.
- Write a concluding statement that sums up the content.

UNIT D

Magnetism and Electricity

Theme: Models

THINK LIKE A SCIENTIST
POLAR LIGHT SHOW .D2

CHAPTER 1

Magnetism D4
Investigation 1   What Are Magnets? D6
Investigation 2   What Are Magnetic Force Fields? D16

CHAPTER 2

Electrical Energy D26
Investigation 1   What Is Static Electricity? D28
Investigation 2   What Is Current Electricity? D36
Investigation 3   How Do Electric Circuits Differ? D44

CHAPTER 3

Electricity at Work D54
Investigation 1   What Are Some Sources of
Electric Current? D56
Investigation 2   How Is Electricity Useful? D66

Using Reading Skills D78
Using Math Skills D79
Unit Wrap-up! D80

THINK LIKE A SCIENTIST

POLAR LIGHT SHOW

This photo shows an aurora seen from Denali National Park, in Alaska. At certain times, auroras such as this one light up the sky in brilliant displays of color over Earth's poles. What causes auroras? Scientists have learned that Earth is a giant magnet that attracts particles of matter streaming from the Sun. The displays of color result from these particles colliding with particles in the atmosphere. Although scientists know what causes auroras, they can't fully explain what causes Earth to be a magnet.

THINK LIKE A SCIENTIST

Questioning In this unit you'll study magnetism and electricity. You'll investigate questions such as these.

- What Are Magnetic Force Fields?
- What Is Current Electricity?

Observing, Testing, Hypothesizing In the Activity "A Magnet's Ends," you'll make observations about how magnets react with each other. You'll test a magnet and infer which end is its north pole.

Researching In the Resource "Properties of Magnets," you'll gather more information about magnets, including kinds of magnets and some uses for magnets.

Drawing Conclusions After you've completed your investigations, you'll draw conclusions about what you've learned—and get new ideas.

Plan and Do a Test • Record and Analyze • Draw Conclusions • Make Observations • Ask a Question • Make a Hypothesis • Plan

D3

CHAPTER 1

MAGNETISM

Where do you find magnets? Perhaps your refrigerator door at home has small magnets that are holding up papers. You may have seen pictures of a giant magnet lifting tons of junked cars in the air. How do these magnets work?

PEOPLE USING SCIENCE

Radiologist The rear doors of an ambulance open. Quickly, Pat is wheeled into the hospital. There are bandages around her head and arm. The doctors need to make sure there are no serious injuries to her head and spine.

Pat is taken to the Magnetic Resonance Imaging (MRI) center. MRI is a technology that uses powerful magnets to produce pictures of the inside of the body. Dr. Ray Cobb, a radiologist, gives Pat the MRI. A radiologist is trained to understand MRI pictures. The pictures help Dr. Cobb identify injuries to muscles and tissues. He can even find problems with blood circulation. In this chapter you'll find out about other ways that magnets help people.

Coming Up

INVESTIGATION **1**

WHAT ARE MAGNETS?

.... **D6**

INVESTIGATION **2**

WHAT ARE MAGNETIC FORCE FIELDS?

.... **D16**

◀ Dr. Ray Cobb studies MRI pictures to identify injuries.

D5

WHAT ARE MAGNETS?

Think about where you might find magnets in each room of your house. But keep in mind that many magnets are out of sight. Just what is a magnet, and what can it do? In Investigation 1 you'll find out.

Activity

Make a Magnet

Make your own magnet. Then find out what kinds of objects it pulls on, or sticks to.

Procedure

1. Open the bag of small objects and spread them on a table. Have each group member collect two other small objects. Include things made of many different materials.

2. In your *Science Notebook,* make a chart like the one shown to record your observations.

Attracted by Magnet or Sticks to Magnet		
Object	**Prediction**	**Actual**

 See **SCIENCE** and **MATH TOOLBOX** page H10 if you need to review **Making a Chart to Organize Data**.

MATERIALS
- bag of small objects
- bar magnet
- nail
- *Science Notebook*

SAFETY
Be careful when handling the nail.

Step 3

3. **Talk with your group** and together **predict** which objects will stick to a magnet. **Record** your predictions in your chart. Then move a magnet close to each object. **Record** your observations in your chart.

4. **Make a chart** like the one you made in step 2. **Predict** whether a nail will attract any of the objects. Then move a nail close to each object. **Record** your observations.

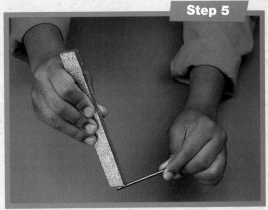
Step 5

5. Stroke the nail with the end of the magnet 30 times. *Stroke in one direction only*.

6. Repeat step 4, using the stroked nail. Make a set of predictions about the stroked nail. **Record** your predictions and, after testing the objects, **record** your observations.

Analyze and Conclude

1. **Compare** your predictions about which objects would be attracted to a magnet with your results.

2. **Compare** your predictions about the nail before you stroked it with a magnet with your results.

3. Explain your observations about the stroked nail. **Hypothesize** how stroking the nail with the magnet affects the nail.

4. What can you **infer** about the objects that were attracted by the magnet and the stroked nail?

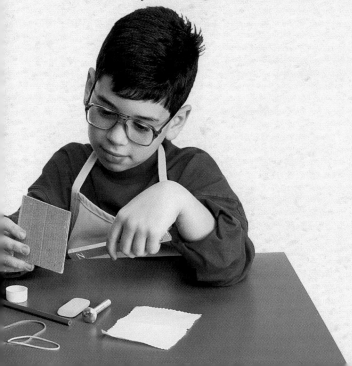

INVESTIGATE FURTHER!

EXPERIMENT

Hold the nail that you stroked with a magnet near a pile of paper clips. If nothing happens, stroke the nail with the magnet 30 times. How many paper clips does the nail pick up?

Suppose you stroke the nail with the magnet 40 times and then 50 times. Will the nail be able to pick up more paper clips? Find out. Make a chart of your results.

Activity

A Magnet's Ends

Both ends of a magnet have "pull." But are both ends of a magnet alike in every way? Find out in this activity.

MATERIALS
- string
- 2 bar magnets
- meterstick
- 2 chairs
- *Science Notebook*

Procedure

1. Tie a string to a bar magnet on which one end is marked *N* and the other is marked *S*. Tie the string to a meterstick placed between two chairs, as shown.

2. **Predict** what will happen if you move the end of another bar magnet marked *N* and *S* close to the hanging magnet. Think about the ways you might arrange the ends of the magnets. **Record** each arrangement and what you **predict** for each arrangement in your *Science Notebook*.

3. **Make a plan** with your group to test your predictions. Then **test** your plan and **record** your observations.

Step 2

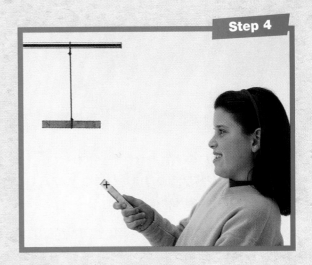

4. Now **test** a bar magnet on which one end is marked *X* and the other end is marked *Y*. Hold one end and then the other end of this magnet near one end of the hanging magnet. **Infer** which end of the magnet you're holding is really *N* and which is really *S*. **Record** your inference and state your evidence. Remove the tape. **Record** whether your inference was correct.

Analyze and Conclude

1. The *N* on the end of a magnet marks its north-seeking pole, or north pole. The *S* on the other end of a magnet marks its south-seeking pole, or south pole. From your observations, **conclude** which poles attract, or pull toward, each other.

2. **Conclude** which poles repel, or push away from, each other. How do you know?

UNIT PROJECT LINK

For this Unit Project you'll invent games, fun devices, and machines. You'll use magnets or electricity in all your inventions. Your first challenge is to invent a magic trick that makes use of magnets. Think about a trick that works because the force of a magnet can be "felt" through various materials. Build a model of your magic trick. Include instructions for others to follow.

Technology Link
For more help with your Unit Project, go to **www.eduplace.com**.

Activity
Pulling Through

A magnet can have a lot of force, or pull. In this activity you'll find out more about how that force works.

MATERIALS
- string
- bar magnet
- meterstick
- 2 chairs
- paper clip
- assorted materials
- *Science Notebook*

Procedure

1. Tie a string around a bar magnet. Hang the magnet from a meterstick between two chairs.

2. Place a paper clip on the palm of your hand. Then move your hand under one end of the magnet until the magnet is just close enough to attract the paper clip.

Force of Magnet Through Materials		
Material	Prediction	Result

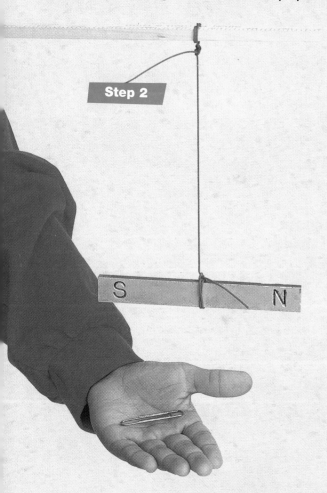

Step 2

3. Talk with your group and together predict whether the magnet can attract the paper clip through materials such as paper, aluminum foil, cloth, plastic, and steel. In your *Science Notebook*, make a chart like the one shown above to record your predictions and observations.

4. Plan a way to find out whether the magnet's force can act through different materials. Test each material, using the plan that you came up with. Record your observations in your chart.

Analyze and Conclude

1. Compare your predictions about whether the force of a magnet acts through different materials with your observations.

2. From your observations, infer whether the force of a magnet can pass through different materials.

Properties of Magnets

Reading Focus What is a magnet, and what can it do?

▲ **How is a magnet being used in each picture?**

What's an easy way to clean up a mixture of metal paper clips and rubber bands spilled on the floor? If you drag a magnet over the floor, the paper clips will stick to the magnet, but the rubber bands won't. Why does this happen?

The Pull of Magnets

The activity on pages D6 and D7 shows how a magnet affects some materials. A **magnet** is an object that attracts, or pulls on, certain materials, mainly iron and steel. A magnet's

property of attracting these materials is called **magnetism** (mag′nə tiz əm).

Paper clips are made of steel, which contains iron. That's why you can pick them up with a magnet. Rubber bands contain no iron or other materials that a magnet attracts.

The photographs above show some uses of magnets. The part of the can opener that lifts the steel lid of the can is a magnet. Using a magnet to pick up pins keeps fingers from being stuck. A magnetic screwdriver makes it easier to hold screws in place.

The steel figures of this toy can be arranged in various ways on a magnet. ▼

Two Kinds of Magnets

Magnets made in factories, including toy magnets, are permanent magnets. A permanent magnet is not easy to make, but it keeps its magnetism for a long time. It may be made from steel that contains iron as well as other metals.

Some objects, such as iron nails, are easy to make into magnets. For example, the activity on pages D6 and D7 shows that you only have to stroke a nail with a permanent magnet to magnetize the nail. But magnets made in this way are temporary magnets. A temporary magnet is one that doesn't keep its magnetism for very long.

▲ Are the magnets on this refrigerator door likely to be temporary or permanent?

Science in Literature

MIND YOUR MAGNETS

"Magnetize a needle by allowing it to lie on a magnet for two minutes. Tie a thread to the center of the magnetized needle and suspend it inside a glass jar. Use a compass to determine which end of the needle points toward the north. Once you have identified the polarity of the needle, it can be used as a compass."

To learn more about this and other magnet activities, read *Magnets: Mind-boggling Experiments You Can Turn Into Science Fair Projects* by Janice VanCleave.

Magnets: Mind-boggling Experiments You Can Turn Into Science Fair Projects
by Janice VanCleave
John Wiley & Sons, 1993

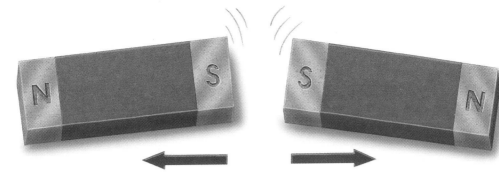

▲ The south poles or north poles of two magnets repel each other.

▲ The south pole of one magnet attracts the north pole of another magnet.

North and South Poles

When a magnet is hung so that it can move freely, one end of it always points toward the north. This is the magnet's north-seeking pole, or **north pole**. If one end points north, you know what direction the other end points toward. It points south. This is the magnet's south-seeking pole, or **south pole**.

What happens if you move the north pole of one magnet near the south pole of another magnet? If both magnets are free to move, they move closer together, and the north and south poles may stick to each other.

What happens if you bring the north pole of one magnet near the north pole of another? The two magnets move farther apart. Here is a rule to remember about how magnets

behave. The unlike poles of magnets attract, or pull toward, each other. The like poles of magnets repel, or push away from, each other. In the activity on pages D8 and D9, the taped-over poles of a magnet can be determined from the way a second magnet moves. ■

Technology Link
CD-ROM

INVESTIGATE FURTHER!

Use the **Science Processor CD-ROM**, *Magnetism and Electricity* (Unit Opening, Shocking Behavior!) to see how objects react when they are charged and to test objects for magnetism.

Maglev Trains

Reading Focus In what ways is a maglev train different from other forms of transportation?

Can a train fly? The maglev train does, in a way. If you visit Europe or Japan, you might ride on a maglev. It may look as if this train runs on a track, but it doesn't. The maglev train floats about 1 cm (0.4 in.) above the track!

It Flies and It's Fast

The maglev's full name tells something about how it works. *Maglev* is short for "magnetic levitation" (lev ə-tā'shən). *Levitation* means "rising

into the air." The maglev uses magnetic force to rise into the air.

Ordinary trains are slowed by friction, the force caused by the wheels rubbing on the track. Because the maglev doesn't touch its track, there's no friction. This means that it can go as fast as 500 km/h (310 mph)!

Ordinary trains go "clackety-clack" along the rails. But speeding on air makes a maglev train ride very quiet, as well as smooth and superfast. What if maglev trains were everywhere? How might this affect people where you live?

This maglev train can travel about 500 km/h. An ordinary train can travel 300 km/h. How long would it take a maglev train to reach a city 1,500 km away? An ordinary train?

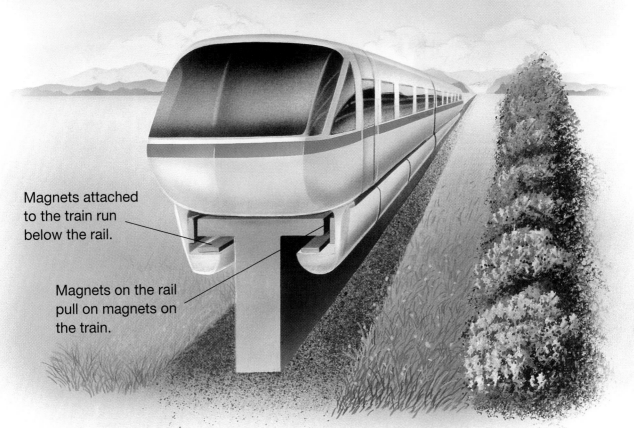

Magnets attached
to the train run
below the rail.

Magnets on the rail
pull on magnets on
the train.

▲ Maglevs are lifted into the air by magnetic forces. There are
powerful magnets on both the train and the rails.

It's Clean

Most buses and cars run by burning
oil or gasoline. So do most trains.
When oil and gasoline burn, they pollute the air. That means those vehicles
make the air dirty by giving off harmful substances.

The maglev runs on electricity.
Power plants that produce electricity
do burn fuels that pollute the air. But
the train itself doesn't pollute the air
because it doesn't burn fuels. Would
you call the maglev an environmentally
friendly train? Explain your answer. ■

━━━━━━ INVESTIGATION 1 WRAP-UP ━━━━━━

REVIEW

1. What happens when you put the unlike poles
of two magnets together?

2. What general types of materials are attracted
to magnets?

**CRITICAL
THINKING**

3. Suppose that a rock sample from Mars is
brought to Earth. Pieces of the rock can be
picked up by a magnet. What metal may be
present in the rock?

4. Two doughnut-shaped magnets are placed
on a pencil. One of the magnets floats above
the other one. What makes this happen?

WHAT ARE MAGNETIC FORCE FIELDS?

You can't see, hear, or smell a magnetic force field. But bring a magnet near an iron object and you can *feel* the force. In Investigation 2 you'll explore the patterns of magnetic force fields.

Activity

Getting Directions

Earth has a magnetic force field around it. In this activity you'll make a magnet and use it to detect Earth's magnetic force field.

Procedure

1. Magnetize a needle by stroking it 30–40 times with one end of a bar magnet. Stroke the needle in the same direction each time.

2. Stick the needle through the center of a plastic-foam ball, as shown.

Step 2

3. Half-fill a bowl with water. Carefully place the foam ball and needle on the water. **Observe** what happens. **Record** your observations in your *Science Notebook*.

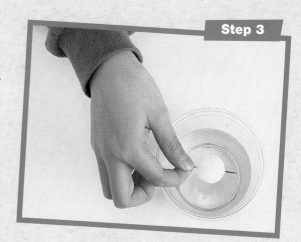

4. Wait until the foam ball is still. **Talk with your group** and together **predict** what will happen if you move the bar magnet near the bowl. **Test** your prediction and **record** your observations.

5. Take away the bar magnet. Give the bowl a quarter turn. Make sure that the foam ball is free to move. Keep turning until you complete a full circle. **Record** your observations.

Math Hint *Remember that a quarter turn measures 90°.*

6. Then repeat steps 4 and 5 to check your results.

Analyze and Conclude

1. Find out from your teacher which direction is north. In which directions did the ends of the needle point?

2. **Compare** your prediction with your observation of what happened when you moved a bar magnet near the bowl.

3. One end of a compass always points in the direction of north. From your observations, **infer** whether or not you have made a compass. Give reasons for your inference.

INVESTIGATE FURTHER!

RESEARCH

When you magnetize an object, the particles that make up the object become tiny magnets called domains. Find out more about magnetic domains at a library. One book you might read is *Magnets: Mind-boggling Experiments You Can Turn Into Science Fair Projects* by Janice VanCleave. Write a report and illustrate it with a drawing of magnetic domains.

Activity

Picture a Magnet's Force

Even though you can't see a magnet's force, you can make a picture of it. In this activity you'll find out how.

Procedure

1. Place a bar magnet on a sheet of newspaper. Put a sheet of white cardboard on top of the magnet.

2. Hold a jar of iron filings over the cardboard. Carefully sprinkle the filings on the cardboard over the magnet.

3. Gently tap the cardboard. Look for a pattern of lines of iron filings. In your *Science Notebook*, **draw** the pattern the lines form.

4. Put a clean sheet of cardboard over a horseshoe magnet. **Talk with your group** and together **predict** the pattern that will form if you sprinkle iron filings on the cardboard. Then **make a drawing** to show your prediction.

Step 1

5. **Test** your prediction. Then **draw** what you see.

6. Put the iron filings back into the jar. Repeat the experiment to check your results.

Analyze and Conclude

1. **Compare** your predictions with your observations of the patterns of the iron filings.

2. The lines made by the iron filings are a picture of **lines of force**. The space in which the lines of force form is a **magnetic field**. What do the magnetic fields you observed tell you about where the magnetic force is greatest?

RESOURCE

Force Fields

Reading Focus What is a magnetic field, and what evidence shows it exists?

◀ **A magnet is strongest at its poles.**

What happens if you dip a bar magnet into a pile of paper clips and then hold the magnet up? Look at the picture. A lot of clips stick to the magnet. Notice where the clips stick—at the magnet's two poles. Why does this happen?

Lines of Force

The drawings made in the activity on page D18 show force fields of bar and horseshoe magnets. When iron filings are sprinkled on cardboard over a magnet, the iron filings form a pattern.

The pattern of filings shows how the force field spreads between the poles of the magnet and around it. The filings are thickest and closest together where the force is strongest.

These lines formed by the iron filings are called **lines of force**. The picture below shows a bar magnet that was sprinkled with iron filings. Actually, it's the same magnet that was used with paper clips in the picture above. Notice how the lines of force are heaviest at the poles, where the magnet also picked up the paper clips.

Pattern formed by lines of force of a bar magnet ▶

A Magnet's Force Field

The space in which the force of a magnet can act is called a **magnetic field**. You can't see a magnetic field. But you have seen some evidence that it exists.

For example, suppose you want to use a magnet to pick up a paper clip. You know that you have to move the clip and the magnet close enough together for the magnet to attract the clip. That's because a magnet attracts only those paper clips—or other objects that contain iron—that come into its magnetic field.

You can see in the photos on pages D19 and D20 that iron filings can make pictures of the lines of force around a magnet. The photos make it seem that the magnetic field is flat. But is the magnetic field really flat?

The magnetic field actually spreads out in all directions throughout the space around the magnet.

Comparing Force Fields

You've found out about several properties of magnets.

- A magnet attracts objects made of iron.
- The force of a magnet is greatest at its poles.
- Like poles of two magnets repel each other.
- Unlike poles of two magnets attract each other.

How are the force fields of magnets related to those properties? Use the pictures on the next page to find out. As you look at each picture, read the description below it.

▲ The pattern of the iron filings around the magnet in this jar of oil shows how a magnetic field spreads out all around a magnet.

INVESTIGATE FURTHER!

EXPERIMENT

Make a permanent display of one or more patterns made by magnets as shown in the pictures on page D21. Use the procedure in the activity on page D18 to make the patterns you choose. Then put on goggles and spray white vinegar over the filings. Let them stand overnight. Brush off the rusted filings and observe what remains. Write captions for your pictures and put the pictures on display.

MAGNETIC FIELDS

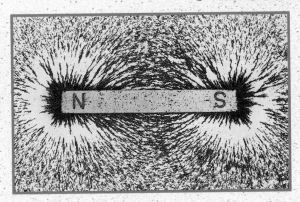

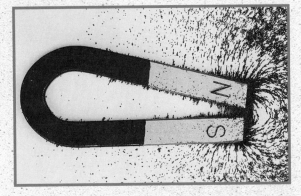

▲ This picture shows the magnetic field of a bar magnet. With your finger, trace the lines of force as they come out of the north pole, curve around the magnet, and enter the south pole.

▲ This picture shows the magnetic field of a horseshoe magnet. Notice how the strongest lines are closer together than they are for the bar magnet. Infer why this is so.

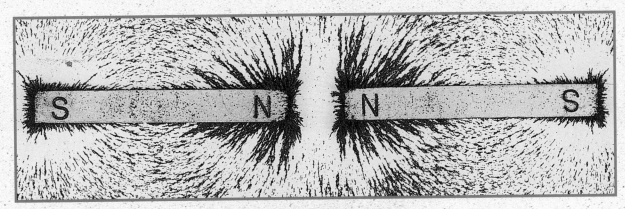

▲ The north poles of these two magnets are facing each other. What do you observe about the lines of force between the two magnets? If you hold two magnets with their north poles together like this, what will you feel?

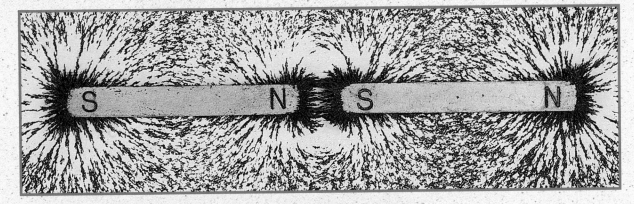

▲ The north pole of the magnet on the left is facing the south pole of the magnet on the right. Notice that the lines of force seem to move straight from one magnet to the other. If you hold two magnets like this, what will you feel?

Earth as a Magnet

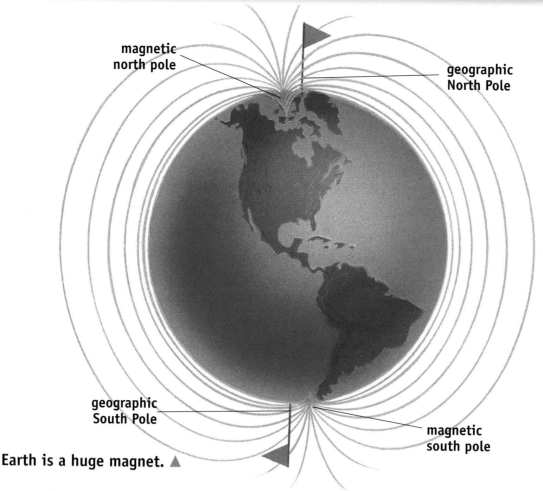

magnetic north pole

geographic North Pole

geographic South Pole

magnetic south pole

Earth is a huge magnet. ▲

Today scientists know that Earth is a giant magnet. However, long before scientists knew anything about Earth's magnetism, they knew about lodestone (lōd′stōn).

Lodestone is a naturally magnetic rock found at or near Earth's surface. The first lodestone was discovered by a sheepherder in Turkey more than 2,000 years ago. The stone attracted iron nails in the sheepherder's shoes. Almost 1,000 years later the Greeks made a discovery. They found that when hung from a string, lodestone always lined itself up in a north-south direction. The same end of the lodestone always pointed north.

D22

A Stone Leads the Way

Chinese sailors found a practical use for lodestone. They floated a small piece of lodestone on some straw in a bowl of water. Since one end of the stone always pointed toward the north, the sailors always knew in which direction they were sailing.

The device used by the Chinese sailors is easy to make. In the activity on pages D16 and D17, a similar device is made with a magnetized needle and a foam ball. The device is a simple compass. A **compass** is a magnetized needle that is allowed to swing freely.

Earth's Magnetism

Since the discovery of lodestones, scientists have learned that Earth's center is made up mostly of iron. They know that the spinning of Earth on its axis has magnetized this iron, turning Earth into a giant magnet. But they can't explain how the spinning causes this.

The "Earth magnet" has poles. It is surrounded by a magnetic field with lines of force like those that can be seen in the activity on page D18. Magnets are affected by Earth's magnetic field. The north-seeking pole of a magnet is attracted to Earth's magnetic north pole. This attraction is what makes a compass work.

Why Two Sets of Poles?

As the drawing on page D22 shows, Earth has two sets of poles— geographic and magnetic. The geographic poles mark the ends of the imaginary line, or axis, around which Earth rotates.

When the first explorers set out for the North Pole, they expected their compass to lead them to the geographic North Pole. But it didn't. Their compass led the explorers to a spot more than 1,600 km (1,000 mi) from the geographic North Pole. This spot marks the location of Earth's magnetic north pole.

A piece of lodestone ▼

▲ This ancient Chinese compass is a spoon that turns so that its handle points south.

▲ An aurora in the northern sky

Magnetism Lights Up the Sky

At certain times of the year, people living in regions near the poles get a special treat. They get to see the northern or southern lights. During these times, the sky above the poles lights up in a display of brilliant colors. The times when these displays occur are also marked by disturbances of radio signals.

These displays, called auroras (ô rôr′əz), are produced when particles of matter from space are captured by Earth's magnetic field. Why are these displays brightest near Earth's magnetic poles? ■

 Internet Field Trip
Visit **www.eduplace.com** to find out more about Earth's magnetism.

INVESTIGATION 2 WRAP-UP

REVIEW

1. What is a magnetic field?

2. Compare Earth to a magnet.

CRITICAL THINKING

3. When a circular magnet is dipped into a pile of paper clips, about the same number of clips sticks to the top as to the bottom. What does this tell you about the magnetic field of that magnet?

4. How could you make a compass with a magnetized nail, a string, a plastic jar with a lid, and some tape?

REFLECT & EVALUATE

Word Power

Write the letter of the term that best completes each sentence. *Not all terms will be used.*

a. compass
b. lines of force
c. lodestone
d. magnetic field
e. magnetism
f. north pole
g. south pole

1. A magnet's property of attracting iron is called ___.
2. The end of a magnet that seeks north is its ___.
3. The space in which the force of a magnet can act is called a ___.
4. A magnetized needle that swings freely is a ___.
5. A naturally magnetic rock is called ___.
6. The end of a magnet that seeks south is its ___.

Check What You Know

Write the term in each pair that best completes each sentence.

1. Lines formed by iron filings near a magnet are (lines of force, poles).
2. The force of a magnet is greatest at its (center, poles).
3. A magnet can be used to pick up (wood, iron).
4. If the south poles of two magnets are brought near each other, the poles (attract, repel) each other.

Problem Solving

1. Suppose that you are lost in the woods. You do not have a compass, but you do have a bar magnet and some string. How can you use the magnet and string to find your way?

2. You have two magnets—one strong and one weak. How could you use paper clips to find out which magnet is stronger?

Study the photograph. Explain whether the magnetic poles that are closest together are like or unlike. In your own words, write how you know this.

CHAPTER 2

ELECTRICAL ENERGY

What does a comic-book artist show by drawing a zigzag line? How can you tell that a character in a cartoon is having a bright idea? Think of some other signs and symbols that stand for electrical energy in action.

Connecting to Science
ARTS

Electric Art Artist David Archer creates pictures with an electric paintbrush. This device produces lightninglike arcs of electricity. Archer uses a wand to direct the arcs so that they hit large blobs of wet paint. The paint forms cloudy shapes on large glass plates. The artist calls these shapes art storms.

Most often, David Archer paints pictures of planets and other bodies in space as he imagines them. His work has appeared in magazines and even in the movies. You may have seen some of this artist's works on a television science-fiction show.

To run his electric paintbrush, David Archer uses household electricity. In this chapter you'll find out more about why electricity is such hot stuff!

INVESTIGATION 1

WHAT IS STATIC ELECTRICITY?
. . . . **D28**

INVESTIGATION 2

WHAT IS CURRENT ELECTRICITY?
. . . . **D36**

INVESTIGATION 3

HOW DO ELECTRIC CIRCUITS DIFFER?
. . . . **D44**

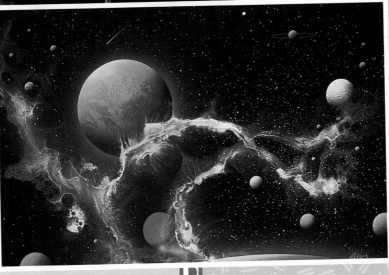

David Archer (*top*) uses an electric paintbrush; one of Archer's paintings (*bottom*).

D27

WHAT IS STATIC ELECTRICITY?

Your clean hair clings to your comb. A shirt you take out of the dryer has socks stuck to it. As you pull up a blanket on a chilly night, you see sparks and feel a slight shock. In Investigation 1 you'll find out how all these events are related.

Activity

Charge!

Sometimes a balloon will stick to another balloon; other times it won't. Try this activity and see if you can figure out why.

MATERIALS

- 2 balloons
- 2 strings (30 cm each)
- metric tape measure
- wool cloth
- plastic wrap
- *Science Notebook*

Procedure

1. Have two members of your group blow up balloons. Tie each balloon tightly with a string.

2. Have two other group members hold the strings so that the balloons hang about 10 cm apart. **Observe** any movement. **Record** your observations in your *Science Notebook*.

See **SCIENCE** *and* **MATH TOOLBOX** page H6 if you need to review **Using a Tape Measure or Ruler.**

Step 1

3. Rub each balloon with a wool cloth. **Predict** what will happen now if you repeat step 2. **Talk with your group** and **record** your prediction. Then repeat step 2.

4. Repeat step 3, but this time rub each balloon with plastic wrap instead of a wool cloth.

5. With your group, **predict** what will happen when a balloon rubbed with wool is brought near a balloon rubbed with plastic wrap. **Test** your prediction and **record** your observations.

Step 3

Analyze and Conclude

1. Rubbing a balloon with wool or plastic wrap gives the balloon an electric charge. From observing the behavior of the balloons, **infer** whether there is more than one kind of electric charge. Explain how you made your inference.

2. **Compare** your prediction about the balloons with your observations after they were rubbed with the wool cloth.

3. **Compare** your prediction about the balloons with your observations after they were rubbed with the plastic wrap.

4. Like charges repel, or push away from, each other. Unlike charges attract, or pull toward, each other. How do your results support these statements?

INVESTIGATE FURTHER!

EXPERIMENT

How does a balloon that has been charged interact with objects that have not been charged? Bring a charged balloon close to some puffed-cereal grains. Then bring another charged balloon near a wall. What can you conclude about the effect of a charged balloon on uncharged objects?

Static Electricity

Reading Focus What is static electricity, and how do objects become charged with static electricity?

You're combing your clean, dry hair. Strands of your hair fly away from each other. At the same time, the strands also stick to your comb. In the activity on pages D28 and D29, rubbing balloons with a wool cloth or plastic wrap causes the balloons to be attracted to or repelled by each other. Why does rubbing materials together cause these effects?

Hair, combs, balloons, wool, and plastic are kinds of matter. All matter is made up of tiny particles. Some of these particles carry units of electricity called **electric charges**.

Positive and Negative Charges

An electric charge can be positive or negative. A plus sign (+) stands for a positive charge, and a minus sign (−) stands for a negative charge. Most matter is neutral. A neutral object has the same number of positive charges as negative charges.

Only negative charges can move from one material to another. If negative charges move from one neutral object to another, the first object then has an overall positive charge. The second one has an overall negative charge. Look at the pictures

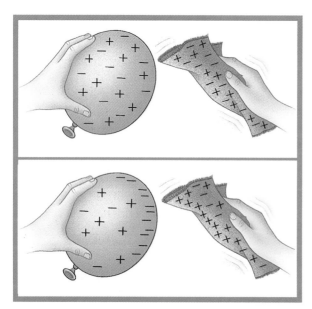

▲ Rubbing a balloon with wool (*top*) gives a negative charge to the balloon (*bottom*). What is the charge on the wool?

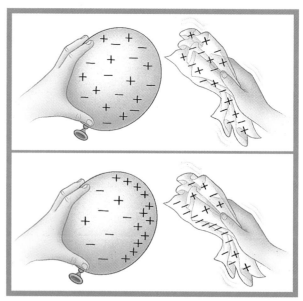

▲ Rubbing a balloon with plastic (*top*) gives a positive charge to the balloon (*bottom*). What is the charge on the plastic?

on page D30. They show balloons becoming charged.

The form of energy that comes from charged particles is called electrical (ē lek′tri kəl) energy. Negative electric charges can move from one object to another. When this happens, an electric charge builds up on both objects. One object will have a positive charge; the other will have a negative charge.

This buildup of electric charges is called **static electricity**. An object charged with static electricity has a buildup of electric charges on its surface. Objects with a buildup of like charges repel, or push away from, each other as shown in the top picture below.

Recall that when you comb your freshly washed and dried hair, your hair sticks to the comb. When the comb is removed, some of the hairs move away from each other. You're rubbing hair, which is one kind of matter, with plastic, which is another kind of matter.

If the air is dry enough, negative charges move from the hair to the comb, giving the comb an overall negative charge. Since the hair loses negative charges, it now has an overall positive charge. As the bottom picture of the balloons shows, objects having unlike charges attract, or pull toward, each other.

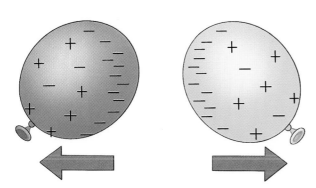

▲ A balloon that has a negative charge repels another one that has a negative charge.

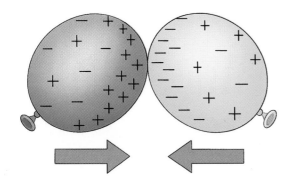

▲ A balloon that has a positive charge attracts one that has a negative charge·

Why do separate strands of the girl's hair repel each other? Why does the comb attract each strand of hair? ▼

You're taking the laundry out of the dryer, and your socks are stuck to your shirt. This is a case of static cling. Why does this happen?

As the dryer whirls, the clothes rub together. When different materials rub together, negative charges move from some materials to others. So the clothes become charged with static electricity. Your wool socks may have a positive charge and your cotton shirt may have a negative charge. So they attract one another.

When cotton is rubbed with wool, negative charges move from the wool onto the cotton. The cotton then has more negative charges than positive charges. And the wool has more positive charges than negative charges. So both socks and shirt become charged with static electricity.

Attracting Neutral Objects

If you charge a balloon by rubbing it with wool, the balloon may stick to a wall. But the wall is neutral. In the

Why is static cling called "static"? ▼

▲ **What evidence is there that the charge on the balloon is the opposite of the charge on the wall?**

activity on pages D28 and D29, the balloons that stick together are both charged. Why does a charged balloon stick to a neutral wall?

The rubbed balloon has extra negative charges that repel the negative charges in the wall. As a result, that part of the wall has extra positive charges. These charges attract the negative charges of the balloon. So the balloon sticks to the wall.

Shock, Spark, and Crackle

Do you want to shock a friend? Walk across a rug and touch your friend's hand. Your friend may get a mild electric shock. There's a catch, though. You'll feel the shock, too. You may even see a spark and hear a slight crackling sound.

What causes the shock, the spark, and the crackle? When you rub your shoes against the rug, negative charges move from the rug onto your shoes. The charges move from your shoes onto your body. Your body is now charged with static electricity.

Charges that build up in this way don't stay on the charged object. Sooner or later the charges move away. Charges may leak harmlessly into the air. Or the charges may "jump" when static electric charges move off a charged object. When that happens, an **electric discharge** takes place. ■

In an electric discharge, negative electric charges move from a charged object to another object. ▼

![computer icon] **Technology Link**
CD-ROM

INVESTIGATE FURTHER!

Use the **Science Processor CD-ROM**, *Magnetism and Electricity* (Unit Opening, Shocking Behavior!) to watch a video about the nature of electric charges and static electricity. See what happens when everyday objects become charged.

Lightning

Reading Focus How do electric charges cause lightning?

Using Math *A flash of lightning contains enough electricity to light a 100-watt light bulb for three months. How many flashes would be needed to light a 100-watt bulb for one year?*

Zap! Boom! Lightning flashes across the sky. Then thunder cracks. The wind is strong and rain starts pouring down—it's a thunderstorm. You may know that lightning causes thunder. But what causes lightning?

During a thunderstorm, positive charges can build up at the top of a cloud. Negative electric charges build up at the bottom of the cloud. These negative charges at the bottom of a cloud repel negative charges in the ground below. That causes the ground, and objects on the ground, to be positively charged.

When negative charges jump between the cloud and the ground, there's a giant electric discharge, or spark. This spark is lightning.

Lightning Safety

Lightning often strikes the tallest object on the ground. That is why you should never stand under a tree during

D34

1 Negative charges on a cloud cause positive charges to build up on the ground and the tree.

2 Lightning strikes when negative charges jump from the cloud to the ground or to the tree.

a lightning storm. Also, you should not play in an open field or swim. Take shelter in a building or an enclosed car.

Using lightning rods is another way to increase lightning safety. A lightning rod is a metal rod about 20 cm (8 in.) long. It is attached to the highest point of a structure. Heavy wires connect the rod to the ground. If lightning strikes the rod, electric charges move through the wires safely to Earth. ■

Internet Field Trip
Visit **www.eduplace.com** to see how scientists are studying lightning.

▲ **How can you stay safe if you're outdoors when lightning starts?**

INVESTIGATION 1 WRAP-UP

REVIEW

1. What is static electricity?

2. How does a neutral object become positively charged?

CRITICAL THINKING

3. How might you use a balloon with a negative charge to find out whether the charge on another balloon is positive or negative?

4. Explain why playing in an open field during a lightning storm is unsafe.

INVESTIGATION 2

WHAT IS CURRENT ELECTRICITY?

In Investigation 1 you saw that electric charges can move from place to place. In Investigation 2 you will find out how this flow of electricity can be controlled.

Activity

On or Off?

You usually take for granted that flipping on a light switch will turn on a light. What else has to happen for the light to go on? Find out in this activity.

MATERIALS
- dry cell (size D) in holder
- light bulb in holder
- 3 insulated wires (stripped on ends)
- thick cardboard
- 2 brass paper fasteners
- paper clip
- *Science Notebook*

Procedure

1. Place all the materials listed above on your desk. With your group, **hypothesize** ways you can connect some of the parts to make the bulb light. **Draw** pictures of these ways in your *Science Notebook*.

Step 1

2. Test each idea that your group has drawn. Circle the drawings you made that make the bulb light.

3. When the bulb lighted, you had made an electric circuit (sur'kit). An **electric circuit** is a path through which electricity can flow.

4. Use the round picture as a guide to arrange a paper clip, two brass fasteners, and two wires on a piece of thick cardboard.

Step 4

5. You have made a switch, which you can use to turn the bulb on or off. Make a drawing to predict how you can connect the switch to the circuit. Test your prediction. Make sure your drawing shows how the parts are connected when the switch works.

Analyze and Conclude

1. Compare your predictions about how to light the bulb—with and without the switch—with your results.

2. An electric circuit through which electricity moves is called a closed circuit. When you disconnect a part of a closed circuit, the circuit is called an open circuit. When you flip a switch to turn on a light, are you opening a circuit, or closing it? Explain your answer.

INVESTIGATE FURTHER!

RESEARCH

What are some different types of switches? How do the switches on electric devices and on the wall work in your home? Why do some switches click and others not click when you turn them on or off? Use resources in a library to find the answers.

Activity

Stop or Go?

Does electricity flow easily through all materials? Try some tests to find out.

- -

Procedure

1. With your group, use a wire to connect a light-bulb holder to a dry-cell holder. Attach a second wire to the light-bulb holder only. Attach a third wire to the dry-cell holder only. *Do not allow the two wires that are attached to the dry cell to touch.*

2. **Predict** what will happen if you touch the free ends of the wires together, as shown. **Record** your prediction in your *Science Notebook*. **Test** your prediction and **record** your results.

3. A material that allows electricity to flow through it is called a **conductor** (kən duk′tər). **Infer** whether the wires in your circuit are conductors. **Record** your inference.

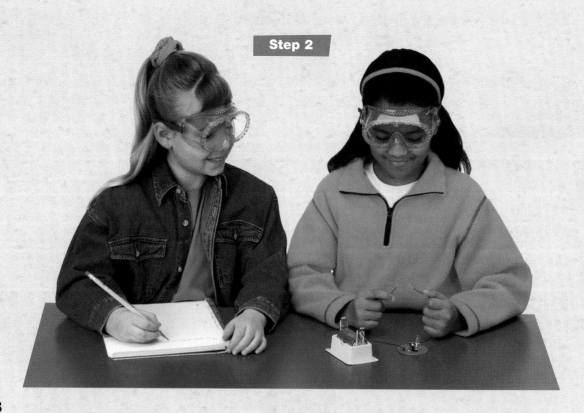

Step 2

4. A material that does not allow electricity to flow through it easily is called an **insulator** (in′sə lāt ər). **Make a chart** like the one shown. **Predict** which objects in the Materials list are conductors and which are insulators. **Record** your predictions in the chart. Then **test** them and **record** your results.

Step 4

Conductor or Insulator		
Object or Material	**Prediction**	**Result**

See **SCIENCE** *and* **MATH TOOLBOX** page H10 *if you need to review* **Making a Chart to Organize Data**.

Analyze and Conclude

1. **Compare** your predictions about which materials electricity would flow through with your results.

2. Which of the objects or materials that you tested are conductors? How do you know?

3. Which of the objects or materials that you tested are insulators? How do you know?

UNIT PROJECT LINK

Invent a way to use the opening and closing of circuits to make a quiz board. Work with your group to write a set of questions and answers. Then decide how to place dry cells, wires, and light bulbs. Test your invention by trying it in front of members of other groups in your class.

Technology Link

For more help with your Unit Project, go to **www.eduplace.com**.

D39

RESOURCE

Electric Current

Reading Focus What are the parts of an electric circuit?

You press a switch and your flashlight lights or your radio plays music. Electrical energy powers your flashlight and radio. You depend on electricity in hundreds of other ways, too. The picture below shows some ways that electricity works for the members of one family.

Charges in Currents

In Investigation 1 you found out about static electric charges. The charges collect on objects and may jump quickly between objects. But these charges can't be used to run electric devices. For electric charges to be useful, they have to flow.

Using Math *This home has four different electric circuits. Each circuit has six outlets, or places to plug in appliances. How many outlets are in the home?*

In the form of electricity used in homes and businesses, electric charges flow steadily, somewhat like currents of water in a stream. An **electric current** is a continuous flow of negative charges. An **electric circuit** is a path along which negative charges can flow. The activity on pages D36 and D37 shows how to put together the parts of an electric circuit.

A simple electric circuit starts with a source of electric charges, such as a dry cell. A wire connects the source to a light bulb or another device. A second wire connects the bulb or the other device back to the source of negative charges.

Open and Closed Circuits

When a circuit is closed, or complete, there is no break in the pathway of negative charges. The charges can flow through a closed circuit. In a closed circuit containing a light bulb, the bulb lights.

When a circuit is open, or incomplete, there's a break in the pathway. Charges can't flow through an open circuit. If you disconnect a wire in a simple circuit, the bulb can't light.

A **switch** is a device that opens or closes a circuit. When you turn a switch to *on*, you close a circuit so it is complete. When you turn a switch to *off*, you open a circuit so it is incomplete. If you add a switch to a circuit, you don't have to disconnect a wire to open the circuit.

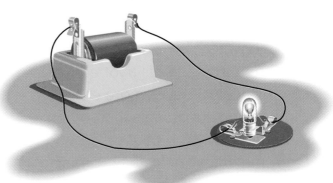
▲ Trace the path of electric charges in this circuit. Start and end at the dry cell. Why does the bulb light?

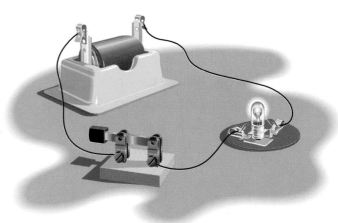
▲ This circuit contains a closed switch. Trace the path of the charges through this circuit. Why does the bulb light?

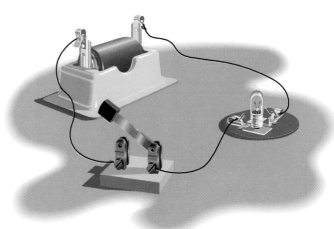
▲ How is this circuit the same as the one in the middle picture? How is it different? Why doesn't the bulb light?

Conductors and Insulators

Have you ever tried running through water? It's hard work, isn't it? Running through air is a lot easier. Electricity also moves more easily through some materials than others.

In the activity on pages D38 and D39, materials are tested for their ability to conduct electricity. Materials that allow electricity to pass through them easily are called **conductors**. Most kinds of metals are good conductors of electricity. Copper is a metal that is used in wires in electrical cords. The wires in the power lines that bring electricity to your house are copper wires, too.

Insulators are materials that don't let electricity move easily through them. Plastics, rubber, wood, paper, cloth, and ceramics are good insulators. The picture shows how a conductor and an insulator are used in an electrical cord.

How a Flashlight Works

What happens inside a flashlight when you turn it on or off? When you turn the switch to *on*, you close the circuit and the bulb lights. When you turn the switch to *off*, you open the circuit, so the light in the bulb goes out. The picture on page D43 shows what's inside one kind of flashlight and how it works.

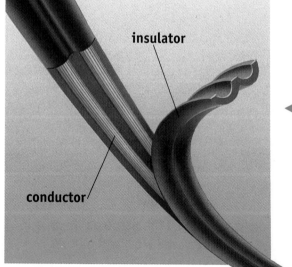

insulator

conductor

◀ Electricity flows through copper wires that are coated with plastic. The electric charges can't get through the plastic covering because the plastic is an insulator.

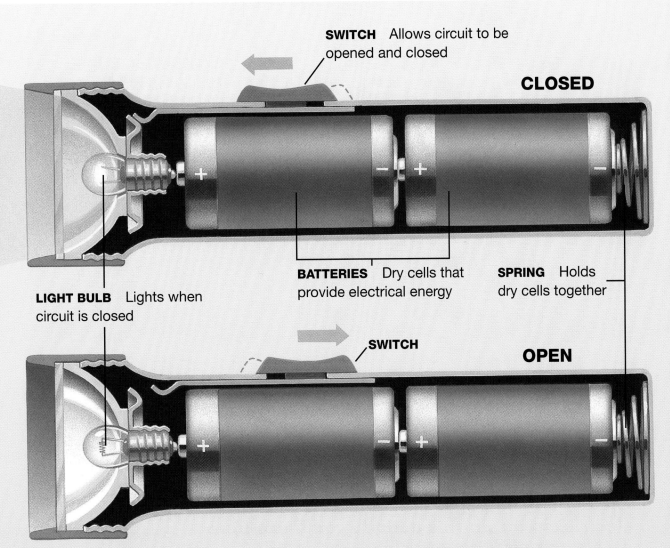

SWITCH Allows circuit to be opened and closed

CLOSED

BATTERIES Dry cells that provide electrical energy

SPRING Holds dry cells together

LIGHT BULB Lights when circuit is closed

SWITCH

OPEN

▲ When the switch is closed, negative charges flow from the batteries through the spring, along the metal case of the flashlight to the metal strip attached to the switch, to the bulb holder, through the light bulb, and back to the batteries.

INVESTIGATION 2 WRAP-UP

REVIEW

1. Make a sketch of a simple electric circuit. Label the parts.

2. Distinguish between conductors and insulators.

CRITICAL THINKING

3. The bulb in a circuit is not glowing. The circuit consists of a light bulb, switch, dry cell, and three wires. What parts of the circuit would you check to find out why the bulb is not glowing?

4. Suppose you set up a circuit, using a plastic paper clip for a switch. Will the circuit work? If not, how could you get the circuit to work?

HOW DO ELECTRIC CIRCUITS DIFFER?

Suppose you want to put up a string of lights for a party, but one bulb is missing from the string. Is this a problem? It depends on how the lights are wired. In this investigation, find out the different ways lights can be wired.

Activity

One Type of Circuit

The activity on pages D36 and D37 shows an electric circuit. In this activity you'll examine an electric circuit more closely.

MATERIALS

- dry cell (size D) in holder
- 3 insulated wires (stripped on ends)
- 2 light bulbs in holders
- colored pencil
- *Science Notebook*

Procedure

1. On your desk, place a dry cell, three wires, and two light bulbs.

2. Find a way to make both bulbs light at the same time. Talk with your group and together predict a way to use the materials to light both bulbs at once. In your *Science Notebook*, draw a diagram that shows the arrangement of materials for your group's prediction.

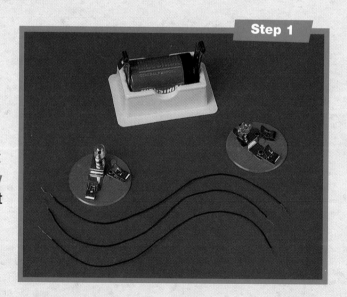
Step 1

3. Work with your group to **test** your prediction. Make sure that the connections are tight. You may change the connections until both bulbs light. Then **draw** a diagram of your complete circuit.

Step 3

4. When both bulbs are lighted, **predict** what will happen if you take one bulb out of its holder. **Record** your prediction. **Test** your prediction and **record** your observations.

Analyze and Conclude

1. The circuit you constructed is called a series circuit. In a **series circuit** there is only one path for an electric current. Place your finger on the dry cell in your drawing. Then, with your finger, follow the path of the electric current through the circuit. Use a colored pencil to show this path on your drawing.

2. Would placing a switch between the bulbs in the circuit affect whether one or both bulbs would light? Explain your reasoning. With your teacher's permission, make and test the circuit.

3. Some strings of lights used for decoration are connected in a series circuit. If one light bulb burns out, **infer** what happens to the other bulbs. Why does this happen?

Technology Link CD-ROM

INVESTIGATE FURTHER!

Use the **Science Processor CD-ROM**, *Magnetism and Electricity* (Investigation 3, Power Play) to learn about the connection between electricity and magnets. You can also watch a video about the uses of electromagnetism.

Activity

Another Type of Circuit

Can you wire a circuit so that one bulb stays lighted when another is missing? Try out your ideas in this activity.

MATERIALS

- dry cell (size D) in holder
- 4 insulated wires (stripped on ends)
- 2 light bulbs in holders
- colored pencils
- *Science Notebook*

- -

Procedure

1. On your desk, place a dry cell, four wires, and two light bulbs.

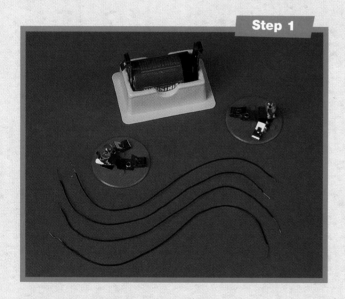

Step 1

2. In the activity on pages D44 and D45, two bulbs are connected in a series circuit. Now you'll connect two bulbs in a different kind of circuit. This circuit will use four wires instead of three. Talk with your group and together plan a way to connect the materials. In your *Science Notebook*, draw a diagram of your group's plan.

3. Predict how the materials will look when connected so that both bulbs light. Work with your group to test your prediction. Make sure that the connections are tight. If you need to, change the connections until both bulbs light. Then record your observations.

Step 3

4. When both bulbs are lighted, draw a diagram of your complete circuit. Then work with your group to predict what will happen to the other bulb if you take one bulb out of its holder. Record your prediction and explain why you predicted as you did. Then work with your group to test your prediction. Record your observations.

Analyze and Conclude

1. The circuit you constructed is a parallel (par′ə lel) circuit. In a **parallel circuit** there is more than one path for an electric current. Starting at the dry cell in your drawing, use your finger to trace each path in your circuit that a current can follow. Use a different-colored pencil for each path in your drawing.

2. Suppose you could choose between a set of lights wired in a series circuit and a set wired in a parallel circuit. Which would you choose? Why?

The Light Bulb

Reading Focus In what ways are incandescent bulbs different from fluorescent bulbs?

What everyday object turns electrical energy into light? It's a light bulb, of course. Light bulbs come in a number of different sizes, shapes, and colors.

There are bulbs for ceiling fixtures and for table lamps. There are bulbs for street lights, for headlights, and even for growing plants.

Many light bulbs are incandescent (in kən des'ənt) bulbs. Look at the diagram of this type of bulb. As electric current passes through the **filament** (fil'ə mənt), the filament gets so hot that it begins to glow, or give off light.

Now look at the fluorescent (floo-ə res'ənt) bulb. In this bulb, ultraviolet light is changed into white light.

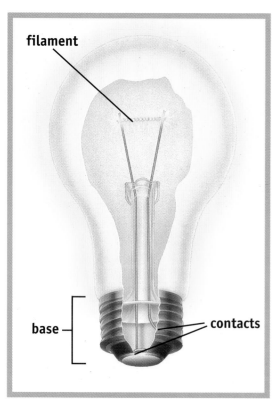

filament

base — contacts

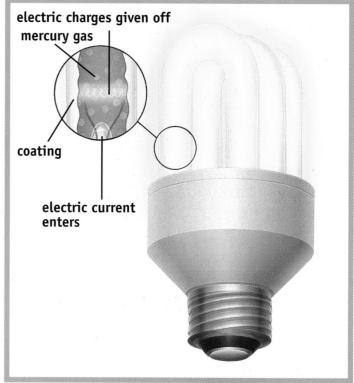

electric charges given off
mercury gas

coating

electric current enters

▲ **INCANDESCENT BULB** The filament is a long, thin wire coil made of the metal tungsten (tuŋ'stən). It glows when electricity passes through it. The contacts at the base conduct electricity.

▲ **FLUORESCENT BULB** As electricity enters the bulb, electric charges bump into particles of mercury gas. The gas gives off ultraviolet light. This light strikes the coating, which gives off white light.

D48

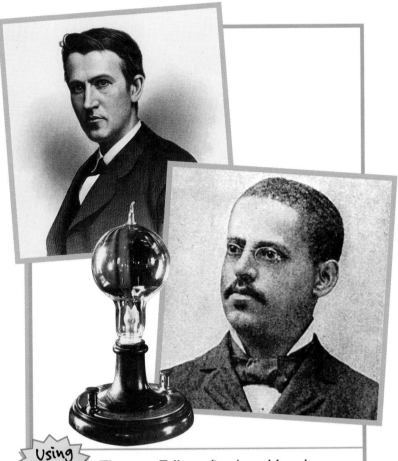

INVESTIGATE FURTHER!

RESEARCH

Count the number of incandescent light bulbs in your house. Estimate how long they are used each day. Add together the number of watts for each bulb. Then contact your electric company or an electrical supply store in your community.

Get information about fluorescent bulbs that could replace the incandescent bulbs in your home. Based on the information you obtain, figure out how much money your family could save by switching to fluorescent bulbs.

Using Math

Thomas Edison (top) and Lewis Latimer (bottom) are shown with an early incandescent bulb invented in the 1870s. About how many years ago was the incandescent bulb invented?

Bulbs and Energy

In incandescent bulbs, electrical energy changes to heat and light. These bulbs produce much more heat than light, so they get very hot. All the heat that incandescent bulbs produce is wasted energy.

In fluorescent bulbs, electricity is used to change one type of light to another. These bulbs produce much less heat and cost less to operate than incandescent bulbs do. Fluorescent bulbs are good for the environment because they don't waste energy.

Invention of the Light Bulb

Thomas Edison, who headed a team of scientists called the Edison Pioneers, invented the light bulb. Edison's first bulb used a filament made of scorched thread. But this bulb was costly and didn't last long.

Lewis Latimer was a member of the Edison Pioneers. Latimer made a greatly improved bulb that used a carbon filament. This bulb cost less and lasted longer than Edison's bulb. Carbon was later replaced by tungsten, which is used in bulbs today. ■

Series and Parallel Circuits

Reading Focus How do series circuits and parallel circuits differ?

You've seen how electricity flows along paths called circuits. You can compare a circuit's path to a path in a maze. In the two mazes shown below, you start at point A, follow some paths, and come back to A. You can turn right or left, but you must move only in the direction of the arrows.

In the first maze there is only one path you can follow. You can move from A to B and then through C to get back to A. In the second maze there are two paths you can follow to make a round trip. Use your finger to trace these paths.

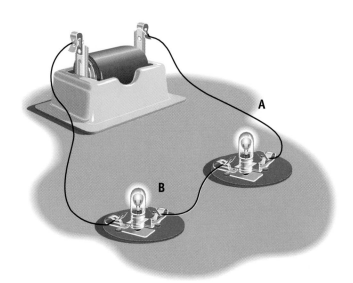

▲ Trace the path of current through this series circuit.

Just One Path

In the activity on pages D44 and D45, a series circuit is made. A **series circuit** is one that has only a single path for current to follow. In a series circuit, all of the parts are connected one after the other in a single loop, or path, as shown in the drawing above.

In this circuit, charges flow from the dry cell through bulb A and bulb B and back to the dry cell. If either bulb is removed from the circuit, the circuit is broken and the current stops.

Mazes that are like two kinds of circuits ▼

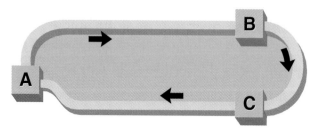

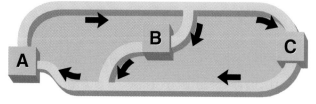

More Than One Path

In the activity on pages D46 and D47, a parallel circuit is made. A **parallel circuit** is one that has more than one path for an electric current to follow, as shown in the picture on the right.

Notice that in path 1, negative charges can flow from the dry cell through bulb A and back to the dry cell. In path 2, negative charges can flow from the dry cell through bulb B and back to the dry cell.

When both bulbs are in place, current will follow both paths, and both bulbs will be lighted. However, if either bulb is removed, current will still

There are two paths a current can follow in this parallel circuit. ▼

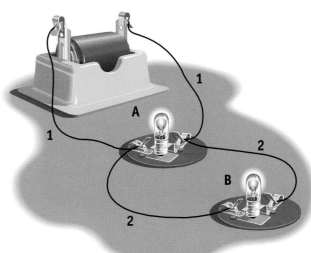

follow the path through the other bulb. So the bulb in this part of the circuit will remain lighted.

Science in Literature

YOUR ELECTRIC VOICE

"When you talk into your phone, your words zip through the telephone wires in electrical form. They travel across the streets all the way to your friend's house. Here, your friend's phone changes the electric signals back into sound waves. And, presto, your friend is listening to the sounds of your voice."

This description comes from *Hello! Hello! A Look Inside the Telephone* by Eve and Albert Stwertka. If you like amusing and unusual stories, this book is for you.

**Hello! Hello!
A Look Inside the Telephone**
by Eve and Albert Stwertka
Illustrated by Mena Dolobowsky
Julian Messner, 1991

▲ This home has just four circuits, but a real home may have as many as twenty circuits.

How Homes Are Wired

All of the lights and electric appliances in your home are linked in circuits. Lamps, toaster ovens, stereo systems, hair dryers, and refrigerators are parts of the circuits. The circuits in home wiring are parallel, not series. Why, do you think, is this so?

Different circuits control electrical outlets in different parts of a home. Each of these circuits is connected to an outside source of electric current.

One circuit in the house shown above controls the outlets in the kitchen. Trace the circuit that controls the outlets in a child's bedroom.

Every home circuit has a fuse or a circuit breaker. These safety devices open circuits that overheat when too much electricity flows through them. A **fuse** contains a metal strip that melts when overheated. A **circuit breaker** is a switch that opens a circuit by turning itself off. ■

INVESTIGATION 3 WRAP-UP

REVIEW

1. Compare a series circuit with a parallel circuit.

2. Why do circuits in homes have fuses or circuit breakers?

CRITICAL THINKING

3. Explain why you can open a series circuit, but not a parallel circuit, by removing one bulb.

4. You want to make a parallel circuit with two light bulbs, a dry cell, and two switches. Draw the way you would connect the parts so that each switch can turn off one bulb at a time.

REFLECT & EVALUATE

Word Power

Write the letter of the term that best matches the definition. *Not all terms will be used.*

1. Circuit that has only one path for electricity to follow
2. Buildup of electric charges on objects
3. Material that lets electricity flow easily
4. A thin wire inside a light bulb
5. Circuit that has more than one path for electricity to follow
6. Safety device that opens a circuit by melting

a. circuit breaker
b. conductor
c. filament
d. fuse
e. insulator
f. parallel circuit
g. static electricity
h. series circuit

Check What You Know

Write the word in each pair that best completes each sentence.

1. A switch that opens a circuit by turning itself off is a (fuse, circuit breaker).
2. A continuous flow of negative charges is an (electric current, electric discharge).
3. A path through which electricity can flow is (a conductor, an electric circuit).
4. A device that opens or closes a circuit is a (switch, cell).

Problem Solving

1. You and a friend are trying to shock each other by rubbing your feet on the carpet. Your friend can shock you, but you aren't able to shock him. Give a reason why this might be so.

2. Suppose that all of the outlets in a room are part of the same circuit. Why is it better to have the outlets wired in a parallel circuit than in a series circuit?

BUILD YOUR PORTFOLIO

Study the drawing. Explain on paper why the drawing is incorrect. Then make a drawing of a circuit that is correct.

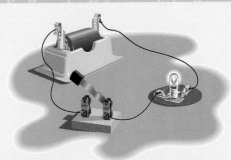

ELECTRICITY AT WORK

You turn on the TV set and the picture appears. Where does the electricity come from to make this happen? How does electricity get to your home? What produces this electricity? In this chapter you'll find out the answers to these questions as you explore the story of electricity.

PEOPLE USING SCIENCE

Electrical Engineer Have you ever wondered what makes your telephone work? When Adelina Mejia-Zelaya was a child, she wondered about such things. She wondered how, by just pressing a button, she could make an elevator or a calculator work. Since that time she has studied much about all kinds of electronic equipment.

Today Adlina Mejia-Zelaya is an electrical engineer. Designing tiny electric circuits is part of her everyday work. Explaining her work, she says, "I design circuits for the computers that make your phone work."

In this chapter you'll learn more about electricity. And you'll explore some of the many ways that electricity can be useful.

Coming Up

INVESTIGATION 1

WHAT ARE SOME SOURCES OF ELECTRIC CURRENT?
. . . . D56

INVESTIGATION 2

HOW IS ELECTRICITY USEFUL?
. . . . D66

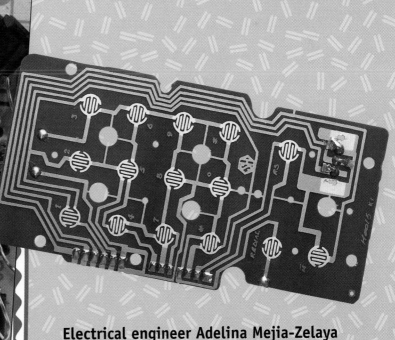

Electrical engineer Adelina Mejia-Zelaya works with tiny electric circuits, such as these.

WHAT ARE SOME SOURCES OF ELECTRIC CURRENT?

You've seen that electricity can flow through wires. A dry cell provided a source of energy for that current. In this investigation you'll find out about some other sources of electrical energy.

Activity

Detect a Current

How can you tell if a current is flowing in a wire? Make a current detector.

MATERIALS
- insulated wire (stripped on ends, 50 cm)
- metric tape measure
- compass
- transparent tape
- dry cell (size D) in holder
- *Science Notebook*

Procedure

Starting from the middle of a 50-cm wire, wrap several turns of wire around a compass so that the wire is either parallel to the compass needle or forms a narrow **X** with the compass needle. Tape the wire in place. You've made a current detector. Connect one end of the wire to a dry cell. With your group, predict what will happen when you connect the free end of the wire to the dry cell. Test your prediction and record your observations in your *Science Notebook*.

Analyze and Conclude

1. What happens when a current flows through the wire?

2. Infer what causes any changes you observe.

Activity

A Magnetic Source

How can you use your current detector to find another source of electric current?

MATERIALS
- insulated wire (stripped on ends, 3 m)
- cardboard tube
- current detector from activity on page D56
- bar magnet
- *Science Notebook*

Procedure

1. Wind 3 m of wire into a coil around a cardboard tube. Leave about 25 cm of wire free at each end of the tube, as shown. Then put your current detector from the activity on page D56 on your work surface.

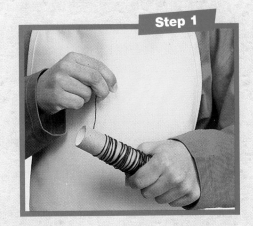

Step 1

2. Talk with your group and infer whether or not there is an electric current in the wire coil. Record your inference in your *Science Notebook*. Then test your inference by connecting the free ends of the current detector to the free ends of the wire coil. Record your observations.

3. Now predict how a magnet moving inside the tube might affect your current detector. Record your prediction. Then test it by moving a bar magnet back and forth quickly inside the tube. Observe the current detector when the magnet is moving and when it is still. Record your observations.

Step 3

4. Now try holding the magnet still and moving the tube back and forth. Record your observations.

Analyze and Conclude

1. Infer what caused the electric current in this activity. What observations support your inference?

2. The device you made with a wire coil and a magnet is called a **generator** (jen'ər āt ər). How might a generator be used to make an electric current?

Producing Electric Current

Reading Focus How do generators and electric cells produce electrical energy?

Where do you get the energy to kick a soccer ball? You get energy from food. Suppose you eat a peanut butter sandwich. The sandwich—and everything else you eat—has chemical energy stored in it. Your body can change that chemical energy into energy of motion.

Electricity From Magnetism

Energy of motion can change to electrical energy. In the activity on page D57, moving a magnet inside a wire coil produces an electric current in the wire. Moving a wire coil in a magnetic field will also produce a current in the coil.

A device in which a wire coil and a magnet are used to produce electricity is called a **generator**. A generator is a device that changes energy of motion into electrical energy.

Getting a Strong Current

The magnet used in the activity is not very strong. And not many turns of wire are used to make the coil. With a current detector you can detect a current produced by such a generator.

But the current isn't even strong enough to light a bulb. How can a stronger current be made?

The stronger the magnet in a generator, the stronger the current produced. Adding more turns of wire to the coil also strengthens the current. So you could make your generator stronger by using a strong magnet and many coils of wire.

Giant generators produce the electricity that flows to the electrical outlets in homes and schools. These generators also produce the electricity that lights cities, powers machinery, and works in other ways. The generators have powerful magnets and huge coils of wire.

Where does the energy of motion that turns large generators come from? The energy may come from a power plant that uses coal or nuclear fuel to heat water. The heated water makes steam, which turns the generator. Sometimes the energy comes from water falling over a dam such as the one shown on the next page. Or the energy may come from wind turning the blades of a windmill.

D58

Using Math

Hoover Dam is 201 m (660 ft) thick at its base and 14 m (45 ft) thick at its top. How much thicker is Hoover Dam at its base than at its top?

Hoover Dam stands in the Black Canyon of the Colorado River. Water falling over the dam provides energy to turn large generators.

▲ Power plant at Hoover Dam

▲ Generators inside the power plant at Hoover Dam

Chemicals and Currents

Batteries are another source of useful electrical energy. A battery is made up of one or more smaller parts called **electric cells**. Energy is stored in chemicals used in an electric cell. When an electric cell is connected to a circuit, this stored chemical energy changes into electrical energy.

There are two basic types of electric cells—wet cells and dry cells. The drawing below shows the operation of a simple wet cell. In this wet cell, strips of the metals copper and zinc hang from the wires of a current detector into a liquid chemical. The zinc metal reacts with substances in the liquid to produce a chemical change. This change separates negative charges from zinc atoms.

The negative charges move through the zinc strip, which then becomes the negative end of the cell. These charges then move through the wire around the current detector to the copper strip. This strip has become the positive end of the cell. As the charges move back into the liquid, the circuit is completed.

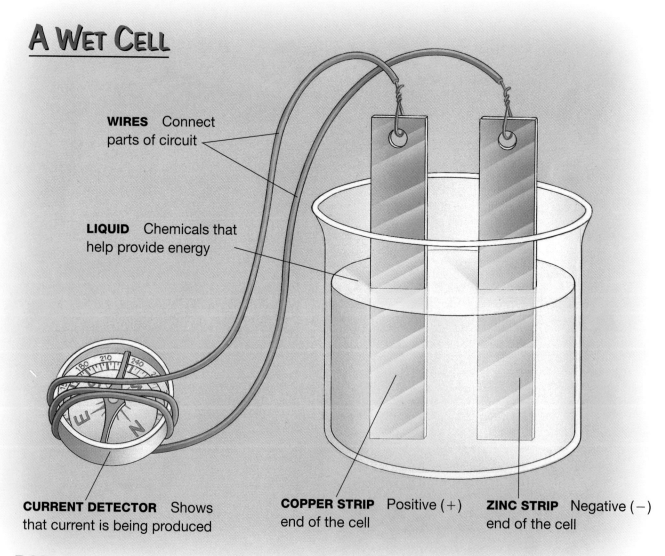

A WET CELL

WIRES Connect parts of circuit

LIQUID Chemicals that help provide energy

CURRENT DETECTOR Shows that current is being produced

COPPER STRIP Positive (+) end of the cell

ZINC STRIP Negative (−) end of the cell

A dry cell like the one used in the activity on page D56 is shown below. Trace the path of charges through the cell and around the current detector.

A zinc case is the negative end of the cell. A chemical paste inside the case has a carbon rod in its center. The carbon rod is the positive end of the cell. Zinc reacts with substances in the paste, separating negative charges from the zinc atoms. These charges move through the wire around the current detector to the carbon rod and back to the paste, completing the circuit. ■

Technology Link
CD-ROM

INVESTIGATE FURTHER!

Use the **Science Processor CD–ROM**, *Magnetism and Electricity* (Investigation 3, Power Play) to experiment with an on-screen magnet and coil. From the same program, you can learn more about the parts of a generator and how a generator works.

A DRY CELL

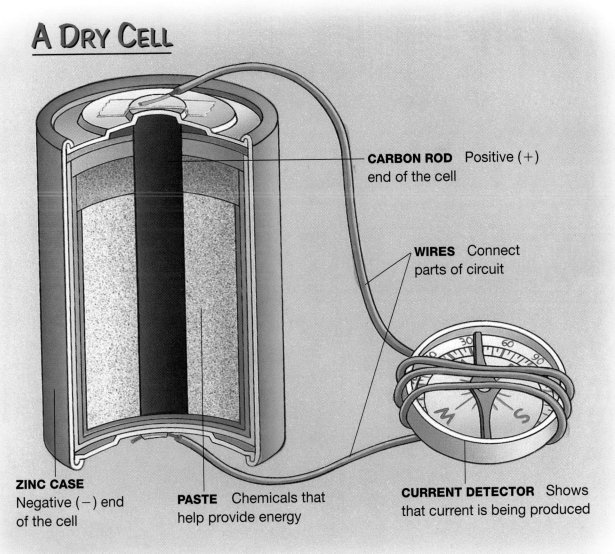

CARBON ROD Positive (+) end of the cell

WIRES Connect parts of circuit

ZINC CASE Negative (−) end of the cell

PASTE Chemicals that help provide energy

CURRENT DETECTOR Shows that current is being produced

From Power Plant to You

Reading Focus How does the electricity from a power plant reach your home?

Most of the electricity you use is as near as a wall switch or an outlet. When you flip a switch or plug in a cord, the electric current is right there. But the generators in the power plant that make this current may be very far away from your home. How does electricity from power plants get to other places where it's used? Study the drawing below to find out.

The Force of Electricity

The generators in power plants push the electricity through heavy-duty power lines that leave the plant.

WHERE YOUR ELECTRICITY COMES FROM

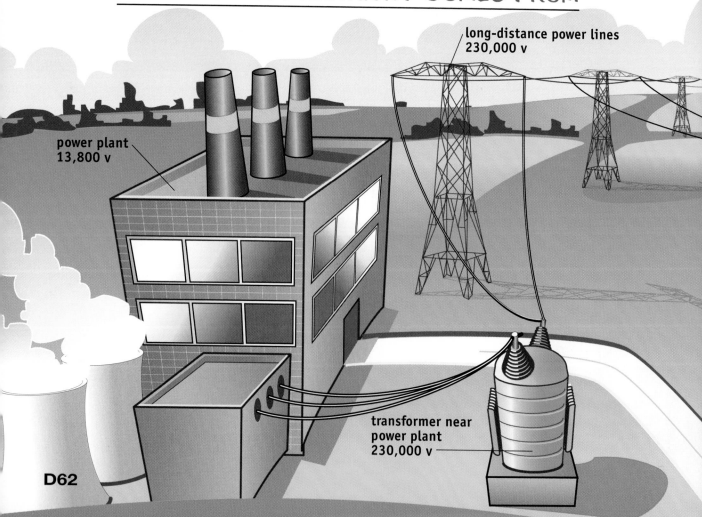

long-distance power lines
230,000 v

power plant
13,800 v

transformer near
power plant
230,000 v

The force that pushes electricity along wires is called **voltage** (vōl'tij). This force is measured in units called volts. The letter v is the symbol for volts.

You can compare voltage to the pressure, or pushing force, of water in a hose. Water can rush from a hose, or flow gently, depending on the pressure. The current in a wire can also be strong or weak, depending on the voltage.

Raising and Lowering Voltage

A transformer (trans fôrm'ər) is a device that changes the voltage of a current. The voltage of the current coming from a power plant is too low to send long distances. A transformer raises the voltage, sending it cross-country to users.

After current makes a long journey from a power plant, its voltage must be lowered. It is too high for use in homes and in most other buildings. So the current is sent through another transformer. Study the drawing to see how voltages are changed as current travels from a power plant to you and to other users of electricity. ■

Using Math

How much greater is the voltage at the transformer near the power plant than the voltage at the substation transformer?

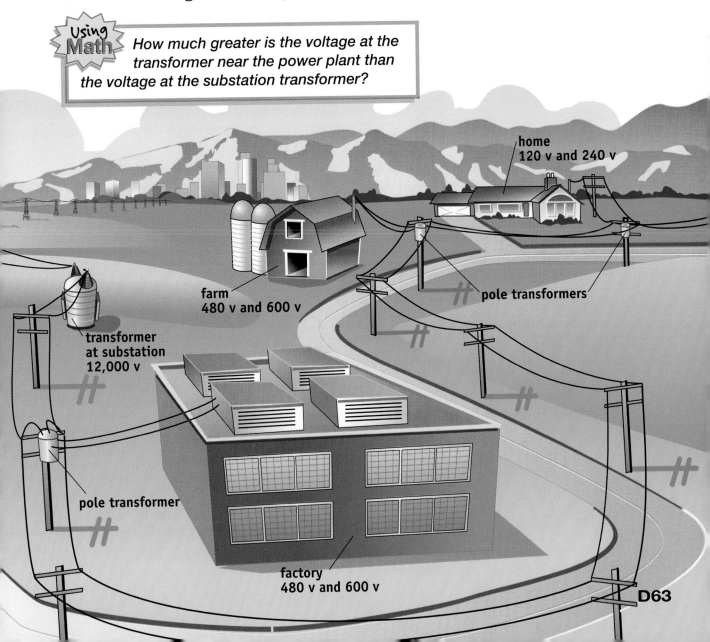

home
120 v and 240 v

farm
480 v and 600 v

pole transformers

transformer at substation
12,000 v

pole transformer

factory
480 v and 600 v

Electricity From Sunlight

RESOURCE

RESOURCE

Reading Focus What is a solar cell, and how is it used in a solar panel?

STS
SCIENCE
TECHNOLOGY
& SOCIETY

Did you ever use a solar calculator? **Solar energy**, or the energy of the Sun, powers the calculator. Inside solar calculators are solar cells. A **solar cell** is a device that changes light into electrical energy. Solar cells are so sensitive they even work on overcast days.

Solar Cells, Clean Energy

About 25 power plants in the United States use solar cells to produce electricity. Solar cells produce electricity in a way that helps keep the environment clean. Burning coal or oil to produce electricity can pollute the air. Using nuclear energy can create toxic wastes that pollute water and land.

Another advantage of using solar energy is that it helps to save fossil fuels. The amount of solar energy Earth receives in 12 hours is equal to the energy produced from burning fossil fuels in one year! Look at the photographs to see some uses of solar cells.

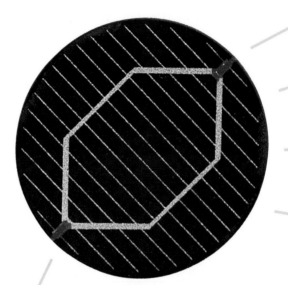

▲ One solar cell produces a tiny amount of electricity. Because of this, many cells are connected in panels.

Solar-powered airplane ▼

▲ Solar-powered car

▲ Solar-powered toy

◀ Solar-powered watch

Solar-powered home ▶

INVESTIGATION 1 WRAP-UP

REVIEW

1. What energy change takes place in a generator? in a dry cell? in a solar cell?

2. Compare how electricity is produced by a generator with how it's produced by an electric cell.

CRITICAL THINKING

3. List and discuss at least two advantages of using solar energy over energy from burning fossil fuels.

4. Certain electric devices, such as cordless telephones, have small transformers that plug into a wall. What do the transformers do?

INVESTIGATION 2

How Is Electricity Useful?

Light and sound come from your TV. Heat comes from your toaster oven. A motor spins inside your toy car. In all these examples, electricity is changed into another form of energy to make it useful. Explore some of these energy changes and how to stay safe around electricity.

Activity

Make It Move

How can you use electricity to make something move? Find out in this activity.

MATERIALS

- insulated wire (stripped on ends, 125 cm)
- metric ruler
- iron nail
- 10 paper clips
- dry cell (size D) in holder
- *Science Notebook*

Procedure

1. Measure about 20 cm from one end of a 125-cm length of insulated wire. From that point, wrap 25 turns of the wire around a nail. You will have a length of free wire at both ends of the nail, as shown.

See **SCIENCE** and **MATH TOOLBOX** page H6 if you need to review *Using a Tape Measure or Ruler*.

Step 1

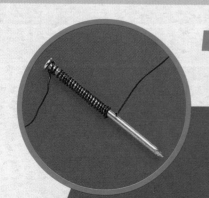

2. Make a small pile of paper clips. **Talk with your group** and together **predict** whether bringing the nail close to the paper clips will have any effect on the paper clips. **Record** your prediction in your *Science Notebook*. **Test** your prediction and **record** your observations.

3. Attach each end of the wire to a different end of a dry cell, as shown.

4. **Predict** what will happen if you now bring the tip of the nail toward the paper clips. **Record** your prediction. **Test** your prediction and **record** your observations.

5. Disconnect the wire ends from the dry cell. Again bring the nail close to the paper clips. **Record** your observations.

6. Wrap 25 more turns of wire around the nail. Leave the nail bare at the end. Repeat steps 3 and 4.

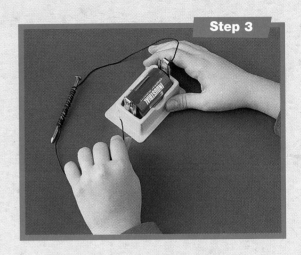
Step 3

Analyze and Conclude

1. **Compare** your predictions about the nail and the paper clips with your observations.

2. A magnet made when an electric current is sent through a wire wrapped around iron is an **electromagnet** (ē lek′trō mag nit). How does adding more turns of wire affect an electromagnet? Give evidence to support your inference.

3. What happens to an electromagnet when the current is turned off? What can you **infer** about electromagnets?

UNIT PROJECT LINK

Have you seen electric devices that run on solar cells, such as solar toys or solar hats with propellers? Ask your teacher for a solar cell. Work with your group to design a solar-powered machine. Display your invention.

Technology Link

For more help with your Unit Project, go to **www.eduplace.com**.

Long Distance, Short Time

Reading Focus What types of devices help us communicate with one another?

How do you communicate (kə myoo'ni kāt) with friends over long distances? Do you talk on the phone? Do you use electronic mail, or E-mail, on a computer? If so, then you use telecommunication (tel i-kə myoo ni kā'shən). This is using electricity for almost instant communication over a long distance.

Electricity has made telecommunication possible, beginning with the invention of the telegraph. Today people link television, telephones, and computers all over the world. These devices work together in a system that provides information, communication, and entertainment. The time line shows some highlights in the field of telecommunication since the 1840s.

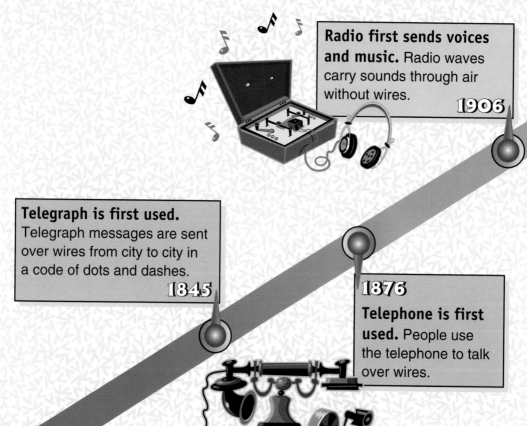

Radio first sends voices and music. Radio waves carry sounds through air without wires.
1906

Telegraph is first used. Telegraph messages are sent over wires from city to city in a code of dots and dashes.
1845

1876
Telephone is first used. People use the telephone to talk over wires.

Communications satellite *Telestar* is sent into space.
Satellites carry live television, radio, telephone calls, and computer data all over the world.
1962

Internet system is in use.
People use the Internet to send information from computer to computer. They use this system to communicate almost instantly throughout the world.
1990s

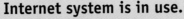

2000
Video phones are used.
Users can see the person they're talking to on a video screen.

1980s
Cellular (sel'yoo lər) **phones and fax machines are in use.** Cellular phones allow people to talk on the phone as they travel. Facsimile (fak sim'ə lē), also called fax, machines are used to send written messages over telephone lines.

1936
Television programs are broadcast.
Television sends clear pictures and sound.

INVESTIGATE FURTHER!

RESEARCH

Analyze television commercials for three phone companies. Infer and then determine which company would save you the most money if you talked to a friend in another state for 17 minutes.

Electric Magnets

Did you ever flip a coin? When the heads side of the coin is up, you can't see the tails side. But you know the tails side is there. In a way, electricity and magnetism are like the two sides of a coin.

In Investigation 1 you found one way that magnetism and electricity are related. Moving a coil of wire in a magnetic field produces electric current. In this way, magnetism produces electricity.

Electricity and magnetism are also related in another way. In the activity on pages D66 and D67, a dry cell and a nail are used to make an electromagnet. An **electromagnet** is a magnet made when electric charges move through a coil of wire wrapped around an iron core, or center. In an electromagnet, electricity is used to produce magnetism.

Properties of Electromagnets

Electromagnets are like natural magnets in some ways. Like natural magnets, they attract materials that contain iron. Electromagnets have a north pole and a south pole. An electromagnet also has a magnetic field, as the drawing above shows.

This electromagnet makes it easy to separate steel from other materials. The magnet is turned on in order to lift the steel. ▶

How are electromagnets different from other magnets? In Chapter 1, a temporary magnet is made by stroking a nail with a bar magnet. Recall that a temporary magnet slowly loses its magnetism over time. An electromagnet is a different kind of temporary magnet. It acts like a magnet only while electric current flows through it. As soon as you turn off the current, it loses its magnetism. As a result, an electromagnet can be turned on or off.

Using Electromagnets

Imagine that you're in charge of a collection center for recycling. People dump bags of cans made of different metals in one big pile. But the cans made of steel and those made of aluminum have to be sent to different places to be recycled. This means that you have to separate the two kinds of cans. One way to do this job is by using a large electromagnet, as the pictures below show.

After the crane swings away from the pile of mixed materials, the magnet is turned off. Then the steel objects fall into a separate pile. ▶

When you push a doorbell, a circuit closes and the electromagnet pulls on the hammer, which strikes the bell. ▶

Many objects in your home have electromagnets in them. These electromagnets are hidden inside loudspeakers, telephones, VCRs, cassette players, and doorbells. All electric motors contain electromagnets, too. Electric motors run refrigerators, clocks, hair dryers, vacuum cleaners, and ceiling fans.

Take another look at the pictures on page D40 in Chapter 2. Electric motors drive many of the devices shown there, too. What other things can you think of that are run by electric motors? ■

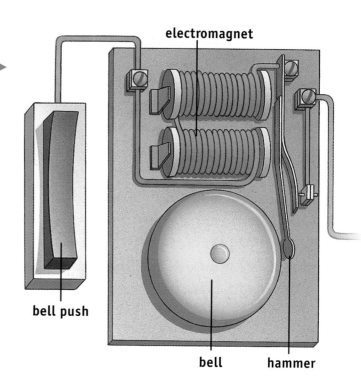

electromagnet

bell push

bell   hammer

Science in Literature

STATION, PLEASE?

"Today the telephone no longer has to depend on wires strung across mountains or under large bodies of water. Because sound waves can now be changed into radio signals, part of the wire circuit can be replaced by radio."

This quotation from *Hello! Hello! A Look Inside the Telephone* by Eve and Albert Stwertka helps you realize how phones have changed communication. Read this book to find out how the first telephones were different from the one you may have today.

Hello! Hello!
A Look Inside the Telephone
by Eve and Albert Stwertka
Illustrated by Mena Dolobowsky
Julian Messner, 1991

RESOURCE

A Car That Plugs In

VD·284 894

STS
SCIENCE TECHNOLOGY & SOCIETY

Do you live in or near a large city? In many cities, air pollution is a serious problem. As you read in Chapter 1, cars that run on gasoline pollute the air. Many cars crowded together can make the air unhealthy. Using electric cars may be one way to solve this problem. These cars run on batteries, which results in less pollution.

Have you ever used a rechargeable battery? Electric cars have rechargeable batteries. As you know, batteries are made up of electric cells. The cells in the batteries of electric cars lose energy, or run down, and stop working after being used a certain length of

time. When the batteries run down, they have to be recharged.

Electric cars aren't used much today. Their batteries must be recharged about once every 96 km (60 mi). Their top speed is about 80 km/h (50 mph). And electric cars cost more to operate than most gas-powered cars.

In the future, many people may drive cars that won't rely only on gasoline. Why? Gasoline is made from oil, and the need to conserve oil is great. The need to clean up the air is just as important.

Internet Field Trip
Visit **www.eduplace.com** to find out more about electric cars.

Using Math

Suppose you traveled 8 km to school each day in an electric car. The car can travel 96 km (60 mi) on one charge of its batteries. How many trips could you make to school on one charge?

Safety Around Electricity

Reading Focus What are some ways to be safe around electricity?

SCIENCE TECHNOLOGY & SOCIETY

In the activities, electric current is sent through wires. But why are those wires safe to touch? The activities use size D dry cells that are marked 1.5 v, which stands for 1.5 volts. A current with such a low voltage has very little energy. But the voltage of the current in the wiring of a house is 110 volts or more. This electric current is dangerous. But you can be safe if you follow certain safety rules.

DON'T use any appliance that has a torn cord or a cord that is worn out. If two bare wires of a cord touch each other while the cord is in use, current will go to the crossed wires and back to its source. This is an example of a short circuit. In a short circuit, wires overheat. Overheated wires can cause a fire. ▶

◀ **NEVER** stick your finger or anything else except an electrical plug into an electrical outlet. Be sure any electrical plug you use is in good condition. Also, always hold a cord by its plug when you pull it from an outlet. What do you think is the reason for this rule?

DON'T overload circuits. Plugging too many appliances into one circuit can overload the circuit. Wires in overloaded circuits can become hot enough to start fires. ▶

◀ **STAY AWAY** from anything with a sign that says "High Voltage." Voltages in electric power lines and electric rails are even higher, and more dangerous, than they are in house current.

DANGER
HIGH VOLTAGE

NEVER touch an electrical cord, appliance, or light switch when you are wet. Unless water is pure, it is a conductor. Electric current can pass through the water and your body more easily than through an appliance. Any water that's in contact with a person's body is not pure. ▶

Have you ever had a power failure in your home? This can happen if a fuse blows or a circuit breaker switches off. As you read in Chapter 2, page D52, fuses and circuit breakers are safety devices. They open circuits when wires get too hot.

What should be done when a fuse blows or a circuit breaker trips, or switches off? First, it's important to find out the cause. Is there an overloaded circuit? Is there a short circuit somewhere? The cause of the overheating should be corrected. Then an adult in your home should replace the fuse or turn the circuit breaker back on. ■

▲ A home circuit-breaker box

▲ A good fuse

▲ A blown fuse

INVESTIGATION 2 WRAP-UP

REVIEW

1. What is an electromagnet?

2. List at least six devices that contain electromagnets.

CRITICAL THINKING

3. What are some advantages of an electric-gasoline combination car? What might the disadvantages be?

4. How would you explain to a group of first graders why radios used in a bathroom should be battery-powered?

REFLECT & EVALUATE

Word Power

Write the letter of the term that best matches the definition. *Not all terms will be used.*

1. A device that uses a wire coil and a magnet to produce electricity
2. A device that produces electric current from energy stored in chemicals
3. A device that changes sunlight into electrical energy
4. A magnet made from a wire wrapped around iron
5. The force that pushes electricity through wires

a. electrical cell
b. electromagnet
c. generator
d. solar cell
e. solar energy
f. voltage

Check What You Know

Write the word in each pair that best completes each sentence.

1. Solar energy is changed to electricity by (an electric cell, a solar cell).
2. When wires get too hot, circuit breakers (close, open) circuits.
3. Doorbells and telephones contain (generators, electromagnets).
4. Electric current can be produced by a (generator, transformer).

Problem Solving

1. A magnet passing through a coil of wire does not produce enough electric current to light a bulb. What are two ways to increase the amount of current?

2. How do you think the energy of the Sun might be used to power a motorcycle?

BUILD YOUR PORTFOLIO

Study the photograph. Name the device shown and describe how it works. Explain how the usefulness of the device would change if it could not be turned on and off.

Drawing Conclusions

Often writers imply, or hint at, more information than they actually state. They give clues and expect readers to figure out the rest, using what they already know. Suppose an author writes, "The children stared out the window." A reader can conclude that something interesting was happening outside—or that the children were bored by what was happening inside.

Consider these questions as you draw conclusions.

- What did the author write?
- What do I know?
- What is my conclusion?

Read the paragraphs. Then complete the exercises that follow.

Invention of the Light Bulb

Thomas Edison, who headed a team of scientists called the Edison Pioneers, invented the light bulb. Edison's first bulb used a filament made of scorched thread. But this bulb was costly and didn't last long.

Lewis Latimer was a member of the Edison Pioneers. Latimer made a greatly improved bulb that used a carbon filament. This bulb cost less and lasted longer than Edison's bulb. Carbon was later replaced by tungsten, which is used in bulbs today.

---

1. Which statement is a conclusion you can draw from the paragraphs? Write the letter of that statement.

   a. Edison was jealous of Latimer's success.

   b. Carbon lasts longer than tungsten and costs less.

   c. People will someday invent a better way to make electric light.

   d. Edison and Latimer should share the credit for the invention of the light bulb.

2. What was the most important clue in helping you draw that conclusion?

D78

Bar Graph

The graph below shows the estimated life span, in hours, of light bulbs of different wattages.

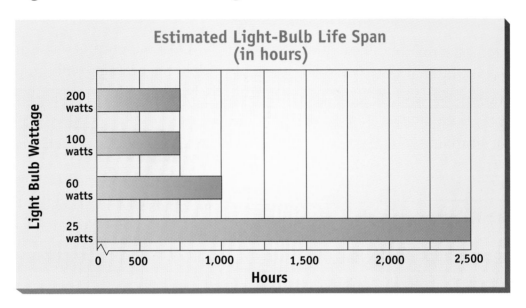

Use the data in the graph to complete the exercises that follow.

1. Which light bulb should last the longest?

2. About how many times longer will a 25-watt light bulb last than a 60-watt bulb?

3. Which bulb, if left on continuously, will last for about one month?

4. Estimate the life span, in days, of a 60-watt light bulb.

5. Estimate the number of months a 100-watt light bulb will last if it is left on for 8 hours a day.

6. Estimate the life span, in hours, of a 150-watt light bulb. Explain your answer.

7. Estimate the life span of a 75-watt light bulb in hours. Explain your answer.

WRAP-UP!

On your own, use scientific methods to investigate a question about magnetism and electricity.

THINK LIKE A SCIENTIST

Ask a Question

Pose a question about magnetism and electricity that you would like to investigate. For example, ask, "What effect does changing voltage have on an electromagnet?"

Make a Hypothesis

Suggest a hypothesis that is a possible answer to the question. One hypothesis is that increasing voltage increases the strength of an electromagnet.

Plan and Do a Test

Plan a controlled experiment to find whether or not increasing voltage increases the strength of an electromagnet. You could start with insulated wire, a metric ruler, an iron nail, paper clips, and dry cells. Develop a procedure that uses these materials to test the hypothesis. With permission, carry out your experiment. Follow the safety guidelines on pages S14–S15.

Record and Analyze

Observe carefully and record your data accurately. Make repeated observations.

Draw Conclusions

Look for evidence to support the hypothesis or to show that it is false. Draw conclusions about the hypothesis. Repeat the experiment to verify the results.

WRITING IN SCIENCE
Giving Instructions

Write a description of how to set up and operate a simple series circuit that includes a light bulb and a switch. Use these guidelines for writing your instructions.

- Keep in mind the person, or audience, who will read your instructions.
- List the materials for making the circuit.
- Write the steps in chronological order.

Weather and Climate

Theme: Constancy and Change

THINK LIKE A SCIENTIST
TORNADO WARNING E2

The Air Around Us E4
CHAPTER 1
Investigation 1   What Is Air? E6
Investigation 2   Why Does Air Move? E16

Observing Weather E24
CHAPTER 2
Investigation 1   What Is Air Pressure? E26
Investigation 2   How Can You Find Wind Speed
and Direction? E34
Investigation 3   How Does Water in the Air
Affect Weather? E42

Weather Patterns E50
CHAPTER 3
Investigation 1   What Can Clouds Tell You About
the Weather? E52
Investigation 2   How Can Maps Help You Predict
Weather? E58
Investigation 3   How Can You Stay Safe During
Dangerous Weather? E64

Seasons and Climate E74
CHAPTER 4
Investigation 1   What Causes the Seasons? E76
Investigation 2   What Factors Affect Climate? E82

Using Reading Skills E94
Using Math Skills E95
Unit Wrap-up! E96

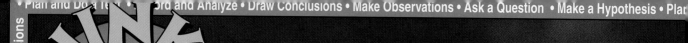

THINK LIKE A SCIENTIST

TORNADO WARNING

Tornadoes, such as this one seen over a Texas prairie, can have wind speeds up to 500 km/h. Tornadoes are the most violent storms on Earth. Hundreds of tornadoes strike the United States each year. Scientists study actual tornadoes, measuring conditions that occur within them. Artificial tornadoes are also studied in laboratory experiments. Yet, scientists still don't fully understand how tornadoes develop.

THINK LIKE A SCIENTIST

Questioning In this unit you'll study tornadoes and other types of storms. You'll investigate questions such as these.

- What Is Air Pressure?
- What Can Clouds Tell You About the Weather?

Observing, Testing, Hypothesizing
In the Activity "Tornado Tube," you'll make observations about the motion of swirling water. You'll also hypothesize about the motion of air in a tornado.

Researching In the Resource "The Fiercest Storms on Earth," you'll gather more information about the nature of tornadoes, and hurricanes too!

Drawing Conclusions
After you've completed your investigations, you'll draw conclusions about what you've learned—and get new ideas.

CHAPTER 1

THE AIR AROUND US

What do you need air for? You need it to breathe, of course. But is air important for anything else? Learning about air is a good way to begin learning about something that affects you every day. That something is weather.

PEOPLE USING SCIENCE

Meteorologist On Sunday, March 11, 1888, a storm stalled over New York City, dumping 53 cm (21 in.) of snow. Wind gusts of 117 km/h (73 mph) piled up 6-m (20-ft) high snowdrifts, stranding New Yorkers in trains and horse-drawn carriages. There had been no warning that a major blizzard was coming. People lost their lives.

On January 7 and January 8, of 1996, almost 70 cm (28 in.) of snow fell on New York City. For that storm, meteorologists (mēt ē ər äl'ə jists) such as Al Roker were able to give people lots of warning. A meteorologist is a scientist who studies the atmosphere and forecasts the weather. Thanks to meteorologists, New Yorkers were spared tragedies like those suffered in the Blizzard of 1888.

Coming Up

INVESTIGATION 1

WHAT IS AIR?
.... E6

INVESTIGATION 2

WHY DOES AIR MOVE?
.... E16

◄ Meteorologist Al Roker not only forecasts the weather but has fun announcing his forecasts on television.

E5

WHAT IS AIR?

Suppose someone asked you to describe the air. Perhaps you'd say, "Air is something that makes your hair blow on a windy day." But what is that "something"? In Investigation 1 you'll find out.

Activity

An Empty Cup

If you had a cup filled with hot chocolate, would you say that the cup is empty? Of course not. But what if you were to drink all the hot chocolate? Would the cup be empty then? Find out!

MATERIALS

- large clear plastic bowl
- water
- plastic-foam peanut
- clear plastic cup
- clear plastic cup with small hole
- *Science Notebook*

SAFETY

Clean up spills immediately.

Procedure

1. Fill a clear bowl with water. Float a plastic-foam peanut in it.

2. Talk with your group and together predict what will happen to the peanut if you cover it with a clear plastic cup and then push the cup under the water to the bottom of the bowl. Write your prediction in your *Science Notebook*. Draw a picture to show your prediction.

Step 1

3. **Test** your prediction. Turn a cup upside down and push it *straight down* over the peanut until the rim of the cup touches the bottom of the bowl. **Record** what happens to the peanut.

Step 4

4. Repeat step 3, using a clear plastic cup that has a small hole in its side, near the base. **Record** your observations.

Analyze and Conclude

1. **Compare** your results in step 3 with your prediction. What happened to the peanut? Write a **hypothesis** to explain why this happened. Give reasons to support your thoughts.

2. What happened to the peanut in step 4? **Hypothesize** why this happened. Based on this hypothesis, **predict** what would happen if you were to cover the hole with a finger or piece of tape and then repeat the experiment.

3. Was the cup empty or not? Explain your answer. What can you **infer** about air from this activity?

INVESTIGATE FURTHER!

EXPERIMENT

Use a straw to blow air into the bottom of the bowl of water you used in this activity. Blow as hard and as steadily as you can. Have a partner observe what happens to the level of the water in the bowl as you blow into the straw. Infer what's causing a change in water level.

Activity

An Ocean of Air

Have you ever gone swimming in the ocean? Can you remember the feeling of water pressing against you? In this activity you'll find out about the "ocean" that presses against you on dry land!

Procedure

1. Lay a wooden slat across your desk so that about one half of the slat hangs over the edge of the desktop.

Math Hint *To find the midpoint of the wooden slat, measure the length of the slat. Divide that measurement by 2.*

Step 2

2. Use the palm of your hand to strike down on the end of the slat that is hanging over. Record what happens in your *Science Notebook*. Then put the slat back in the same position as before.

3. Place a sheet of newspaper over the part of the slat that is on the desk. Strike the slat as you did in step 2. Record your observations.

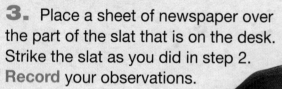

Step 3

4. Place a slat on the desk in the same position you placed it in step 1. Cut the newspaper in half. Lay one half of the paper over the part of the slat that is on the desk. With other group members, **predict** what will happen when you strike the slat this time. **Record** your prediction and then test it. Be sure to strike the slat as you did in step 2. **Record** your observations.

Step 4

Analyze and Conclude

1. **Compare** what you observed in step 2 with what you observed in step 3. **Describe** the difference in your results.

2. **Describe** what happened in step 4. How does it **compare** with your prediction?

3. Think about what was holding down the newspaper when you struck the slat in step 3. **Infer** whether that same "thing" was holding down the half sheet of newspaper in step 4. Do you think this "thing" has weight? Give reasons for your answer.

Technology Link
CD-ROM

INVESTIGATE FURTHER!

Use the **Science Processor CD-ROM**, *Weather and Climate* (Investigation 1, Up, Up, and Away) to take an imaginary weather-balloon ride. Find out about the layers of the atmosphere. Ride the balloon higher and higher to learn which gases you'll find at each layer.

It's Got Us Covered

Reading Focus What gases make up air, and how do they make life possible?

▲ Air is matter, just as all of the objects shown are matter.

You feel it when a gentle breeze touches your face. You hear it rustling leaves. You see its force bend tree branches. What is this thing that hints of its presence but is tasteless, odorless, and unseen? It's the air.

It's a Mix of Matter

Air is made up of matter. Like objects that you can see, air takes up space and has weight. The activity on pages E6 and E7 shows that air takes up space. When the cup was pushed down over the plastic-foam peanut, the water did not rise to fill the cup. That's because the cup was already filled with air. The activity on pages E8 and E9 demonstrates the effect of the weight of air when a wooden slat covered with newspaper is struck. The weight of the air holds the newspaper down over the slat as it is struck.

Air is a mixture of gases. Like all matter, these gases are made up of tiny particles that are in constant motion.

The circle graph on the next page shows the mixture of gases that make up air. The largest part of air is made up of **nitrogen** (nī′trə jən). The second most plentiful gas is **oxygen** (äks′i jən). The small portion of air that's left is made up of other gases, including **carbon dioxide** (kär′bən dī äks′īd) and **water vapor**.

Is the amount of nitrogen in Earth's air closer to $\frac{1}{2}$ or $\frac{3}{4}$?

GASES IN AIR

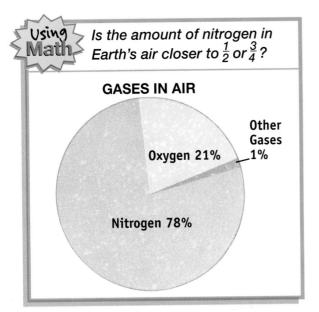

Oxygen 21%

Other Gases 1%

Nitrogen 78%

A Life-Support System

Life on Earth depends on the gases in air. For example, all animals need oxygen from the air to use the energy that is in the food they eat. Plants need carbon dioxide in order to make food. Study the picture below to see how air provides a life-support system for the living things on Earth. Look for one way in which oxygen, which is used by animals, is added to air.

▼ **The gases in air make life possible.**

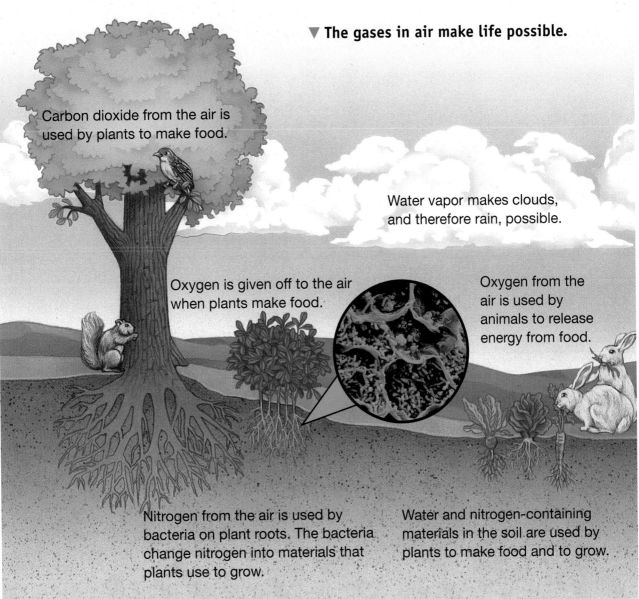

Carbon dioxide from the air is used by plants to make food.

Water vapor makes clouds, and therefore rain, possible.

Oxygen is given off to the air when plants make food.

Oxygen from the air is used by animals to release energy from food.

Nitrogen from the air is used by bacteria on plant roots. The bacteria change nitrogen into materials that plants use to grow.

Water and nitrogen-containing materials in the soil are used by plants to make food and to grow.

E11

Earth's Blanket of Air

Imagine that you are riding in a space shuttle. You look down and see patterns of clouds in constant motion above Earth. These clouds are part of a blanket of air that surrounds Earth. This blanket of air, made up of gases, liquids, and some solid matter, is called the **atmosphere**. The atmosphere reaches from the ground to about 700 km (435 mi) above Earth's surface.

As you can see in the diagram on the next page, the atmosphere is made up of four main layers. The farther a layer is from Earth's surface, the farther apart are the particles of air in that layer.

Of the four main layers, the one farthest from Earth's surface is the thermosphere (thur′mō sfir). The particles of air in this layer may be as far apart as 10 km (6 mi)!

Only the lowest layer of the atmosphere has enough air to support life. This layer, called the **troposphere** (trō′pō sfir), starts at Earth's surface and goes up about 8 km–16 km (5 mi–10 mi) above the surface. Most of the oxygen, nitrogen, carbon dioxide, and water vapor in the atmosphere is found in this layer.

In the lower part of the troposphere, particles that make up air are packed close together. But you would need a supply of oxygen to help you breathe

Science in Literature

Lightning and Other Wonders of the Sky
by Q. L. Pearce
Illustrated by Mary Ann Fraser
Julian Messner, 1989

A FROGGY DAY

"On June 16, 1882, the people of Dubuque, Iowa, were pelted with hailstones that had tiny frogs trapped inside. These unfortunate animals were probably sucked into the clouds from nearby streams and ponds by strong updrafts, then quickly frozen and covered with layers of ice."

This story comes from *Lightning and Other Wonders of the Sky* by Q. L. Pearce. You will be amazed at what can happen in the world of weather. Read this book to learn about all sorts of weather wonders!

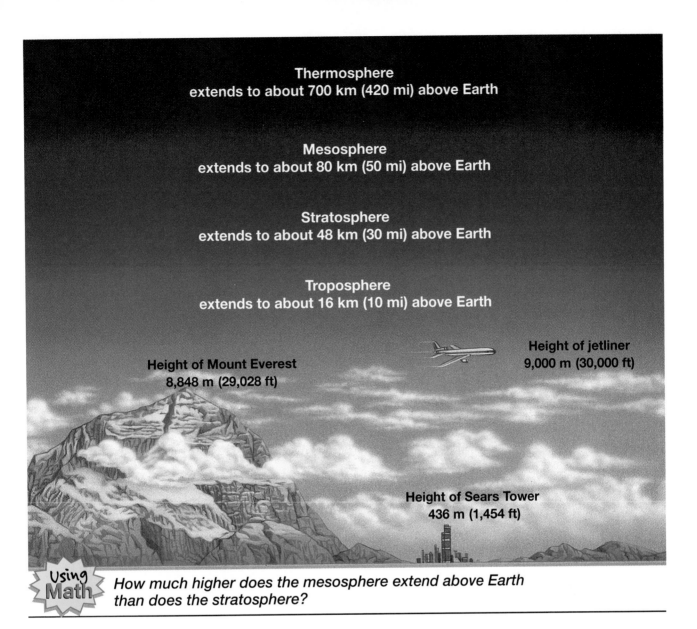

Thermosphere
extends to about 700 km (420 mi) above Earth

Mesosphere
extends to about 80 km (50 mi) above Earth

Stratosphere
extends to about 48 km (30 mi) above Earth

Troposphere
extends to about 16 km (10 mi) above Earth

Height of Mount Everest
8,848 m (29,028 ft)

Height of jetliner
9,000 m (30,000 ft)

Height of Sears Tower
436 m (1,454 ft)

Using Math
How much higher does the mesosphere extend above Earth than does the stratosphere?

at the top of Mount Everest. The troposphere is the only layer that supports life. This layer is also where weather occurs.

Sometimes a Wet Blanket

What's the weather like today where you live? Is it wet and chilly? Hot and dry? *Hot, wet, cold, dry, cool, warm, windy, chilly, rainy, foggy, sunny,* and *cloudy* are all words used to talk about weather. Those words are actually ways of describing what's happening in the atmosphere.

Weather is the condition of the atmosphere at a certain place and time. It can change from minute to minute. Air temperature and the amount of water vapor in the air greatly affect weather. Without the atmosphere, there would be no weather. What place do you know of where there is no weather? ■

Internet Field Trip

Visit **www.eduplace.com** to explore the atmosphere.

Not Too Warm, Not Too Cold

Reading Focus How is Earth's atmosphere like the glass of a greenhouse?

SCIENCE TECHNOLOGY & SOCIETY

Have you ever visited a gardener's greenhouse? A greenhouse is usually made of glass. The glass lets in sunlight, which warms the ground and other surfaces inside the greenhouse. As these surfaces warm, they release heat into the air. The glass keeps this heat from escaping. This is similar to the way the inside of a car heats up when sunlight shines through closed windows. The air inside the greenhouse stays warm enough for plants to grow throughout the year.

Earth's Greenhouse

In some ways, Earth's atmosphere acts like the glass of a greenhouse. It allows the Sun's rays to pass through it and heat Earth's land and water. Some of the heat from the warmed Earth then goes back into the atmosphere as invisible rays. Some of these heat rays escape into space. But most are trapped by water vapor, carbon dioxide, and other gases of Earth's atmosphere. So the atmosphere warms up.

The gases send some of this heat back toward Earth's surface, as shown

Plants are grown in a greenhouse like this one. ▼

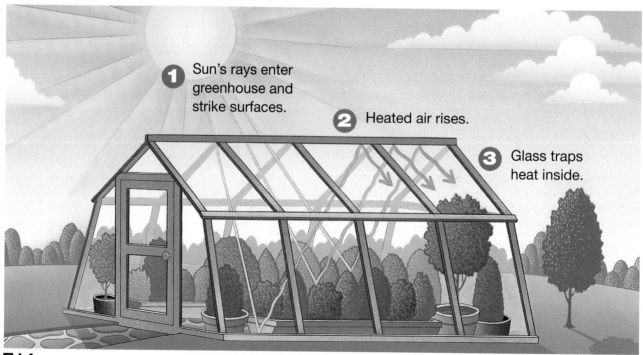

1 Sun's rays enter greenhouse and strike surfaces.

2 Heated air rises.

3 Glass traps heat inside.

E14

in the diagram below. So the air in the lower atmosphere stays warm enough for life to exist. This process in which heat from Earth is trapped by the atmosphere is called the **greenhouse effect**.

Without the greenhouse effect, Earth would be a much colder place. For example, the Moon has no atmosphere. Without an atmosphere, there is no greenhouse effect. So the Moon's surface gets much colder than any place on Earth, as low as $-173°C$ ($-279°F$). The atmosphere keeps Earth's average surface temperature at about $14°C$ ($57°F$).

The amount of carbon dioxide in the air is increasing. Because of this fact, some scientists think that the greenhouse effect may be increasing, raising Earth's average surface temperature. ■

The greenhouse effect on Earth ▼

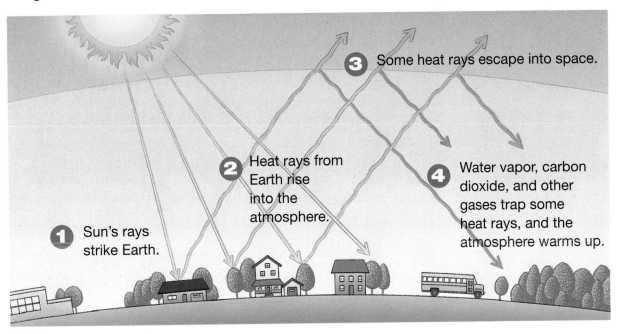

3 Some heat rays escape into space.

2 Heat rays from Earth rise into the atmosphere.

1 Sun's rays strike Earth.

4 Water vapor, carbon dioxide, and other gases trap some heat rays, and the atmosphere warms up.

— **INVESTIGATION 1 WRAP-UP** —

REVIEW

1. What is air made of?

2. Which gas makes up about 78% of air?

CRITICAL THINKING

3. Give evidence to show one way in which the atmosphere is like other matter.

4. Could there be life on Earth without the greenhouse effect? What might happen if Earth lost its atmosphere?

WHY DOES AIR MOVE?

Imagine that it's summertime in a big city. The air feels hot and still. What would the air feel like by the seashore or near a large lake? It's likely there would be a nice cool breeze. Why? Find out in Investigation 2 what makes the air move.

Activity

Warming the Air

What happens when the Sun's rays strike your body? Some of the light energy changes to heat and warms your body. Earth's surface is warmed by the Sun, too. Does this heating of Earth's surface change the air above it? Find out!

MATERIALS
- goggles
- cardboard tube
- aluminum foil
- meterstick
- rubber band
- thermometer
- timer
- *Science Notebook*

SAFETY /////
Wear goggles when doing step 1. Be careful when handling glass thermometers.

Procedure

1. Wrap a cardboard tube in a piece of aluminum foil. Do not cover the ends. Attach the tube to a meterstick, using a rubber band, as shown. Push the tube and rubber band along the meterstick until the bottom edge of the tube is at the 10-cm mark on the meterstick. In your *Science Notebook*, **make a chart** like the one shown.

Type of Surface	Temperature (°C)

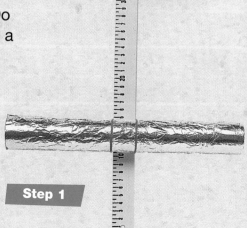
Step 1

E16

2. Go outdoors to a grassy area. Hold the meter-stick with the zero end touching the ground. Have a group member slide a thermometer into the tube. Wait at least three minutes and then **read** the thermometer. **Record** the temperature of the air.

Step 2

3. **Predict** how the temperature of the air over other types of surfaces will vary. Repeat step 2 over three very different surfaces, such as concrete, bare soil, and gravel. **Measure** the air temperature for three minutes each time. **Record** your data.

UNIT PROJECT LINK

For this Unit Project you'll make a class weather station and record weather-related data. In the outside area set aside for your weather station, use a rubber band to attach a thermometer to a milk carton. For two weeks, record the temperature in the morning, at noon, and late in the afternoon.

Technology Link

For more help with your Unit Project, go to **www.eduplace.com**.

Analyze and Conclude

1. Make a bar graph of the temperatures you recorded.

See **SCIENCE** and **MATH TOOLBOX** page H3 if you need to review **Making a Bar Graph.**

2. **Compare** your results in step 3 with your predictions. How did the temperatures you recorded vary? What can you **infer** about the temperature of the surfaces from the temperature of the air above them?

3. Make a **hypothesis** to explain how the air over Earth's surface is affected by the Sun's warming of that surface.

Activity

Making an Air Scale

Does temperature affect the way air moves? In this activity you'll find out!

MATERIALS

- string
- scissors
- 2 metersticks
- 2 large brown bags
- tape
- high desk or table
- heavy books
- lamp with light bulb
- thermometer
- *Science Notebook*

SAFETY

The light bulb used in this activity will get hot. Avoid touching the bulb.

Procedure

1. Cut one 20-cm and two 10-cm lengths of string. Tie one end of the long string to the center of a meterstick.

2. Open two large paper bags fully. Turn each bag upside down. Tape one end of a 10-cm string to the center of one bag bottom. Do the same with the other bag. Tape the free end of each string to opposite ends of the meterstick. The open end of each bag should hang toward the floor.

3. On a high table, place a second meterstick between two books in a stack of heavy books. About one third of the meterstick should hang over the edge of the table. Tape the string from the center of the first meterstick to the end of this meterstick. The bags should hang freely and be in balance with one another.

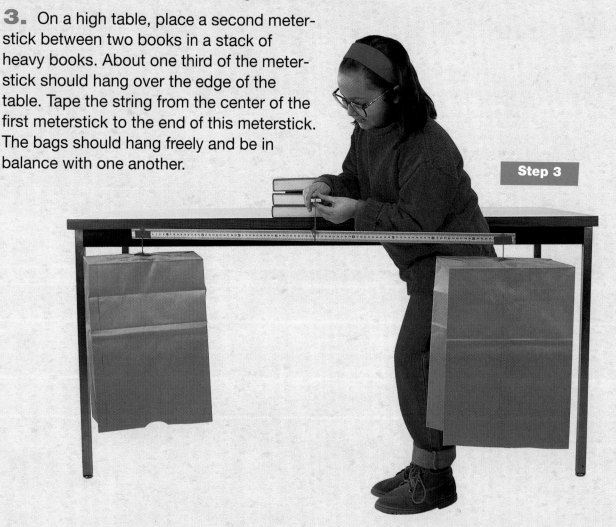

Step 3

E18

4. Put a lamp below one of the bags, as shown. **Talk with your group** and **predict** what will happen to the bag when the lamp is turned on. **Record** your prediction in your *Science Notebook*. **Measure** and **record** the temperature inside the two bags.

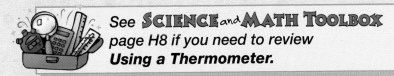

See **SCIENCE** *and* **MATH TOOLBOX** *page H8 if you need to review* ***Using a Thermometer.***

5. Turn on the lamp and **observe** what happens. Again **measure** the temperature inside the two bags. **Record** your data and observations. Let the lamp cool. Then repeat your measurements to check your results.

Analyze and Conclude

1. **Describe** what happened to the bag over the lamp. How does this result **compare** with your prediction?

2. **Compare** the temperature of the air in the two bags in steps 4 and 5. **Infer** the effect of temperature on the weight of the air in each of the bags. Give reasons for the inference you make.

Hot-Air Balloon

Reading Focus What must you do to raise and lower a hot-air balloon?

The hot-air balloon shown below doesn't look like a paper bag, does it? But it *does* work like the paper-bag scale described on pages E18 and E19. Read and find out why.

4 The pilot controls how high the balloon rises. To make the balloon rise higher, the pilot burns more fuel to heat the air more. To lower the balloon the pilot lets the air cool.

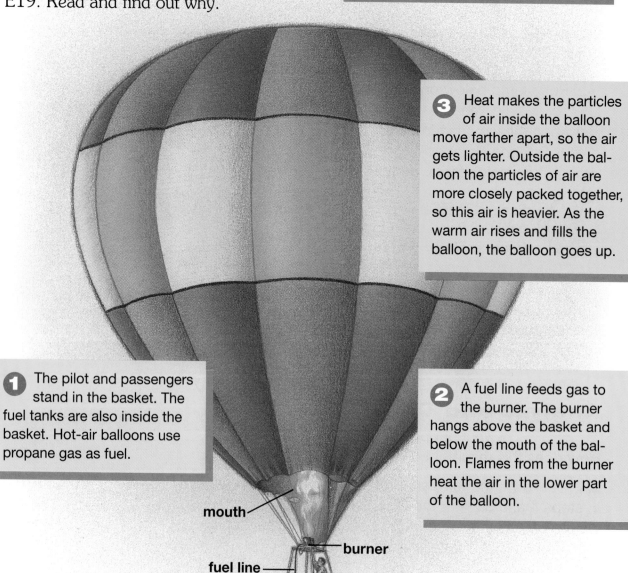

3 Heat makes the particles of air inside the balloon move farther apart, so the air gets lighter. Outside the balloon the particles of air are more closely packed together, so this air is heavier. As the warm air rises and fills the balloon, the balloon goes up.

1 The pilot and passengers stand in the basket. The fuel tanks are also inside the basket. Hot-air balloons use propane gas as fuel.

2 A fuel line feeds gas to the burner. The burner hangs above the basket and below the mouth of the balloon. Flames from the burner heat the air in the lower part of the balloon.

mouth

burner

fuel line

basket

Feeling the Air

Reading Focus What causes wind or moving air?

The activity on pages E16 and E17 shows that some surfaces on Earth are warmed more than others. This leads to greater warming of the air over some surfaces than over others.

Moving Air

Look at the photos on this page. They show some of the different materials that make up Earth. In general, dark-colored materials heat up more rapidly than light-colored materials do. So the air above dark-colored surfaces is warmer than the air above light-colored surfaces.

The activity on pages E18 and E19 shows how heating the air in a paper bag makes that bag lighter than an unheated bag. The bag with the heated air moves upward.

When an area of air is warmed, the particles of the warm air spread out. The warm air becomes lighter than the cooler air above it. The warm air rises and the cooler air sinks. The movement of air is called **wind**. Wind is caused by the uneven heating of Earth's surface.

Although you can't see air, you can *feel* it when the wind blows! Wind can be gentle or strong. It can set a leaf softly on the ground or blow down an entire tree.

▲ **Which of these surfaces, do you think, heats up most rapidly?**

RESOURCE

Cooler air over land moves out toward the water and takes the place of the rising air.

Warm air over the water rises.

LAND BREEZE

cool land

warm sea

Warm air over the land rises.

Cooler air over the water moves toward land and takes the place of the warmer air that has risen.

SEA BREEZE

warm land

cool sea

▲ The uneven heating of land and water causes land and sea breezes.

Land and Sea Breezes

Let's look at the movement of air between two very different areas on Earth's surface: water and land. Land loses heat faster than water. So at night, the air over land cools off more than does the air over water. Land also heats up faster than water. So during the day, the air over land is heated more than is the air over water. Thus, land and water are heated unevenly.

How does it feel when you walk barefoot on the hot sand at a beach? Your feet may feel as if they are burning. But when you go into the cool water, your feet stop burning. Your body may feel a cool breeze when you come out of the water. Such breezes can make a shoreline a very comfortable place to be in hot weather. Look at the drawings to learn more about what causes land and sea breezes. ■

───── **INVESTIGATION 2 WRAP-UP** ─────

REVIEW

1. Which heats up more rapidly—a dark surface or a light surface?

2. Which loses heat faster—land or water?

CRITICAL THINKING

3. What is the link between the uneven heating of Earth's surface and air movement?

4. Would you expect the temperature near a ceiling to be the same as or different from the temperature near the floor? Explain.

REFLECT & EVALUATE

Word Power

Write the letter of the term that best completes each sentence. *Not all terms will be used.*

a. air
b. atmosphere
c. nitrogen
d. oxygen
e. troposphere
f. water vapor
g. weather
h. wind

1. Water that is in the form of a gas is called ___.
2. The gas that makes up the largest part of air is ___.
3. The condition of the atmosphere at a certain place and time is known as ___.
4. The gas that makes up about 21% of air is ___.
5. The blanket of air that surrounds Earth is the ___.
6. The lowest layer of air surrounding Earth is the ___.

Check What You Know

Write the word in each pair that best completes each sentence.

1. Land loses heat (faster, slower) than water does.
2. The layer of air farthest from Earth's surface is the (stratosphere, thermosphere).
3. When air is heated, it (sinks, rises).
4. Weather occurs in the (stratosphere, troposphere).

Problem Solving

1. Why is carbon dioxide important to the survival of life on Earth? Name one other gas in Earth's atmosphere and explain its importance to living things.

2. You're in a spaceship that takes you high above the troposphere. What would the weather be like there? Explain your answer.

PORTFOLIO

Study the drawing. In your own words, explain how a greenhouse works. Then explain how a greenhouse is similar to Earth's atmosphere.

CHAPTER 2

OBSERVING WEATHER

Have you ever noticed that the leaves on trees sometimes flip upside down in the wind? When the leaves turn like this, some people think it's a sign that rain is on the way. What signs do you observe in nature that make you think it's about to rain?

• •

Connecting to Science
CULTURE

Weather Sayings Long ago, people lived closer to nature. Their very lives depended on the weather. Here are some old-fashioned weather sayings from different countries. What weather sayings do you know?

Windy March and rainy April
Bring a flowery and beautiful May.
From Spain

If woolly worms are fat and black
*   in late fall,*
Expect bad weather.
If they are light brown,
Expect a mild winter.
From the United States

Red sky at night,
Sailor's delight.
Red sky in morning,
Sailors take warning.
From England

When spiders weave their
*   webs by noon,*
Fine weather is coming soon.
From Japan

Coming Up

INVESTIGATION 1

WHAT IS AIR PRESSURE? E26

INVESTIGATION 2

HOW CAN YOU FIND WIND SPEED AND DIRECTION? E34

INVESTIGATION 3

HOW DOES WATER IN THE AIR AFFECT WEATHER? E42

◀ What other weather sayings, rhymes, or songs do you know that tell about the weather?

E25

INVESTIGATION ①

WHAT IS AIR PRESSURE?

Air pushes down on Earth's surface. Air pushes up and sideways, too. How does the way that air pushes against things affect weather? You'll begin to find out in this investigation.

Activity

It's a Pressing Problem

Air pressure is the push of air against its surroundings. Is air pressure always the same, or can it change? How can you find out?

MATERIALS

- plastic soda bottle with cap (2 L)
- 2 small plastic dish tubs
- hot tap water
- ice water
- timer
- *Science Notebook*

SAFETY /////

Be careful when using hot water. Clean up spills immediately.

Procedure

1. Unscrew the cap of an empty plastic bottle. Wait a few seconds. Tightly screw the cap back on.

2. Fill a plastic dish tub with hot water from the tap. Fill a second plastic dish tub with ice water.

3. Talk with your group and predict what will happen to the capped bottle when it is put into hot water and then into cold water. Explain why you made the prediction you did. Record your prediction in your *Science Notebook*.

E26

4. Lower the bottle into the tub of hot water. Hold as much of the bottle as you can below the water level. Keep it there for one minute. Remove the bottle and **record** your observations.

 See **SCIENCE** *and* **MATH TOOLBOX** *page H12 if you need to review* ***Measuring Elapsed Time.***

5. Repeat step 4 with the tub of ice water.

Step 5

Analyze and Conclude

1. **Describe** what happened to the bottle after step 4 and after step 5.

2. **Compare** your results with your prediction. **Talk with other groups** about their results.

3. **Infer** what the results have to do with **air pressure**—the push of air against its surroundings. **Explain** what led you to this inference.

INVESTIGATE FURTHER!

EXPERIMENT

Fill the plastic bottle with hot water. Let the water sit in the bottle for one minute. Hypothesize what will happen if you empty the bottle and then quickly screw the cap back on tightly. Test your hypothesis. Compare your results with those from the activity.

Activity

Measuring Air Pressure

To find out how hot or cold the air is, you use a thermometer. But how can you measure air pressure? In this activity you'll make a barometer to measure air pressure.

Procedure

1. Cut a large balloon lengthwise. Stretch it over the open top of a coffee can. Secure it with a rubber band. Tape the edge of the balloon to tightly seal the air inside the can.

2. Cut one end of a plastic straw to form a point. Tape the uncut end to the center of the stretched balloon. You have now made a **barometer** (bə räm′ət ər), a device that measures air pressure.

Step 1

3. Tape a cardboard strip on a wall so that the bottom of the strip is level with the table, as shown on the next page. Place your barometer next to the strip so that the straw pointer just touches it.

4. In your *Science Notebook*, **make a chart** like the one shown.

Date	Time	Air Pressure Reading	Weather Conditions

See **SCIENCE** *and* **MATH TOOLBOX** page H10 if you need to review *Making a Chart to Organize Data.*

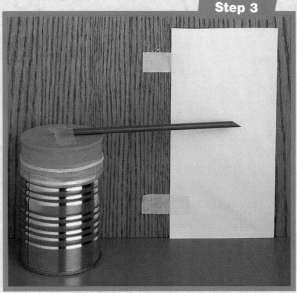

5. Each day for one week, take a barometer reading. Draw a line on the cardboard where the straw is pointing. Label the line with the date, time, and weather conditions, such as *cloudy*, *windy*, or *rainy*.

6. Record this data in your chart. Under the heading *Air Pressure Reading*, record whether the pressure is higher, or lower, than the day before. The higher the line is on the cardboard, the higher the pressure.

Analyze and Conclude

1. Describe how the pointer moved from day to day. Explain how you could tell whether the air pressure was high or low.

2. Compare the readings on your barometer to your observations about the weather.

3. Talk with your group and form a hypothesis about how your barometer can help predict the weather.

Torricelli's Barometer

Reading Focus What events led to the making of the first barometer?

A **barometer**, a device that measures air pressure, is made in the activity on pages E28 and E29. More than 350 years ago, the very first barometer was made by accident.

A scientist named Evangelista Torricelli (tôr ə chel′ē) was trying to make a vacuum (vak′yo͞om), a space in which there is no air or any other kind of matter. He used a large bowl and a long glass tube that was open at one end and closed at the other.

Torricelli filled the tube with a heavy liquid metal, called mercury, and turned the tube upside down in the bowl. Some mercury flowed out of the tube, leaving a space at the top. The space was the vacuum Torricelli wanted to investigate.

Torricelli wondered why *all* of the mercury didn't flow out of the tube. He also questioned why the height of the mercury changed from day to day. He inferred that air was holding up the mercury in the tube.

As the diagram shows, air pushes down on the surface of the mercury in the bowl. This air pressure keeps some of the mercury inside the tube. And because air pressure keeps changing, the mercury level keeps changing.

◄ Mercury barometers very similar to Torricelli's are still used today.

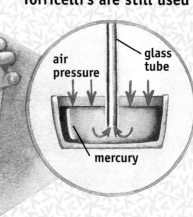

air pressure

glass tube

mercury

All About Pressure

Reading Focus What causes air pressure to differ from place to place?

You live in an atmosphere in which the billions of particles that make up air are in constant motion. These particles move in all directions—up, down, and sideways. When air particles bump into things—a tree, a dog, a pencil, a person, or other air particles—they push. The push of air against its surroundings is called **air pressure**.

You can see the effect of air pressure when you blow up a balloon. When the opening is tied shut, air pushes in all directions at once against the inside of the inflated balloon.

▲ **Blow up a balloon to feel air pressure at work.**

Gravity Rules

Look at the drawing. Are the particles of air closest together near sea level or at the top of the mountain? Do you know why?

Air is matter. Like all matter, particles of air are pulled toward Earth's surface by a force called gravity. The closer you are to sea level, the more particles of air there are squeezed into a given space. Suppose you climbed to the top of the highest mountain, Mount Everest. Three quarters of all the air particles in the atmosphere would be below you.

▼ **The particles of air are closest together near sea level.**

Internet Field Trip

Visit **www.eduplace.com** to learn more about Earth's atmosphere and air pressure.

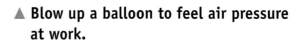

E31

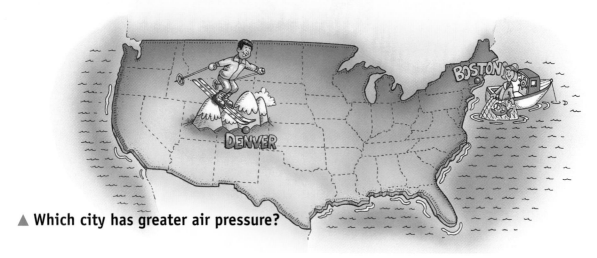

▲ **Which city has greater air pressure?**

Who's Under Pressure?

What difference does it make how many particles of air are squeezed into a given space? A lot! The closer the air particles are to each other, the more pressure the air has.

Denver is called the Mile High City because it is about a mile above sea level. Boston is just above sea level. In which city are people under greater air pressure? If you said Boston, you're right! People who live at sea level are at the "bottom" of Earth's atmosphere. All the air of the atmosphere is above them.

People in Denver are also under pressure. But the higher you go, the less air there is above you. The higher you go, then, the farther apart the particles of air are. So the air pressure in Denver is lower than in Boston.

Measuring Air Pressure

Air pressure is measured with a barometer. There are two main kinds of barometers—mercury barometers and aneroid barometers.

A mercury barometer works like Torricelli's barometer described on page E30. A column of mercury in a tube rises and falls as air pressure changes.

An aneroid barometer is made with a sealed metal can. The can expands or contracts when air pressure changes. This barometer is similar to the one that is made in the activity on pages E28 and E29.

Air pressure is usually measured in inches of mercury. Air pressure varies from place to place. It can also vary in the same place. At sea level when the temperature is 0°C, the height of the column of mercury is 29.92 in. (75.99 cm). This is called

Using Math

Suppose the air pressure, according to this aneroid barometer, is 30.06 in. How much higher is this air pressure than standard air pressure?

standard air pressure. As air pressure changes, the height of the mercury column changes.

Air Pressure and Temperature

The activity on pages E26 and E27 shows that air pressure in a bottle increases when the air inside is heated. Air pressure in the atmosphere changes with temperature as well. But air pressure in the atmosphere works in the opposite way from air pressure in a closed space, such as a bottle.

When air in the atmosphere is warmed, air pressure gets lower because the particles of air can move away from each other. When air is cooled, air pressure gets higher because particles move closer together.

Areas where pressure is higher than the surrounding air are called **high-pressure areas**. Areas where pressure is lower than the surrounding air are called **low-pressure areas**. The difference in air pressure between such areas can cause winds. ∎

Which "block" of air has greater pressure? ▼

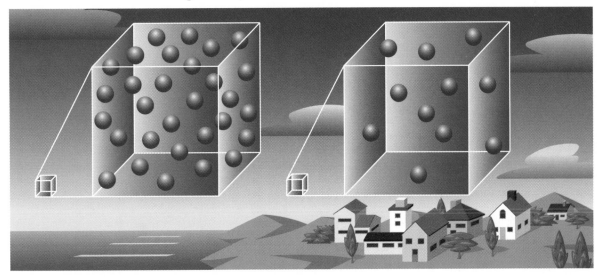

_____ **INVESTIGATION 1 WRAP-UP** _____

REVIEW

1. What is air pressure, and how is it measured?

2. Are particles of air in a given space closer together at sea level or at the top of a mountain?

CRITICAL THINKING

3. You carry a barometer with you to the top of a very tall building. You notice that the barometer reading goes down as you ride up to the 107th floor. Explain what happened and why.

4. Explain how pressure would change as the air temperature falls.

HOW CAN YOU FIND WIND SPEED AND DIRECTION?

Look out a window to observe a flag, a tree, or some leaves on the ground. What can these observations tell you about the wind? In Investigation 2 you'll discover even better ways to measure wind speed and find wind direction.

Activity

A Windy Day

Which way is the wind blowing? In this activity you'll build a wind vane to find out!

Procedure

1. Draw a large cross with its center on a hole in the middle of a wooden board. Mark the end of each line of the cross with one of the letters *N, E, S,* and *W* to stand for *north, east, south,* and *west.*

Math Hint *Each angle of the cross should be 90° in order to form a right angle.*

2. Remove the rubber bulb from a dropper. Carefully push the pointed end of the dropper into the hole in the wooden board.

3. Tape the middle section from a plastic bottle to a wire hanger. Then insert the straightened end of the wire hanger into the dropper.

MATERIALS

- goggles
- wooden board with hole in center
- marker
- dropper
- middle section from plastic soda bottle (1 L)
- wire hanger (with hook straightened)
- tape
- cardboard
- scissors
- magnetic compass
- *Science Notebook*

SAFETY /////

Wear goggles during this activity.

4. Cut out an arrowhead and arrow tail from cardboard. Attach these to the hanger as shown. You have made a wind vane.

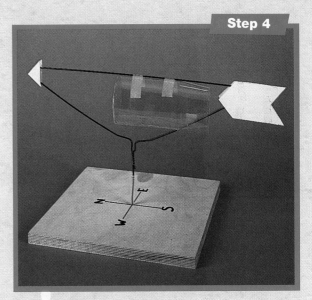

5. Place the wooden board in an open area outdoors. Use a compass to find north. Then turn the wooden board so that *N* is in the direction of north.

6. **Observe** such things as flags and leaves to see how they move in the wind. **Discuss** your observations **with your group** members. **Infer** the direction from which the wind is blowing.

7. A **wind vane** is a device that shows the direction from which the wind is blowing. The arrow of your wind vane will point in the direction from which the wind is blowing. Use the wind vane to **find** the wind direction and **record** it in your *Science Notebook*.

8. **Make a chart** like the one shown. For one week, **observe** and **record** the wind direction. **Record** other weather conditions at the same time.

Date/Time	Wind Direction	Weather Conditions

See **SCIENCE** and **MATH TOOLBOX** page H10 if you need to review **Making a Chart to Organize Data.**

Analyze and Conclude

1. **Compare** your findings in step 7 with the inference you made in step 6.

2. Use the data in your chart to **infer** whether the wind comes from the same direction on warm days as it does on cool days. What connections do you see between the direction of the wind and other weather conditions over a period of time? What patterns do you see? Explain.

Activity

How Fast the Wind Blows

Have you heard a weather reporter talk about the speed of the wind? Perhaps you've wondered how wind speed is measured. In this activity you'll build an anemometer, a device to measure wind speed.

Procedure

1. Staple one end of a plastic straw to the outside of a paper cup, near the rim. Do the same thing with three other straws and paper cups. Each straw should be sticking out to the *right* of its cup.

2. Place two cups on their sides with the straws pointed toward each other. The open ends of the cups should be facing in opposite directions. Overlap the tips of the straws about 1 cm and tape them together.

3. Repeat step 2 with the other two cups. Then crisscross the two pairs of straws, as shown. Tape the two pairs of straws together at their midpoints. Mark the bottom of one cup with an *X*.

Step 1

Step 3

4. Your teacher will insert a straight pin through the center of the cross and into the top of a pencil eraser. Don't push the pin all the way in. Your anemometer (an ə mäm′-ət ər) is complete.

5. Test your anemometer by holding the pencil and blowing into the cups. The cups should spin freely. You can watch for the cup marked *X* on the bottom to tell when the anemometer has made one complete spin.

6. **Talk with your group** members and **hypothesize** how your anemometer can be used to measure wind speed. **Record** and **explain** your hypothesis in your *Science Notebook*.

7. **Make a chart** like the one shown. Take your anemometer outside. **Count** how many times it spins in one minute. **Record** the number of spins at different times of the day or at the same hour each day for one week. **Record** other observations about weather conditions at the same time.

Date	Time	Spins in 1 min	Weather Conditions

Analyze and Conclude

1. Study the data in your chart. **Compare** differences in wind speed at different times and under different weather conditions. **Describe** any patterns you see.

2. **Compare** the hypothesis you made in step 6 with your results.

Technology Link CD-ROM

INVESTIGATE FURTHER!

Use the **Science Processor CD-ROM**, *Weather and Climate* (Investigation 2, Windswept) to find out how wind speed is used to assess severe weather conditions.

Which Way Is the Wind Blowing?

Reading Focus How can you find wind direction and wind speed?

Wind is moving air. In Chapter 1 you saw that the uneven heating of Earth results in the uneven heating of air. Recall that differences in air temperature affect air pressure. Winds occur when there are differences in air pressure between two areas of air that are near each other. Winds move from areas of high pressure to areas of low pressure.

Finding Wind Direction

The direction of the wind is the direction from which it is blowing. A wind blowing from the east to the west is called an east wind.

A **wind vane** is a device that shows wind direction. Most wind vanes are shaped like a long arrow with a tail. When the wind blows,

the arrow points into the wind. If the arrow points south, the wind is a south wind.

Another instrument used to find wind direction is a windsock. A **windsock** is a cloth bag that is narrow at one end and open at both ends. Air enters the wide end and causes the narrow end to point away from the direction that the wind is blowing. This is opposite to what the wind vane does.

Measuring Wind Speed

What makes some winds stronger than others? The greater the difference in air pressure between two areas, the stronger the winds produced. Also, the closer the areas are, the stronger the winds produced.

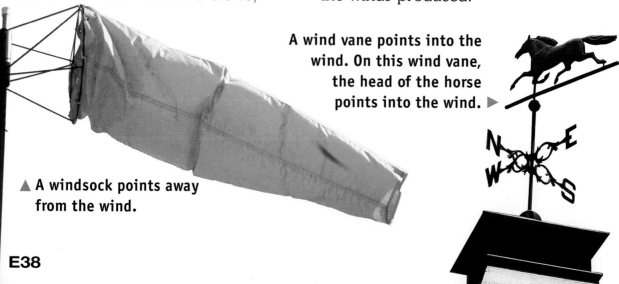

A wind vane points into the wind. On this wind vane, the head of the horse points into the wind. ▶

▲ A windsock points away from the wind.

An **anemometer** is a device used to measure wind speed. It often consists of cups on spokes attached to a pole. Scientists use an anemometer like the one shown below to record wind speed in kilometers per hour (km/h). The activity on pages E36 and E37 uses spins per minute to record wind speed.

If you don't have special devices to measure wind speed, you can try to figure out wind speed using the Beaufort (bō'fərt) scale. In 1805 a British naval officer named Sir Francis Beaufort made a scale that divides wind strength into 12 different categories. Part of the Beaufort scale is shown below. ■

THE BEAUFORT SCALE

Beaufort Number	Speed in km/h (mph)	Description	Observations on Land
2	6–11 (4–7)	light breeze	leaves rustle, wind felt on face; wind vanes move
4	20–28 (13–18)	moderate breeze	dust and paper blow; small branches sway
6	39–49 (25–31)	strong breeze	umbrellas hard to open; large branches sway
8	62–74 (39–46)	gale	walking is very difficult; twigs break off trees
10	89–102 (55–63)	whole gale	much damage to buildings; trees uprooted
12	117 and up (72 and up)	hurricane	violent, widespread destruction

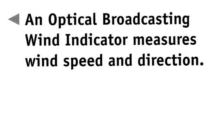

◄ **An Optical Broadcasting Wind Indicator measures wind speed and direction.**

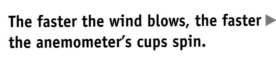

The faster the wind blows, the faster ▶ the anemometer's cups spin.

Wind Power

Reading Focus How can people use wind energy to do work?

STS
SCIENCE
TECHNOLOGY
& SOCIETY

The activity on pages E36 and E37 shows how to make a device called an anemometer, which measures wind speed. The harder the wind blows, the faster an anemometer will spin. What if all that spinning energy could be put to work?

Early Wind Machines

Windmills are machines that put the wind to work. They were first used in the Middle East, perhaps as long ago as the seventh century. In those early windmills, a wheel made of cloth sails was attached to a tall structure.

As the wind blew, the sails spun. The turning motion was used to grind grain.

In the fourteenth century, the Dutch began using windmills to pump water out of low-lying land. The traditional Dutch windmill has four arms attached to cloth sails or wooden blades. The sails or blades spin like the propeller of a plane. They can turn only when the wind blows directly at them.

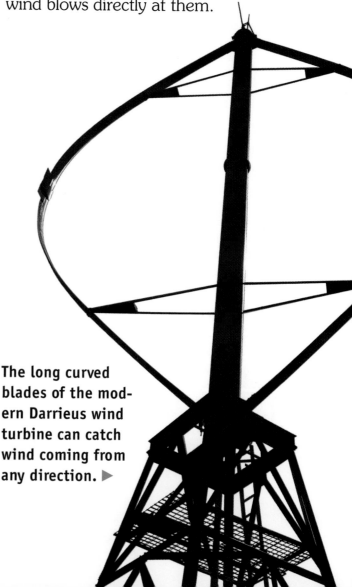
The long curved blades of the modern Darrieus wind turbine can catch wind coming from any direction. ▶

▲ Many modern windmills work the same way as this traditional Dutch windmill.

Today's Windmills

Modern windmills are designed to work at much higher wind speeds than are traditional ones. They are usually made of aluminum or other light metals. Some modern windmills, called wind turbines (tur′binz), are used to produce electricity.

The largest wind turbines are over 90 m (300 ft) tall. The blade tips travel as fast as 400 km/h (250 mph). The wind turbine operates a generator that produces the electricity.

Worldwide Use of Wind Energy

Wind power may be one of the answers to today's energy needs. Unlike many other sources of energy, wind can't be used up and it doesn't pollute the air. Also, wind turbines can be built fairly quickly.

But wind power is not a perfect answer to energy needs. The direction and speed of the winds change over

▲ **Wind farm in Altamont Pass, California**

time and from place to place. Sometimes, of course, the wind doesn't blow at all. Wind power works best where wind speeds are high and fairly steady. Wind turbines are placed in areas where there are few trees, houses, or other things that might block the wind.

A wind farm is a system of 50 or more wind turbines working together. Each turbine turns a generator. The Altamont Pass wind farm has over 5,000 turbines. It produces enough electricity to supply several towns in California. Wind farms are being developed in other states as well as in Europe, India, China, and other parts of the world. ■

INVESTIGATION 2 WRAP-UP

REVIEW

1. Name one device used to find wind direction and one device that measures wind speed.

2. In which direction does an east wind blow?

CRITICAL THINKING

3. Most people would agree that wind turbines offer benefits as an energy source for producing electricity. Identify two problems in using wind turbines as a source of energy.

4. Compare how a windsock works with how a wind vane works.

HOW DOES WATER IN THE AIR AFFECT WEATHER?

Water vapor is a very important gas in Earth's atmosphere. In Investigation 3 you'll find out how the amount of water vapor in the air affects weather.

Activity

Make a Rain Gauge

Rainfall is measured with a device called a rain gauge. Make one in this activity.

MATERIALS

- flat wooden stick
- metric ruler
- marker
- aluminum soda can, top removed
- plastic soda bottle (2 L), cut in half
- *Science Notebook*

Procedure

1. Place a flat wooden stick on your desk. Use a metric ruler and a marker to draw a line 3 cm from the lower end. Label this line 1 *cm*. Draw another line on the stick 3 cm above the 1-cm line. Label this second line 2 *cm*. Then draw another line 3 cm above the 2-cm line. Label this third line 3 *cm*.

2. Divide the space between the lower end of the stick and the line labeled 1 *cm* into ten equal parts. Repeat this for each of the other two spaces. Your stick should look like the one shown.

Step 2

Math Hint Each of the ten equal parts has a measure of $\frac{3}{10}$ cm or 3 mm.

3. Place an aluminum can, with the top removed, inside the bottom half of a cut plastic soda bottle.

4. Turn the top half of the bottle upside down. Insert the neck of the bottle into the can, as shown. The top half of the bottle will serve as a funnel. You've made a rain gauge (gāj).

5. In your *Science Notebook*, **make a chart** like the one shown.

Date	Amount of Rainfall

6. Put your rain gauge outdoors where it won't be disturbed. Use your chart to **record** the amount of rainfall every day for one month. To **measure** rainfall, put the marked wooden stick along the inside wall of the can. Then empty the can. Be sure to measure rainfall the same way each time. You might want to add your readings and then find the total rainfall for the month. You can use a calculator to help you.

 See **SCIENCE** and **MATH TOOLBOX** *page H4 if you need to review **Using a Calculator.***

Analyze and Conclude

1. How would you measure the rainfall if the water overflowed the can?

2. How could you use your rain gauge to measure snowfall?

3. **Talk with your group** and **predict** how the amount of rainfall where you live will vary during different seasons in the coming year. What information will you need in order to make such a prediction?

Step 4

UNIT PROJECT LINK

Choose one of each weather device you have made—barometer, wind vane, anemometer, rain gauge—to put in your class weather station. Explain each choice you made. Use the devices to collect more weather data.

 **Technology Link**

For more help with your Unit Project, go to **www.eduplace.com**.

Snow Around the World

Reading Focus How does snow affect people's lives around the world?

Over 2,000 years ago, the Chinese scholar Han Ying observed that snowflakes have six points. About 1,700 years passed before people in other places discovered this fact.

You don't have to know about the shape of a snowflake to know how much fun, or how much trouble, snow can be. Take a look at some ways that people around the world deal with "the white stuff."

▲ **UNITED STATES** In 1880 Wilson A. Bentley began photographing snow crystals through a microscope. He took thousands of pictures, but not one snowflake looked exactly like another.

◀ **JAPAN** Sapporo, a city in northern Japan, has long winters with lots of snow. Every February the city holds a week-long snow festival in which groups compete in a snow-statue contest. The sculptures made are very large. Trucks bring in 40,000 tons of extra snow in order to make them.

Using Math *Explain how you could use mental math to find how many pounds of extra snow are brought in for the festival.*

E44

LAPLAND   Cars aren't practical in regions with heavy snowfall. The Saami (sär′mē) are a people who live in the northern parts of Norway, Sweden, Finland, and Russia. Instead of using cars, they train reindeer to pull sleds over the snow. ▶

◀ **THE ALPS**   The northern side of the Alps Mountain range receives about 305 cm (120 in.) of snow a year. People who live there must find ways to avoid avalanches (av′ə lanch əz). An avalanche is a sudden sliding of snow down a mountain. Some avalanches weigh thousands of tons and move at speeds of 160 km/h (100 mph).

THE ARCTIC   The Inuit (in′ᴏᴏ wit) live in the Arctic, which is frozen under snow and ice for as long as nine months a year. To survive, Inuits join together to fish and to hunt. Snow is so much a part of Inuit life that their language has more than two dozen words to describe different kinds of snow. ▶

The Water Cycle

Reading Focus What role does water vapor play in the weather?

Water is not only found in oceans, lakes, and rivers. Water is also found in air as an invisible gas—water vapor. The movement of water into the air as water vapor and back to Earth's surface as rain, snow, or hail is called the **water cycle**, shown below.

The Sun's energy heats bodies of water, causing some water to evaporate into the air. When water **evaporates**, it changes from a liquid to a gas.

As the water vapor in the air cools, it **condenses**, or changes from a gas to liquid water. The water may freeze and become ice or snow depending on the temperature of the air.

Clouds are formed as water vapor in the air condenses. A **cloud** is billions of tiny drops of water that condensed from the air. A cloud that touches Earth's surface is called **fog**. As the drops of water in clouds grow larger, they become heavier. Finally they fall to Earth. Any form of water that falls from the air is called **precipitation** (prē sip ə tā'shən).

Snow, rain, and hail that fall from the air are part of the water cycle. The water that falls to Earth becomes part of the bodies of water on Earth's surface. As the Sun's energy causes evaporation, the water cycle continues.

THE WATER CYCLE

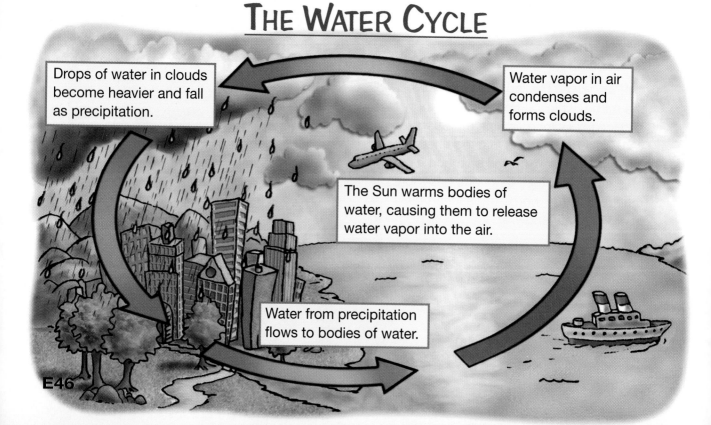

Drops of water in clouds become heavier and fall as precipitation.

Water vapor in air condenses and forms clouds.

The Sun warms bodies of water, causing them to release water vapor into the air.

Water from precipitation flows to bodies of water.

Measuring Precipitation

You've probably heard the amount of rainfall given in weather reports. How do weather forecasters know the amount? They use a rain gauge much like the one made in the activity on pages E42 and E43. A **rain gauge** is a device that measures precipitation.

It's Relative

The amount of water vapor in the air is called **humidity** (hyo͞o mid′ə tē). There is a limit to the amount of water the air can hold. But that limit can change. The amount depends on the temperature of the air. The warmer the air, the more water vapor it can hold.

The **relative humidity** is the amount of water vapor the air is holding compared to the amount it *could* hold at that temperature. If the air is holding all the water vapor it can at a certain temperature, the relative humidity is 100 percent.

When the temperature outside is high but the humidity is low, the sweat on your skin evaporates quickly. The evaporating sweat carries heat away and you feel cooler.

At the same temperature but with high humidity, the water on your skin can't evaporate quickly. Even though the temperature is the same, you feel warm and uncomfortable.

Science in Literature

A Fatal Fog

"In some ways, fog may be the most dangerous of all clouds. If thick enough, fog can prevent you from seeing more than a few feet in front of you . . . . In 1977, thick fog contributed to the worst air disaster in history—two huge passenger jets crashed into each other on a runway in the Canary Islands."

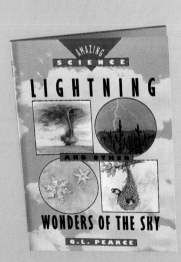

Lightning and Other Wonders of the Sky
by Q. L. Pearce
Illustrated by Mary Ann Fraser
Julian Messner, 1989

This excerpt comes from *Lightning and Other Wonders of the Sky* by Q. L. Pearce. Fog is just one way clouds can cause disasters. Read the book to learn about a pilot who parachuted from a plane into a thundercloud.

Rain is water drops that are larger and fall faster than drizzle. ▼

▲ Drizzle is very fine drops of water smaller than 0.5 mm (0.02 in.) in diameter.

Hail is particles of ice usually ranging from the size of a pea to the size of a golf ball. Some hailstones are even larger. ▼

▲ Snow is a solid form of precipitation made of ice crystals.

INVESTIGATION 3 WRAP-UP

REVIEW

1. Describe the water cycle.

2. What is used to measure precipitation?

CRITICAL THINKING

3. Imagine that it's a cold winter day. You are outside, talking with a friend. Why can you see your breath as you talk?

4. How can the relative humidity increase if the amount of water vapor in the air remains unchanged?

REFLECT & EVALUATE

Word Power

Write the letter of the term that best matches the definition. *Not all terms will be used.*

1. Device that shows wind direction
2. Movement of water into the air as vapor and back to Earth's surface as a liquid or solid
3. Device used to measure air pressure
4. Amount of water vapor in the air
5. Water that falls to Earth's surface as snow, rain, or hail

a. air pressure
b. anemometer
c. barometer
d. humidity
e. precipitation
f. water cycle
g. wind vane

Check What You Know

Write the term in each pair that best completes each sentence.

1. A device that measures wind speed is called (a barometer, an anemometer).
2. When there is a great difference in air pressure between two areas, winds are (slight, strong).
3. Billions of drops of water condensed in the air form a (cloud, lake).
4. As the temperature decreases, the humidity (increases, decreases).

Problem Solving

1. Explain why an aluminum can "sweats" when you take it out of the refrigerator on a hot day.
2. How can you use a wind vane and an anemometer to help you fly a kite?
3. Suppose you want to find wind speed, wind direction, and air pressure. Which instruments would you use? Explain how each instrument works.

Study the drawing. It shows air pressure readings in inches of mercury. They were taken in different places at the same time on the same day. Explain in writing why the air pressure readings are different.

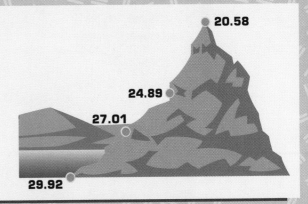

20.58

24.89

27.01

29.92

CHAPTER 3

WEATHER PATTERNS

When you listened to the radio, the weather forecaster said it was going to be sunny for your outdoor field trip. But then it rained all day. In this chapter you'll find out what goes into predicting the next day's weather.

PEOPLE USING SCIENCE

Research Meteorologist You might think that studying weather is not very exciting. But seeing how Anton Seimon learns about storms will change your mind. He flies in a plane above, around, and even into storms.

Anton Seimon is a research meteorologist. He studies storms to better understand how they form and to help other people predict storms. He uses instruments such as thermometers and radar for gathering weather data. He sometimes drops packages of instruments from the plane into a storm that is too strong to fly into. "Studying the information we collect is almost as exciting as flying into a storm," he says.

Coming Up

INVESTIGATION 1

WHAT CAN CLOUDS TELL YOU ABOUT THE WEATHER?
. . . . E52

INVESTIGATION 2

HOW CAN MAPS HELP YOU PREDICT WEATHER?
. . . . E58

INVESTIGATION 3

HOW CAN YOU STAY SAFE DURING DANGEROUS WEATHER?
. . . . E64

Anton Seimon flies in a plane such as this one into the storms he studies. ▼

N43RF

UNITED STATES DEPT OF COMMERCE

WHAT CAN CLOUDS TELL YOU ABOUT THE WEATHER?

You're about to head out the door. You notice thin, wispy white clouds high in the sky. Should you take an umbrella or your sunglasses? Find out how clouds can help you predict the weather.

Activity

Kinds of Clouds

Are there different types of clouds in the sky? Discover the answer in this activity.

MATERIALS

• *Science Notebook*

SAFETY

Never look directly at the Sun.

Procedure

Choose three different times of day to carefully observe clouds. Write a description in your *Science Notebook* of how the clouds look and where they appear in the sky. Then draw pictures of the clouds. With your group, classify the clouds you saw. Share your results with other groups.

Analyze and Conclude

1. How many different cloud shapes did you see? Did any of the clouds change shape?

2. What colors were the clouds? How high were they in the sky?

3. Explain how your group classified the clouds.

Activity

Cloudy Weather

Can the types of clouds in the sky help you predict what the weather will be? In this activity you'll find out.

MATERIALS
- thermometer
- *Science Notebook*

SAFETY
Be careful when handling glass thermometers. Never look directly at the Sun.

Procedure

1. Think about the types of clouds you've seen in the sky. Predict which types of clouds may occur in certain types of weather. Record your predictions in your *Science Notebook*.

2. Make a chart like the one shown.

Date	Time	Cloud Description	Weather Conditions

3. Twice a day for one week, observe the types of clouds you see. Record a description of the clouds in your chart.

4. Record the weather conditions at the same time you make your cloud observations. Note whether it is sunny, cloudy, rainy, or snowy. Use a thermometer to measure the temperature of the air.

See SCIENCE and MATH TOOLBOX page H8 if you need to review *Using a Thermometer*.

Step 4

Analyze and Conclude

1. Compare your findings with the predictions you made. What might the weather be like tomorrow?

2. Compare differences in cloud types at different times and for different weather conditions. Hypothesize how clouds might be used to predict the weather.

The Weather From Space

Reading Focus What kinds of information do weather satellites provide?

SCIENCE TECHNOLOGY & SOCIETY

Clouds are one factor scientists use to forecast the weather. **Weather satellites** are devices in space that are used to take pictures of clouds and to collect other weather information. One important type of weather satellite is called GOES, short for the term *Geostationary Operational Environmental Satellite*. This type of satellite travels at the same speed that Earth spins. So a GOES can keep track of weather over the same area day and night.

Weather satellites send images of the clouds over Earth to weather stations on the ground. The satellites also measure moisture in the atmosphere. They provide information about winds as well as the temperature of land and of water. Such data can help farmers know when cold, icy weather is coming. Having this information helps farmers know when they must protect their crops.

GOES can also be used to warn people when big storms are on the way. Weather satellites can track storms over long distances. In 1996, Hurricane Fran was tracked from space for thousands of kilometers over several days.

Using Math ▸ A GOES is shown here with a satellite image of Earth. A GOES orbits at a distance of 36,000 km above a fixed spot on Earth's surface. How many meters is this?

NOAA
NESDIS
NCDC/SDSD

RESOURCE

Watching the Clouds Go By

Reading Focus What are the three main types of clouds, and what type of weather is likely to occur with each?

▲ **Cumulus clouds**

Imagine that you are in a place with no newspapers, radio, or TV. How can you tell what the weather is going to be? Believe it or not, the answer is right outside your window. Just take a look at the sky. The types of clouds that you see can help you predict the coming weather.

But where do clouds come from? Like a magic trick, clouds appear out of the air. That's because they form in air. Look at the diagram to see how a cloud forms.

Cloud Families

As you know, clouds can occur in many different shapes and sizes. The activity on page E52 suggests ways to classify, or group, clouds. In 1803 a scientist named Luke Howard found a way to classify clouds by the way they looked. He classified the clouds into three main families. These families are cumulus (kyōō′myōō ləs) clouds, stratus (stra′təs) clouds, and cirrus (sir′əs) clouds.

Cumulus clouds are puffy clouds that look like cauliflower. They form when large areas of warm, moist air rise upward from Earth's surface.

Stratus clouds are like flat gray blankets that seem to cover the sky. Stratus clouds form when a flat layer of warm, moist air rises very slowly.

A cloud forms when warm, moist air rises, expands, and cools. ▼

3 Water vapor condenses into tiny drops of water that come together to form a **cloud.**

2 As the warm air rises, it expands and cools.

1 A large area of warm, moist air forms above the ground.

E55

TYPES OF CLOUDS

CIRRUS CLOUDS Often a sign that rainy or snowy weather is on its way

CIRROCUMULUS CLOUDS Thin, high clouds that mean changing weather

CIRROSTRATUS CLOUDS Thin milk-colored sheets that often mean rain is on the way

ALTOCUMULUS CLOUDS Fluffy gray clouds that can grow into rain clouds

ALTOSTRATUS CLOUDS Mean that stormy weather is coming soon

CUMULONIMBUS CLOUDS Thunderheads that bring thunder-storms with rain, snow, or hail

CUMULUS CLOUDS Appear in sunny summer skies

STRATOCUMULUS CLOUDS Mean that drier weather is on the way

STRATUS CLOUDS Low clouds that often bring drizzle

NIMBOSTRATUS CLOUDS Thick dark blankets that may bring snow or rain

▲ Stratus clouds

▲ Cirrus clouds

Cirrus clouds look like commas or wisps of hair high in the sky. Cirrus clouds form when the air rises high enough for ice crystals to form.

Sometimes scientists talk about nimbostratus or cumulonimbus clouds. *Nimbus* is a Latin word that means "rain." When you see *nimbus* or *nimbo-* in a cloud name, you know the cloud is a rain cloud.

Clouds are also grouped by height above the ground. Some clouds are close to the ground, some are high in the sky, and some are in between. Clouds that form high in the sky have the prefix *cirro-* in front of their family name. Clouds that form at a medium height have the prefix *alto-* in front of their family name.

Weather Clues From Clouds

The activity on page E53 explains how to use types of clouds to help predict the weather. You may have noticed that certain types of clouds appear in the sky before a rainstorm. Or you may have seen that other types of clouds show up before fair weather.

Different types of clouds give clues about the weather to come. Examine the different cloud types that are shown on page E56. Which cloud types might tell that rain is coming? Which might tell that the weather will be changing soon? ■

Internet Field Trip

Visit **www.eduplace.com** to learn more about cloud types.

INVESTIGATION 1 WRAP-UP

REVIEW

1. What are the three families of clouds?

2. How does a cloud form?

CRITICAL THINKING

3. You are going to a picnic when you notice that the sky is filled with a layer of gray clouds. Should you go to the picnic, or should you stay inside? Explain.

4. How can clouds seen from the ground help people predict the weather? What kinds of information do weather satellites provide?

HOW CAN MAPS HELP YOU PREDICT WEATHER?

You've probably used maps to find cities and streets. But you can also use a map to find out about weather. Investigation 2 will show you how.

Activity

Weather Maps

How can a weather map be used to predict the weather? Find out in this activity.

MATERIALS
• weather maps
• *Science Notebook*

Procedure

1. Look on weather map 1 for a high-pressure area, marked with the letter *H*. Find the same high-pressure area on map 2. Note whether the *H* is in the same place or if it has moved. If it has moved, note in what direction it moved. Now repeat this with map 3. In your *Science Notebook*, describe what happened to the high-pressure area over the three-day period.

2. Look on the weather maps for a low-pressure area, marked with the letter *L*. Note whether the *L* is in the same place on all three maps or if it has moved. If it has moved, note in what direction it moved. Record what happened to the low-pressure area over the three-day period.

WEATHER MAP SYMBOLS

	Rain
	Snow
	High Pressure
	Low Pressure
	Wind Direction
49/32	High and Low Daily Temperatures (°F)
	Clear Skies
	Partly Cloudy
	Cloudy
	Warm Front
	Cold Front

E58

Step 3

3. Look on map 1 for the lines with the little triangles and half circles. These lines show fronts. A **front** is a place where two masses, or areas, of air meet. Cold fronts are shown by the lines with triangles. Warm fronts are shown by the lines with half circles. Find the fronts on maps 2 and 3. Note whether the fronts are always in the same place or if they move. **Record** your observations.

4. **Predict** what weather map 4 will look like. **Draw** a picture of your prediction. Your teacher will give you a copy of weather map 4 so that you can check your prediction.

Analyze and Conclude

1. How do the locations of high-pressure areas, low-pressure areas, and fronts on weather map 4 compare with your prediction?

2. **Hypothesize** how weather maps can help you predict the weather.

UNIT PROJECT LINK

For five days, use the weather devices in your class weather station to measure weather conditions. Use your observations and a weather map to predict the weather each day. Keep track of how often you make the correct prediction. Do your predictions improve over time?

 Technology Link

For more help with your Unit Project, go to **www.eduplace.com**.

Weather Wisdom

Reading Focus How have people from different countries used plants and animals to help predict weather?

People have been predicting the weather since long before forecasts appeared on television or in newspapers. But not everyone looks at weather devices such as barometers and thermometers. Instead, some people observe how plants and animals behave. Look at the map below to see some of the signs people have used in different parts of the world to predict the weather.

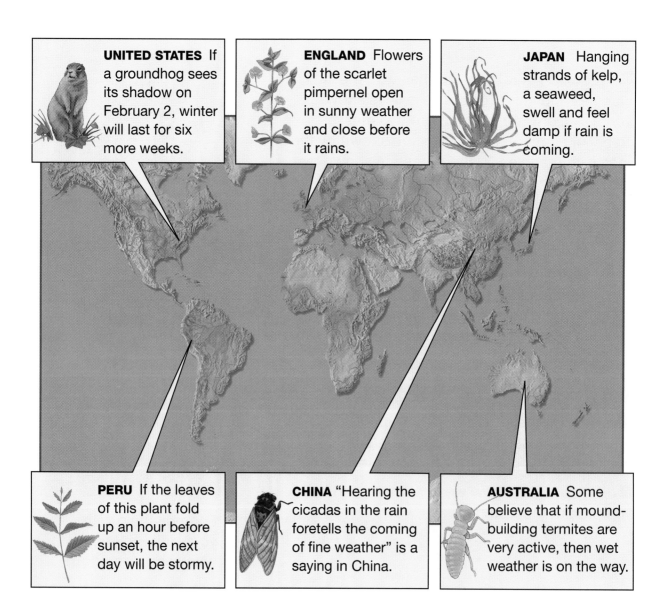

UNITED STATES If a groundhog sees its shadow on February 2, winter will last for six more weeks.

ENGLAND Flowers of the scarlet pimpernel open in sunny weather and close before it rains.

JAPAN Hanging strands of kelp, a seaweed, swell and feel damp if rain is coming.

PERU If the leaves of this plant fold up an hour before sunset, the next day will be stormy.

CHINA "Hearing the cicadas in the rain foretells the coming of fine weather" is a saying in China.

AUSTRALIA Some believe that if mound-building termites are very active, then wet weather is on the way.

Weather in the News

Reading Focus How does a weather forecaster predict the weather?

A **weather forecaster** is someone who makes predictions about the weather. Maybe you've heard a weather forecaster predict bright, sunny skies when, in fact, it rained all day. How do people predict the weather? Why is it such a tough job?

The Weather Detectives

Being a forecaster is a bit like being a detective trying to solve a mystery. First, the forecaster must gather clues, or information, about the current weather. The forecaster gets information from all over the world. The information comes from weather balloons, weather satellites, and weather stations on land and on ships at sea. It tells about such things as wind speed and direction, cloud type, air pressure, temperature, moisture in the air, and precipitation.

Once forecasters have gathered the information, they have to decide what it means. They are like detectives who must sort through the many clues they have uncovered. Fortunately, the forecaster gets to use computers to help solve the "mystery." All the different pieces of information are put into a computer. The computer then puts all the pieces together and produces different types of weather maps, like the ones shown below.

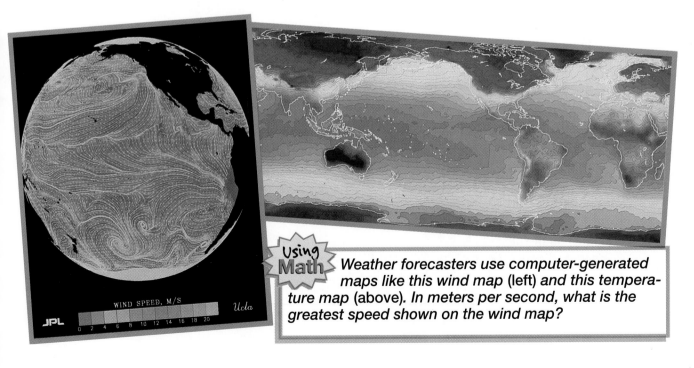

WIND SPEED, M/S

JPL   0 2 4 6 8 10 12 14 16 18 20   Ucla

Using Math *Weather forecasters use computer-generated maps like this wind map (left) and this temperature map (above). In meters per second, what is the greatest speed shown on the wind map?*

Weather Clues

The weather map activity on pages E58 and E59 shows the symbols used for cold fronts and warm fronts and for high- and low-pressure areas. These fronts and areas are clues that a weather forecaster uses to make a prediction. But what do these clues actually mean?

You know that air surrounds Earth. Now imagine that the air is divided into large bodies, or areas. Some of these areas are warm, and other areas are cold. Each different body of air is called an air mass. An **air mass** is a body of air that has the same general temperature and air pressure throughout.

Often different air masses move so that they contact each other. A **front** is a place where two different types of air masses meet. A **cold front** forms

COLD FRONT When a cold air mass meets a warm air mass, the cooler air pushes under the warm air. This forces the warm air mass to rise. Clouds form in the warm air as it is forced upward. ▶

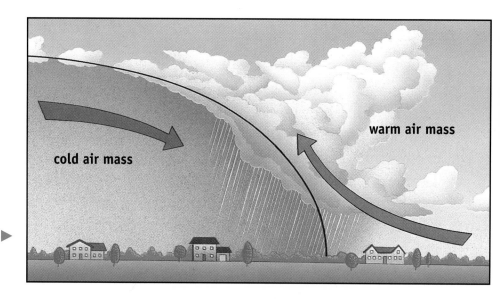

WARM FRONT When a warm air mass moves into a cold air mass, the warmer air rides up over the cooler air. Clouds form as the air rises and cools. ▶

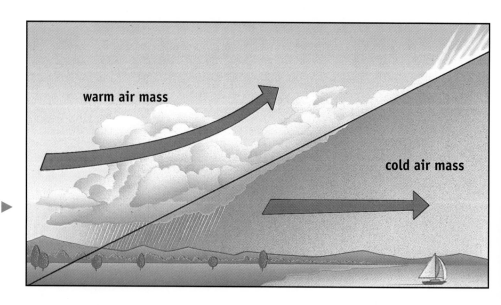

An approaching front darkens the sky ▶ and brings stormy weather.

when a cold air mass moves into a warm air mass. Cold fronts often produce thunderstorms. A **warm front** forms when a warm air mass moves into a cold air mass. Warm fronts often bring light rain.

Weather forecasters also look at air pressure to predict weather changes. In a high-pressure area, or high, the air pressure is higher than in the air surrounding it. High-pressure areas usually bring dry, clear weather.

In a low-pressure area, or low, the air pressure is lower than in the surrounding air. Low-pressure areas usually bring wind, clouds, and rain.

Now the forecaster has enough clues to help solve the mystery. So the forecaster can make a weather prediction. Weather predictions are not always correct. Sometimes weather conditions change so quickly that the information forecasters have isn't up-to-date. And sometimes weather doesn't follow "normal" patterns.

Scientists are developing new ways to gather weather information. These new methods will help forecasters improve their predictions. ■

Technology Link CD-ROM

INVESTIGATE FURTHER!

Use the **Science Processor CD-ROM**, *Weather and Climate* (Investigation 3, Forecasting) to predict the weather as weather forecasters do.

INVESTIGATION 2 WRAP-UP

REVIEW

1. What kind of weather often occurs at a cold front? at a warm front?

2. What are four types of information that appear on weather maps?

CRITICAL THINKING

3. Suppose you are a weather forecaster for your town. What data would you gather to make a prediction about the next day's weather?

4. Can weather forecasters always be right in their predictions?

HOW CAN YOU STAY SAFE DURING DANGEROUS WEATHER?

The weather may range from calm and quiet to stormy and even dangerous. In Investigation 3 you'll find out about different kinds of dangerous weather and how you can stay safe.

Activity

Storm Safety

In this activity, find out how you can plan ahead and be prepared for severe weather.

MATERIALS
- weather safety reference materials
- *Science Notebook*

Procedure

With your group, make a Weather Safety booklet. In your *Science Notebook,* list the types of severe weather that may occur in your area. These may include thunderstorms, lightning, snowstorms, hurricanes, or tornadoes. Find out which radio and TV stations to listen to in case of severe weather and what safety measures you should take. Record what you learn in your Weather Safety booklet.

Analyze and Conclude

1. Where should you go if you are warned that severe weather is about to strike your area?

2. What things should you do or not do during severe weather?

Activity

Tornado Tube

Have you ever seen a tornado? These dangerous twisting storms can cause a lot of damage. If you have never seen a tornado, don't worry. In this activity you'll be making a model of one.

Procedure

1. Fill a plastic soda bottle about two-thirds full of water.

Math Hint *To estimate two thirds of the bottle, first measure the height of the bottle. Round the height to the nearest whole number. Divide the height by 3. Then multiply the quotient by 2.*

2. Screw one end of a tornado tube onto the bottle. Make sure the end fits tightly. Then screw an empty bottle into the other end of the tube. Make sure it also is screwed in tightly.

3. Turn the bottle with the water in it upside down. Hold on to the tornado tube. Quickly move the bottles in five or six circles so that the water inside swirls. **Observe** as the water drains from one bottle into the other. **Record** your observations in your *Science Notebook*.

Step 3

Analyze and Conclude

1. **Describe** the motion of the water as it moved from one bottle to the other.

2. **Hypothesize** how the movement of air in a tornado is similar to the movement of air and water in your model.

Light and Sound Show

Reading Focus What causes a thunderstorm?

KABOOM! You hear a sharp crack of thunder. A **thunderstorm** is a storm that produces heavy rain, strong winds, lightning, and thunder. Every year there are about 16 million thunderstorms around the world. These storms occur along cold fronts and in places where the local weather is very hot and humid.

Stormy Weather

Thunderstorms begin to form when warm, moist air rises from Earth's surface. Sometimes strong winds several kilometers above the surface make the air rise even faster and higher than usual, forming cumulonimbus clouds, or thunderheads. A single thunderhead may be several kilometers wide and up to 10 km (6 mi) high.

Swirling winds within the clouds carry water droplets and ice crystals up and down several times. This action causes the droplets and crystals to grow in size. When the raindrops and ice crystals become large enough and heavy enough, rain or hail begins to fall.

Using Math *This time-exposure photo shows a series of lightning flashes. Lightning strikes somewhere on Earth about 100 times every second. How many times does lightning strike each minute?*

Lightning and Thunder

Water and ice particles inside a thunderhead are thrown together by strong winds. This action produces static electricity. The energy from the static electricity is released as a flash of light and heat, called lightning. As a lightning bolt moves through the air, the air around it can become as hot as 30,000°C (54,000°F). This is more than five times as hot as the surface of the Sun!

As a lightning bolt flashes, it heats the air in its path. The air expands very rapidly, causing the rumbling we call thunder.

Although you might not think so, lightning and thunder happen at the same time. But we see lightning before we hear thunder, because light travels faster than sound.

Thunderstorm Problems

Although thunderstorms cool the air and ground, they can also cause problems. Sometimes there is so much rain from a sudden thunderstorm that floods occur. Sudden and violent floods are called **flash floods**. Heavy rain or hail from thunderstorms can damage crops and destroy property.

Lightning can injure and even kill people. It can cause fires. It can damage power lines and stop the flow of electricity. It can also interfere with radio and TV signals. ■

Science in Literature

MAKING RAIN TO ORDER

"'Good afternoon, ladies and gentlemen,' the stranger said . . . . 'My name is Professor Fergus Fahrenheit, and I represent the Wonder-Worker Weather Company. I understand you folks are in need of some rain. Well, ours is of the very best quality; and with every order we throw in a free silk umbrella.'"

Professor Fergus Fahrenheit and His Wonderful Weather Machine
by Candace Groth-Fleming
Illustrated by Don Weller
Simon & Schuster, 1994

This speech starts the action in *Professor Fergus Fahrenheit and His Wonderful Weather Machine* by Candace Groth-Fleming. Find out how the professor tries to help a town get rain.

Staying Safe in a Storm

Reading Focus How can you stay safe during severe weather?

In the past, people weren't able to predict when storms, hurricanes, or tornadoes would occur. But today, with the help of tools like weather satellites, scientists can better predict the weather.

The activity on page E64 explains how to be prepared for severe weather. What kinds of safety precautions would you include for thunderstorms, hurricanes, and tornadoes? Here are some precautions you should follow.

STAYING SAFE DURING A FLASH FLOOD

Flash floods can result from thunderstorms or hurricanes. Here are things you can do to keep yourself safe during a flood.

- Stay away from rivers, streams, creeks, and sewer drains. Water in these bodies can move very quickly.

- Don't try to walk or drive through water if you can't see the ground beneath the water.

- If a flood occurs, move to higher ground as quickly as possible.

STAYING SAFE FROM LIGHTNING

If you are outdoors:

- Go indoors. If you can't, stay away from tall buildings and trees. Lightning usually strikes the tallest objects.

- Avoid metal objects, such as metal baseball bats.

- Stay in a car, with windows up.

If you are indoors:

- Stay away from metal doors and large windows.

- Do not use the telephone.

- Unplug any TV, VCR, or computer.

In the mountains outside Tucson, Arizona, a flash flood turns an arroyo, or dry gully *(left)*, into a dangerous rush of muddy water *(below)*.

STAYING SAFE DURING A HURRICANE

If you are caught in a hurricane, here are some things you can do.

- Get as far away from ocean beaches as possible. The huge waves produced by hurricanes are very dangerous.

- Stay inside in a basement, under a stairwell, or in another sheltered area.

- Stay away from windows. Hurricane winds can break glass, causing injury to people.

- Listen to local TV and radio stations.

STAYING SAFE DURING A TORNADO

If a tornado is sighted in your area, follow these precautions.

- If you are outside, try to stay in a ditch or other low area. This will help protect you from flying objects.

- If you are inside, try to stay in a basement or a storm cellar. If there is no basement or storm cellar, stay in a closet or bathroom.

- Stay away from windows and doors that lead outside. These can be blown apart by the winds of a tornado.

The Fiercest Storms on Earth

Reading Focus How are hurricanes and tornadoes alike, and how are they different?

What are hurricanes and tornadoes? What causes these storms? Why are they known as the fiercest storms on Earth?

Hurricanes—The Largest Storms

Hurricanes have different names in different parts of the world. They are called cyclones in the Indian Ocean and typhoons in the west Pacific Ocean. **Hurricanes** are large, violent storms that form over warm ocean water.

To be called a hurricane, the storm must have winds of at least 117 km/h (70 mph). Some hurricanes have winds of more than 240 km/h (144 mph)! Hurricanes are classified according to strength. The weakest hurricane is a level 1 and the strongest is a level 5. Look back at the Beaufort scale on page E39. How does the Beaufort scale describe hurricanes?

Hurricanes start out as small thunderstorms over an ocean. Several of these storms may join to form a larger storm. This storm grows bigger as it takes in heat and moisture from warm ocean water. As the storm grows, the wind increases. This causes

These satellite photos of Hurricane Andrew show the storm's location as it moved from Florida to Louisiana. The photos were taken over a three-day period in August 1992. ▼

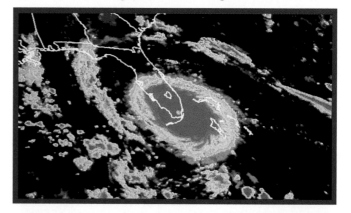

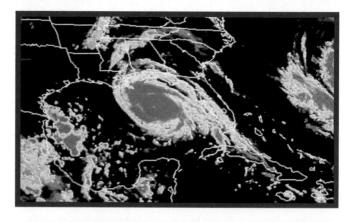

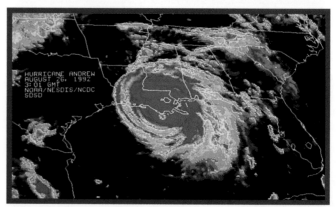

the clouds to spin. The diagram on this page explains how a hurricane forms.

In the middle of a hurricane is a hole, called the *eye* of the hurricane. Within the eye the weather is calm. There is little wind and no rain. Sometimes people are fooled into thinking that a hurricane is over when the eye is overhead. But it isn't over. The other half of the storm is on its way.

Hurricanes are the largest storms on Earth. A hurricane can cover a circular area as wide as 600 km (360 mi). A storm this size could cover both the states of Alabama and Mississippi at one time.

Hurricanes on the Move

Once a hurricane forms, it begins to travel. As it moves, the winds blow harder. The winds can rip up trees, blow off roofs, and produce giant ocean waves. These waves can wash away beaches and sink boats. Rain can cause flooding. Hurricanes don't last long once they reach land. The storm loses its source of energy over land or cold ocean water.

Internet Field Trip

Visit **www.eduplace.com** to find out more about hurricanes and tornadoes.

4 A circular wall of clouds with heavy rains and strong winds develops around the eye. As the warm air moves up, it spreads out.

5 In the eye the air sinks slowly, the winds are light, and there are no clouds.

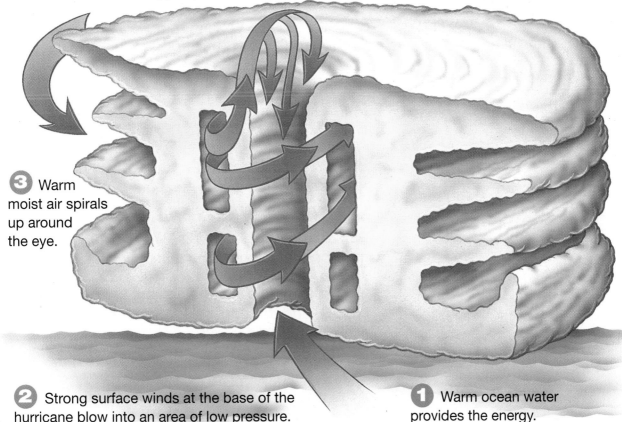

3 Warm moist air spirals up around the eye.

2 Strong surface winds at the base of the hurricane blow into an area of low pressure.

1 Warm ocean water provides the energy.

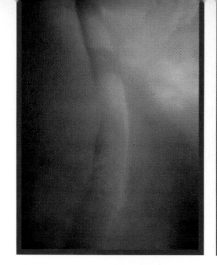

▲ A tornado may skip across the ground like someone playing leapfrog. Whatever it touches is likely to be destroyed.

Twister!

Sometimes a thunderstorm produces a tornado. A **tornado**, also known as a twister, is a funnel-shaped storm of spinning wind. The activity that is on page E65 uses water in a bottle to model a tornado. The spinning water is shaped like a tornado. But unlike the water, air in a tornado spins upward.

Tornadoes can develop without warning. They form when a column of warm air begins to spin. As air flows up into this swirling column, it spins very fast, forming the well-known funnel-shaped cloud.

Even though tornadoes don't cover as much area as hurricanes, they can be just as dangerous. The speed of the winds in the center of a tornado can be as high as 500 km/h (300 mph). This is twice the speed of the winds in the worst hurricane!

In tornadoes the air pressure is very low. The strong winds blowing into these low-pressure areas can sweep objects into the tornado, including dirt, trees, and roofs of buildings. The winds may be strong enough to move and destroy large trees, cars, trains, and houses. ■

INVESTIGATION 3 WRAP-UP

REVIEW

1. Describe the safety precautions you should take if you are outside during a thunderstorm.

2. What causes lightning? Why do you see the flash before you hear the thunder?

CRITICAL THINKING

3. Make a table to compare hurricanes, thunderstorms, and tornadoes. How are they similar? How are they different?

4. What type of dangerous weather is most likely to occur in your region? What precautions should you take if that type of weather occurs?

REFLECT & EVALUATE

Word Power

Write the letter of the term that best matches the definition. *Not all terms will be used.*

a. cirrus clouds
b. cold front
c. cumulus clouds
d. front
e. hurricane
f. stratus clouds
g. tornado
h. warm front

1. Where a cold air mass moves into a warm one
2. High, thin, feathery clouds made up of ice crystals
3. A large violent storm that forms over warm ocean water
4. A place where two masses of air meet
5. A low flat cloud that often brings drizzle
6. A funnel-shaped storm of spinning wind

Check What You Know

Write the term in each pair that best completes each sentence.

1. When a low-pressure area moves into a region, the weather will likely be (rainy, dry).
2. Hurricanes form over (deserts, oceans).
3. The air pressure inside a tornado is very (high, low).
4. Water vapor in the air condenses into tiny drops of water that form a (front, cloud).

Problem Solving

1. Imagine that you can use only two instruments to forecast tomorrow's weather. Which two would you choose? Explain your reasoning.

2. Describe two safety precautions people can take for each of the following types of dangerous weather: thunderstorms, hurricanes, and tornadoes.

BUILD YOUR PORTFOLIO

Study the drawing. Then write an explanation of how hurricanes form.

CHAPTER 4

SEASONS AND CLIMATE

Do you live in the northern part of the United States? If so, you may go sledding in winter and swimming in summer. If you live in southern California or Florida, you may not have as great a change between seasons. But every place on Earth has seasons.

Connecting to Science
CULTURE

Algonquin Moon The Algonquins, a Native American people, gave a name to each full moon to keep track of the seasons. Crow Moon is the name given to spring because that is when the crows return. April is the month of Sprouting Grass Moon. At the peak of spring is Flower Moon. In June comes Strawberry Moon. The heat of summer begins Thunder Moon, and August is the time of Sturgeon Moon. Summer ends with Harvest Moon. October's moon is the Hunter, and chilly November is the month of Frost Moon. The winter brings Long Nights Moon and then the howling winds of Wolf Moon. By February, food is scarce. That month's moon is named Hunger. How would you name the moon for the seasons where you live?

Coming Up

INVESTIGATION 1

WHAT CAUSES THE SEASONS?

. . . . **E76**

INVESTIGATION 2

WHAT FACTORS AFFECT CLIMATE?

. . . . **E82**

◀ The Algonquins might call this moon the Long Nights Moon.

WHAT CAUSES THE SEASONS?

Which activities do you like to do in summer? in winter? How do the differences in weather during summer and winter affect what you do? In Investigation 1 you'll find out what causes summer and winter!

Activity

Sunshine Hours

Do the number of hours of sunlight change from season to season? Gather data to find out.

MATERIALS
- graph paper
- yellow crayon
- *Science Notebook*

Procedure

1. The table shows the times the Sun rises and sets in the middle of each month. Interpret the data in the table to predict whether the number of hours of sunlight is greater in winter or in summer. Discuss your prediction with your group and then record it in your *Science Notebook*.

2. Using graph paper, set up a graph like the one shown on page E77. Note that *Time of Day* should be on the left side and *Month of Year* should be along the bottom. Then make a line graph using the data in the table.

Sunrises and Sunsets (Standard Time) for the Middle of Each Month		
Month	Sunrise (A.M.)	Sunset (P.M.)
Jan.	7:20	5:00
Feb.	6:55	5:34
Mar.	6:11	6:07
Apr.	5:23	6:38
May	4:44	7:09
June	4:31	7:30
July	4:44	7:27
Aug.	5:12	6:56
Sept.	5:41	6:09
Oct.	6:11	5:20
Nov.	6:45	4:44
Dec.	7:15	4:36

3. On your graph, mark a dot to show the time the Sun rises for each month. Connect the dots.

4. Mark another dot to show the time the Sun sets for each month. Connect these dots.

5. Use a yellow crayon to color the space between the two lines on your graph paper. Keep the graph in your *Science Notebook*.

Analyze and Conclude

1. What does the yellow space on your graph represent?

2. Interpret your graph. Are the number of hours of sunlight greater in summer or in winter? Compare your results with your prediction.

3. Use the data on your graph to infer why the temperature of the air in summer tends to be higher than the temperature of the air in winter.

Changing Seasons

> **Reading Focus** How does the tilt of Earth's axis affect surface temperatures and the seasons?

▲ **How do the changing seasons affect what you do?**

It's the first day of summer! You and your friends are planning a trip to the nearest swimming pool. At the same time, students your age in Australia are spending the first day of winter in school. How can it be summer in one part of the world and winter in another? And why are there different seasons at all?

The Tilting Earth

As Earth moves, or revolves, around the Sun, different places on Earth's surface are heated differently by the Sun. To understand why this

happens, imagine Earth has a line running through it, like the one shown in the picture on page E79. This imaginary line is called Earth's **axis** (ak′sis).

Earth spins, or rotates, around its axis. It takes Earth about 24 hours, or one day and night, to complete this turn.

There is a second imaginary line. It circles the middle of Earth. This line is called the **equator** (ē kwāt′ər). Find the equator in the picture on page E79. The half of Earth that is above the equator is called the

Northern Hemisphere. The half below the equator is called the **Southern Hemisphere**.

When Earth revolves around the Sun, its axis is not straight up and down. Instead, Earth's axis is tilted slightly. The tilt of Earth's axis stays almost the same throughout the year. So as Earth revolves around the Sun, at times the Northern Hemisphere is tilted toward the Sun, and at times it is tilted away from the Sun.

AXIS Earth's axis is an imaginary line that runs from the North Pole through Earth's center to the South Pole.

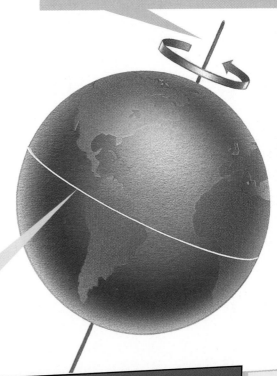

EQUATOR The equator divides Earth into the Northern Hemisphere and the Southern Hemisphere.

Science in Literature

OUT OF THIS WORLD!

The Third Planet: Exploring the Earth From Space
by Sally Ride and Tam O'Shaughnessy
Crown Publishers, 1994

"The Space Shuttle streaks through space at 17,500 miles per hour. It crosses the United States in just a few minutes, and circles the whole planet in just an hour and a half . . . . I could take pictures of giant glaciers in Alaska one minute and of the shallow waters off the Florida coast 15 minutes later."

Here astronaut Sally Ride describes what it's like to look down on Earth from a spacecraft. Her quotation is from the book *The Third Planet*, which she and Tam O'Shaughnessy wrote together. The photographs are out of this world!

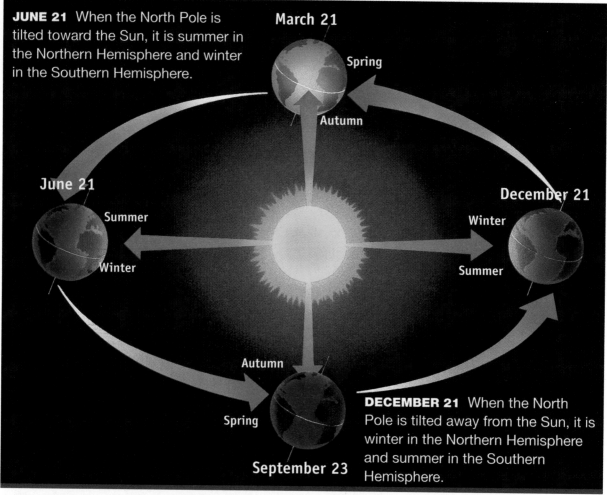

JUNE 21 When the North Pole is tilted toward the Sun, it is summer in the Northern Hemisphere and winter in the Southern Hemisphere.

March 21
Spring
Autumn

June 21
Summer
Winter

December 21
Winter
Summer

Autumn
Spring
September 23

DECEMBER 21 When the North Pole is tilted away from the Sun, it is winter in the Northern Hemisphere and summer in the Southern Hemisphere.

▲ **The seasons change as Earth revolves around the Sun.**

UNIT PROJECT LINK

Use your weather station to collect data for a two-week period during different seasons of the year. Compare data such as high and low temperatures, amounts of precipitation, and air pressure for each season. Discuss the patterns in seasonal weather you observe.

TechnologyLink
For more help with your Unit Project, go to **www.eduplace.com**.

Seasons in the Sun

Study the picture above. As Earth revolves around the Sun, there are changes in the way the Sun's rays strike Earth's surface. These changes cause the temperature of Earth's surface and atmosphere to change. This leads to the change in seasons.

Remember that the tilt of Earth's axis does not change much. What *does* change is the position of the axis in relation to the Sun's position.

The picture on page E81 shows that, during the winter, sunlight strikes Earth at a slant. When light strikes at

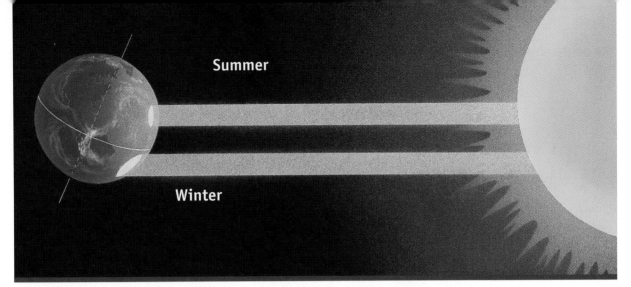

Summer

Winter

▲ The Sun's rays strike Earth at a greater slant during winter.

a slant, it spreads out and covers more area. The greater the slant, the less the ground in this area is heated. This is the main reason that temperatures are colder in winter than in summer.

In summer, sunlight strikes Earth more directly. The light does not spread out as much and covers less area than it does in winter. So the ground is heated more. This is the main reason that temperatures are warmer in summer.

The number of hours of daylight also affects the temperature. When the North Pole is tilted toward the Sun, the Sun appears high in the sky. Then there are more hours of daylight. The longer the Sun shines on an area, the more energy that area can absorb and the warmer the temperatures become.

When the North Pole is tilted away from the Sun, the Sun appears low in the sky. Then there are fewer hours of daylight. Because the Sun has less time to heat an area, temperatures there are cooler. Which season, according to the table in the activity on pages E76 and E77, has the most hours of daylight? ■

INVESTIGATION 1 WRAP-UP

THINK IT WRITE IT

REVIEW

1. Give two reasons why the Sun heats an area more in summer than it does in winter.

2. Make and label a drawing to show the positions of the Northern Hemisphere in summer and in winter. Include the Sun in your picture.

CRITICAL THINKING

3. Suppose the North Pole is tilted toward the Sun. Compare daylight hours at the North Pole and South Pole. Explain your answer.

4. In what season is your birthday? What will the weather likely be on that day in your region? in Australia? Explain your answer.

INVESTIGATION 2

WHAT FACTORS AFFECT CLIMATE?

Climate is the average weather conditions of a place over a long period of time. In Investigation 2 you'll find out what factors cause Earth to have different climates.

Activity

Microclimates Everywhere!

Temperature and wind are important factors in determining climate. Why might two places close to each other have different climates? Investigate to find out.

MATERIALS
- goggles
- cardboard tube
- aluminum foil
- meterstick
- rubber band
- thermometer
- wind vane
- magnetic compass
- *Science Notebook*

SAFETY //////
Wear goggles when doing step 2. Be careful when handling thermometers.

Procedure

1. In your *Science Notebook*, make a chart like the one shown.

Building Side	Temperature (°C)	Wind Direction

2. Cover the outside of a cardboard tube with aluminum foil. Fasten the tube to a meterstick with a rubber band as shown. Move the tube so that the lower edge of the tube is at the 30-cm mark.

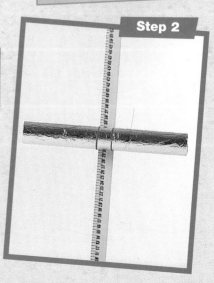

Step 2

3. **Predict** whether temperature and wind direction are the same, or different, on each of the sides of your school building.

Step 4

4. Take a thermometer and a wind vane outside your school. Stay close to one side of the building and **measure** the temperature 30 cm from the ground. Use a magnetic compass to help **determine** the wind direction, too. **Record** this data in your chart.

 See **SCIENCE** and **MATH TOOLBOX** page H8 *if you need to review* **Using a Thermometer.**

5. Repeat step 4 for the other sides of the building. **Record** all data in your chart.

Analyze and Conclude

1. **Compare** your prediction in step 3 with your results. What differences, if any, did you find on different sides of your school?

2. Different sides of a building have different microclimates. *Micro-* means "very small." From your study, how would you **define** *microclimate*?

3. Which microclimate was the warmest? Which was the coolest? **Infer** why temperature would vary on different sides of the building.

4. Was the wind direction different on different sides of the building? What factors affect the way the wind blows on one side of your school building?

INVESTIGATE FURTHER!

EXPERIMENT

Predict what would happen if you repeated this experiment over a longer period of time. Would you get the same results? Discuss your predictions with your group. Repeat the experiment once a month for the next three months. How did your predictions compare with your results?

E83

Florida Is Not North Dakota

Reading Focus What causes climate and what are three main types of climate?

What is the weather in your area normally like in the summer? What is the weather like in the winter? People in different parts of the world will have different answers to these questions. That's because different places have different climates. The **climate** of an area is the average weather conditions over a long period of time.

Hot or Cold, Wet or Dry

Two important parts of an area's climate are its average temperature and

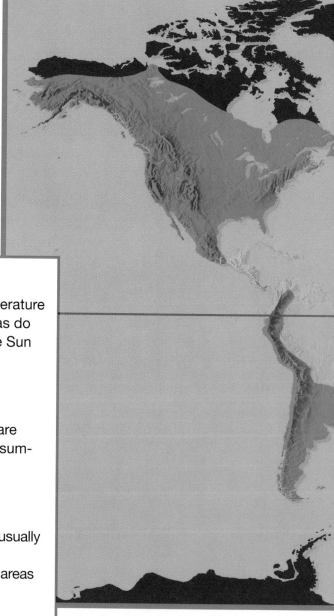

POLAR CLIMATE
In the Arctic and Antarctic, the temperature is usually below freezing. These areas do not receive as much energy from the Sun as other parts of Earth.

TEMPERATE CLIMATE
Between the equator and the poles are areas that generally have warm, dry summers and cold, wet winters.

TROPICAL CLIMATE
The places closest to the equator are usually hot and rainy for most of the year. Temperatures are high because these areas receive the most energy from the Sun.

E84

its average yearly rainfall. The average temperature of an area depends a great deal on how far the area is from the equator. In general, areas close to the equator are warmer than areas farther from the equator. For example, North Dakota is farther from the equator than Florida is, so North Dakota is usually colder than Florida. The map below shows the location of three main types of climates. They are polar, tropical, and temperate.

Areas with a **tropical climate** are usually hot and rainy year-round. Areas with a **temperate climate** generally have summers that are warm and dry and winters that are cold and wet. Areas with a **polar climate** are usually very cold. Which climate do you think you live in?

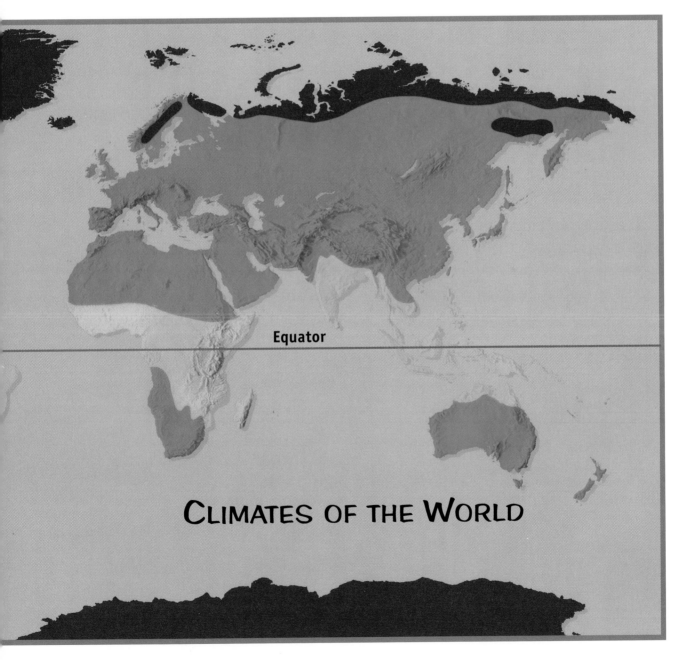

Equator

CLIMATES OF THE WORLD

Air pattern over land near a large body of water ▼

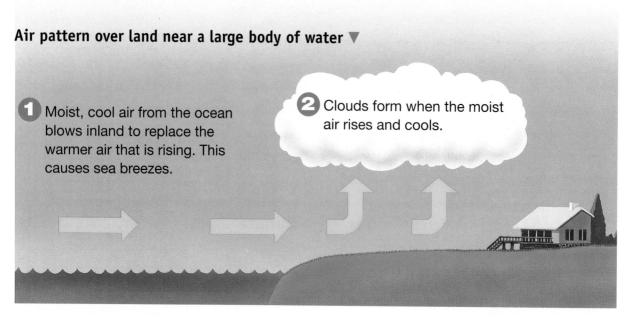

1 Moist, cool air from the ocean blows inland to replace the warmer air that is rising. This causes sea breezes.

2 Clouds form when the moist air rises and cools.

Climate Controls

The activity on pages E82 and E83 shows how to investigate the microclimates around your school building. Factors such as the amount of sunlight and the type of ground cover affect the temperature of an area. Factors such as the placement of buildings and trees affect the way the wind blows in an area.

Just as certain things affect microclimates, certain features, such as oceans and mountains, can affect the climate in an area. In the diagrams on this page and the next, you can see how oceans and mountains affect climate.

If you live near an ocean or large lake, your climate may be cloudier and wetter than the climate of places farther from the water. The summers in your area may be cooler, and the winters may be warmer.

An area in the middle of the plains or far from any large body of water

Air pattern over plains ▼

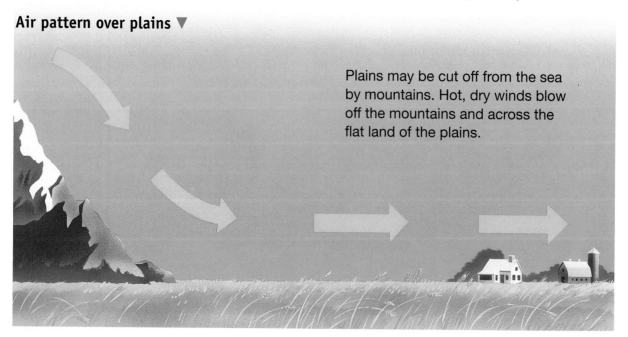

Plains may be cut off from the sea by mountains. Hot, dry winds blow off the mountains and across the flat land of the plains.

will likely have a different climate. These areas probably will have little rain, hot summers, and cold winters.

If you live near a mountain on the side least protected from the wind, your area may often have strong winds and lots of rain. But if you live near a mountain on the side most protected from the wind, your climate will probably be dry.

El Niño

The cool waters of the Pacific Ocean off the coast of South America become warmer about every four years. This causes weather patterns to change around the world! Scientists refer to this huge area of warm ocean water and the changes in weather patterns that it causes as El Niño.

Severe effects of El Niño occurred in 1997–1998. During the spring of 1998, rainfall was much heavier than normal in the eastern United States. California also had heavy rains and flooding. But, in the southern United States and parts of Asia, drought was the effect of El Niño. El Niño also helped cause forest fires that occurred in Indonesia that year.

Scientists still don't understand all of the factors that produce El Niño. Nor can they accurately predict its effects, but they continue to study El Niño and the weather changes it brings. ■

Air pattern over a mountain ▼

2 These clouds bring heavy rain. As the air passes over the mountaintop and flows down the other side, it becomes warmer and drier.

1 When moist air meets a mountain, the air is forced upward. As the air rises, it cools and forms clouds around the peak.

Clues to Earth's Climate

Reading Focus What are three ways scientists learn about climate changes in Earth's past?

The world's climate has gone through many changes. These changes have lasted from just a few years to thousands of years. Scientists who study Earth's climate look for clues to find out why these changes in climate have taken place.

Tree Rings

One way that scientists learn about climate changes is by studying trees. Most trees grow a new ring every year. You can see the tree rings in the picture. If a ring is wide, the weather affecting that tree was probably moister and warmer than normal that year. That means that the tree probably got plenty of nutrients and grew quickly. If a tree ring is narrow, the weather was probably drier and colder than normal that year. That means that the tree probably didn't get enough nutrients and grew slowly. By studying tree rings, scientists can track warm and cold periods several thousand years into Earth's past.

◄ Tree rings can help scientists determine changes in Earth's climate.

▲ Finding fossils in unexpected places may indicate changes in Earth's climate.

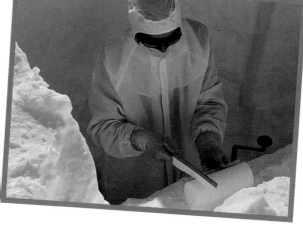

▲ A scientist saws off a piece of an ice core for testing.

Fossil Clues

Another way that scientists learn about climate changes is by studying fossils. Fossils are imprints or remains of animals and plants that lived in the past. Finding fossils in unusual places can be a clue that the climate in an area has changed. For example, some fossilized camel bones were found in the Arctic. Scientists hypothesize that these fossils show that the Arctic was once much warmer than it is now. Fossils can give clues to what Earth's climate was like millions of years ago.

Ice Cores

A third method that scientists use to find out about past climates is to drill holes in glaciers and pull out long columns of ice, or ice cores. Scientists then analyze these ice cores. Finding traces of certain chemicals can give clues about past climate changes. The scientist shown above in the photo on the right is wearing surgical clothing to keep the ice core from getting dirty.

Covered in Ice

Great changes in Earth's climate usually occur very slowly. At times, Earth has been much warmer than it is now. At other times, Earth has been much colder than it is now. Then sheets of ice called glaciers covered large areas of the world. These cold periods are called **ice ages**. The last ice age ended about 10,000 years ago. During that time, glaciers covered much of Earth's land, including large parts of the United States! ■

Technology Link
CD-ROM

INVESTIGATE FURTHER!

Use the **Science Processor CD-ROM**, *Weather & Climate* (Investigation 4, Where on Earth?) to see how the climate in your area is different from those in other places.

Weather Records

Reading Focus What are four kinds of weather records?

Have you ever thought that a certain rainstorm was the worst one you'd ever seen? Or, on a hot day, have you ever thought that it couldn't get any hotter? Imagine what it would be like to live someplace that had no rain for 400 years. Think about how it would feel to live someplace that only gets sunlight for half the year. Find out where these places are as you read about some of the windiest, wettest, driest, hottest, and coldest places on Earth!

The Windiest Place
- Winds coming off Commonwealth Bay, Antarctica, can reach 320 km/h (200 mph).

The Fastest Wind Gust
- A wind speed of 415 km/h (250 mph) was recorded on April 12, 1934, on Mount Washington in New Hampshire. This area is known for unpredictable and dangerous weather.

Mount Washington, New Hampshire ▶

STOP
THE AREA AHEAD HAS THE WORST WEATHER IN AMERICA. MANY HAVE DIED THERE FROM EXPOSURE, EVEN IN THE SUMMER. TURN BACK NOW IF THE WEATHER IS BAD.
WHITE MOUNTAIN NATIONAL FOREST

The Coldest Place
- Polus Nedostuphosti (Pole of Cold), Antarctica, has an average temperature of −58°C (−72°F). This area near the South Pole gets sunlight for only about half the year.

The Lowest Temperatures
- The lowest recorded temperature on Earth was −88°C (−127°F) in Vostok, Antarctica, on July 22, 1983.
- In the United States a low temperature of −62°C (−80°F) was recorded on January 23, 1971, in Prospect Creek, Alaska.

South Pole, Antarctica ▶

The Hottest Place
- Dallol, Ethiopia, has an average temperature of 34°C (94°F). Dallol is very close to the equator and is shielded from the Indian Ocean by mountains.

The Highest Temperatures
- The highest temperature recorded on Earth was in Al-Aziziyah, Libya, where the temperature reached 58°C (136°F) on September 13, 1922.
- The highest temperature recorded in the United States was 57°C (134°F) on July 10, 1913, in Death Valley, California.

◀ **Death Valley, California**

The Wettest Places

- Mawsynram, in India, has about 1,186 cm (474 in.) of rainfall per year.
- The state of Louisiana averages 142 cm (56 in.) of rainfall per year.

  In these areas the warm, wet winds blow in off the water. As the winds blow over the land, the air rises and cools. This creates thick clouds and heavy rains.

The Greatest Rainfall

- In one day, from March 15 through March 16, 1952, nearly 187 cm (74 in.) of rain fell in Cilaos, on the island of Réunion, in the Indian Ocean.

▼ **Mawsynram, India**

The Atacama Desert, Chile ▲

The Driest Places

- Arica, Chile, averages less than 0.01 cm (0.004 in.) of rainfall per year. Chile is near very cold water, so the winds blowing toward land are usually dry and don't form many clouds.
- In the state of Nevada, about 23 cm (9 in.) of rain falls per year. Much of Nevada is sheltered from ocean winds by the Sierra Nevada, a mountain range. The winds that come down from the mountains contain little water vapor.

The Longest Dry Spell

- Desierto de Atacama (the Atacama Desert) in Chile had almost no rain for 400 years! This dry spell ended in 1971.

INVESTIGATION 2 WRAP-UP

REVIEW

1. What are the two main factors that affect the climate of an area? Discuss each type of climate.

2. How are tree rings clues to climate changes?

CRITICAL THINKING

3. What would you conclude if you found the fossilized bones of an Arctic animal near the equator?

4. Suppose your business is landscaping. How can you use your knowledge of microclimates?

REFLECT & EVALUATE

Word Power

Write the letter of the term that best matches the definition. *Not all terms will be used.*

1. Climate of places in the Arctic and Antarctic
2. Climate of places closest to the equator
3. Climate with warm, dry summers and cold, wet winters
4. An imaginary line running around the middle of Earth
5. An imaginary straight line running through Earth from the North Pole to the South Pole.

a. axis
b. equator
c. ice ages
d. polar climate
e. temperate climate
f. tropical climate

Check What You Know

Write the term in each pair that best completes each sentence.

1. The greater the slant of the Sun's rays striking Earth, the (more, less) the Earth's surface is heated.
2. A very wide tree ring is likely to form in a year with (much, little) rainfall.
3. The average weather conditions in an area over a long period of time is its (weather, climate).
4. If you live in a tropical climate, the weather is hot and (wet, dry).

Problem Solving

1. You and a friend live in different cities. The cities are the same distance from the equator, but they have very different climates. What are some of the factors that might explain this difference?

2. Your cousin is packing shorts and bathing suits for his trip to Sydney, Australia, on July 3. During his two-week stay, he expects to spend time enjoying warm beaches. What advice would you give him about his trip? Explain.

Study the drawing. Explain in writing how the tilt of Earth's axis and the slant of the Sun's rays cause the seasons.

Detecting the Sequence

Sequence is the order in which things happen. Sometimes a paragraph contains signal words such as *first*, *then*, *next*, and *later*. When a passage doesn't contain signal words, look for other clues, such as numbers in the text or numbered steps in a diagram.

Look for these clues to detect the sequence.

- Signal words: *first, then, next, later*
- Numbers in the text
- Numbered steps in a drawing

Read the following paragraph. Then complete the exercises that follow.

Earth's Greenhouse

In some ways, Earth's atmosphere acts like the glass of a greenhouse. It allows the Sun's rays to pass through it and heat Earth's land and water. Some of the heat from the warmed Earth then goes back into the atmosphere as invisible rays. Some of these heat rays escape into space. But most are trapped by water vapor, carbon dioxide, and other gases of Earth's atmosphere. So the atmosphere warms up.

1. **Which statement tells what happens first, after the Sun's rays pass through Earth's atmosphere? Write the letter of that statement.**

   a. It heats Earth's land and water.

   b. Some of the heat from Earth goes into the atmosphere.

   c. Some heat is trapped by water vapor.

   d. Heat rays escape into space.

2. **What clues helped you keep track of the sequence?**

Using
Math **Line Graph**

This line graph shows the change in temperature during a 12-hour period at Logan Airport in Boston, Massachusetts.

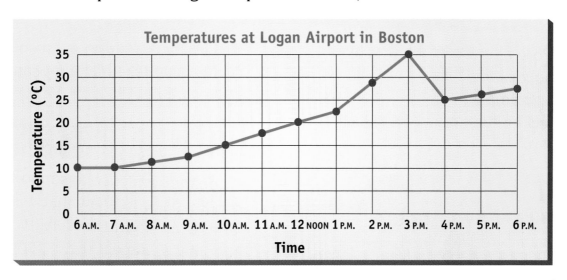

Use the data in the graph to complete the exercises that follow.

1. How many degrees did the temperature change between 6 A.M. and 3 P.M.?

2. What was the difference in temperature between 3 P.M. and 6 P.M.?

3. What was the highest temperature recorded? At what time did that temperature occur?

4. The temperature cooled during a brief thunderstorm in the 12-hour period. Between what hours did the storm take place? How do you know?

5. Make a line graph that shows the data in the table.

Average Monthly Rainfall for New Orleans											
Month	Jan.	Feb.	Mar.	Apr.	May	June	July	Aug.	Sept.	Oct.	Nov.	Dec.
Rainfall (mm)	100	225	100	425	100	200	75	150	150	100	100	200

WRAP-UP!

On your own, use scientific methods to investigate a question about weather.

THINK LIKE A SCIENTIST

Ask a Question

Pose a question about weather that you would like to investigate. For example, ask, "How does wind affect air temperature in a location?"

Make a Hypothesis

Suggest a hypothesis, or possible answer to the question. One hypothesis is that wind will lower air temperature in a location.

Plan and Do a Test

Plan a controlled experiment to find the effect wind has on the air temperature in a location. You could start with two pans holding equal amounts of the same kind of soil, a desk fan, and two thermometers. Develop a procedure that uses these materials to test the hypothesis. With permission, carry out your experiment. Follow the safety guidelines on pages S14–S15.

Record and Analyze

Observe carefully and record your data accurately. Make repeated observations.

Draw Conclusions

Look for evidence to support the hypothesis or to show that it is false. Draw conclusions about the hypothesis. Repeat the experiment to verify the results.

WRITING IN SCIENCE
Letter of Request

Write a letter or an e-mail to ask the National Weather Service for a list of materials they offer to students. When you receive the list, write a letter requesting the items you want. Use these guidelines to write your letters of request.

- Include the parts of a business letter.
- Explain clearly what you are requesting.

SCIENCE and MATH TOOLBOX

Using a Hand Lens..H2

Making a Bar Graph..H3

Using a Calculator..H4

Finding an Average..H5

Using a Tape Measure or Ruler........................H6

Measuring Volume..H7

Using a Thermometer....................................H8

Using a Balance..H9

Making a Chart to Organize Data..............H10

Reading a Circle Graph..............................H11

Measuring Elapsed Time..............................H12

Measurements..H14

Using a
Hand Lens

A hand lens is a tool that magnifies objects, or makes objects appear larger. This makes it possible for you to see details of an object that would be hard to see without the hand lens.

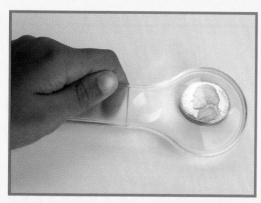

▲ Place the lens above the object.

▲ Move the lens slowly toward you.

Look at a Coin or a Stamp

1. Place an object such as a coin or a stamp on a table or other flat surface.

2. Hold the hand lens just above the object. As you look through the lens, slowly move the lens away from the object. Notice that the object appears to get larger.

3. Keep moving the lens until the object begins to look a little blurry. Then move the hand lens a little closer to the object until the object is once again in sharp focus.

If the object starts to look blurry, move the lens toward the object. ▶

Making a Bar Graph

A bar graph helps you organize and compare data.

Make a Bar Graph of Animal Heights

Animals come in all different shapes and sizes. You can use the information in the table to make a bar graph of animal heights.

Heights of Animals	
Animal	**Height (cm)**
Bear	240
Elephant	315
Cow	150
Giraffe	570
Camel	210
Horse	165

1. Draw the side and the bottom of the graph. Label the side of the graph as shown. The numbers will show the height of the animals in centimeters.

3. Choose a title for your graph. Your title should describe the subject of the graph.

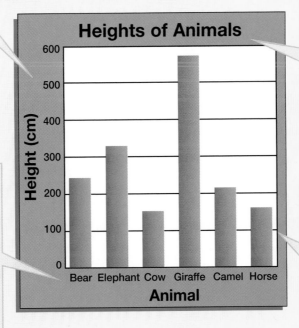

Heights of Animals

2. Label the bottom of the graph. Write the names of the animals at the bottom so that there is room to draw the bars.

4. Draw bars to show the height of each animal. Some heights are between two numbers.

Using a Calculator

After you've made measurements, a calculator can help you analyze your data.

Add and Multiply Decimals

Suppose you're an astronaut. You may take 8 pounds of Moon rocks back to Earth. The table shows the weights of the rocks. Can you take them all? Use a calculator to find out.

Weight of Moon Rocks	
Moon Rock	Weight of Rock on Moon (lb)
Rock 1	1.7
Rock 2	1.8
Rock 3	2.6
Rock 4	1.5

1. To add, press:

$\boxed{1}\ \boxed{.}\ \boxed{7}\ \boxed{+}\ \boxed{1}\ \boxed{.}\ \boxed{8}\ \boxed{+}$

$\boxed{2}\ \boxed{.}\ \boxed{6}\ \boxed{+}\ \boxed{1}\ \boxed{.}\ \boxed{5}\ \boxed{=}$

Display: (7.6)

2. If you make a mistake, press the clear entry key (CE/C) once. Enter the number again. Then continue adding. (Note: If you press CE/C twice, it will clear all.)

3. Your total is 7.6 pounds. You can take the four Moon rocks back to Earth.

4. How much do the Moon rocks weigh on Earth? Objects weigh six times as much on Earth as they do on the Moon. You can use a calculator to multiply.

Press: $\boxed{7}\ \boxed{.}\ \boxed{6}\ \boxed{\times}\ \boxed{6}\ \boxed{=}$

Display: (45.6)

5. The rocks weigh 45.6 pounds on Earth.

clear entry

divide

multiply

plus

equal

Finding an Average

An average is a way to describe a group of numbers. For example, after you have made a series of measurements, you can find the average. This can help you analyze your data.

Rainfall	
Month	Rain (mm)
Jan.	102
Feb.	75
Mar.	46
Apr.	126
May	51
June	32

Add and Divide to Find the Average

The table shows the amount of rain that fell each month for the first six months of the year. What was the average rainfall per month?

1. Add the numbers in the list.

$$
\begin{array}{r}
102 \\
75 \\
46 \\
126 \\
51 \\
+\ 32 \\
\hline
432
\end{array}
\Big\} \ \text{6 addends}
$$

2. Divide the sum (432) by the number of addends (6).

$$
\begin{array}{r}
72 \\
6 \overline{)432} \\
-\ 42 \\
\hline
12 \\
-\ 12 \\
\hline
0
\end{array}
$$

3. The average rainfall per month for the first six months was 72 mm of rain.

Using a
Tape Measure
or Ruler

Tape measures and rulers are tools for measuring the length of objects and distances. Scientists most often use units such as meters, centimeters, and millimeters when making length measurements.

Use a Tape Measure

1. Measure the distance around a jar. Wrap the tape around the jar.

2. Find the line where the tape begins to wrap over itself.

3. Record the distance around the jar to the nearest centimeter.

Use a Metric Ruler

1. Measure the length of your shoe. Place the ruler or the meterstick on the floor. Line up the end of the ruler with the heel of your shoe.

2. Notice where the other end of your shoe lines up with the ruler.

3. Look at the scale on the ruler. Record the length of your shoe to the nearest centimeter and to the nearest millimeter.

Measuring Volume

A graduated cylinder, a measuring cup, and a beaker are used to measure volume. Volume is the amount of space something takes up. Most of the containers that scientists use to measure volume have a scale marked in milliliters (mL).

Measure the Volume of a Liquid

1. Measure the volume of juice. Pour some juice into a measuring container.

2. Move your head so that your eyes are level with the top of the juice. Read the scale line that is closest to the surface of the juice. If the surface of the juice is curved up on the sides, look at the lowest point of the curve.

3. Read the measurement on the scale. You can estimate the value between two lines on the scale.

▲ The bottom of the curve is at 35 mL.

This beaker has marks for each 25 mL. ▶

This graduated cylinder has marks for every 1 mL. ▶

▲ This measuring cup has marks for each 25 mL.

Using a Thermometer

A thermometer is used to measure temperature. When the liquid in the tube of a thermometer gets warmer, it expands and moves farther up the tube. Different scales can be used to measure temperature, but scientists usually use the Celsius scale.

Measure the Temperature of a Cold Liquid

1. Take a chilled liquid out of the refrigerator. Half fill a cup with the liquid.

2. Hold the thermometer so that the bulb is in the center of the liquid. Be sure that there are no bright lights or direct sunlight shining on the bulb.

3. Wait a few minutes until you see the liquid in the tube of the thermometer stop moving. Read the scale line that is closest to the top of the liquid in the tube. The thermometer shown reads 21°C (about 70°F).

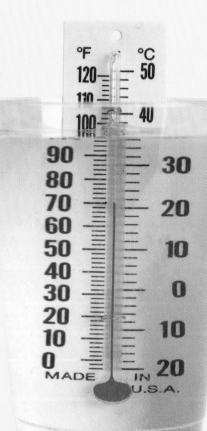

Using a
Balance

A balance is used to measure mass. Mass is the amount of matter in an object. To find the mass of an object, place it in the left pan of the balance. Place standard masses in the right pan.

Measure the Mass of a Ball

1. Check that the empty pans are balanced, or level with each other. When balanced, the pointer on the base should be at the middle mark. If it needs to be adjusted, move the slider on the back of the balance a little to the left or right.

2. Place a ball on the left pan. Then add standard masses, one at a time, to the right pan. When the pointer is at the middle mark again, each pan holds the same amount of matter and has the same mass.

3. Add the numbers marked on the masses in the pan. The total is the mass of the ball in grams.

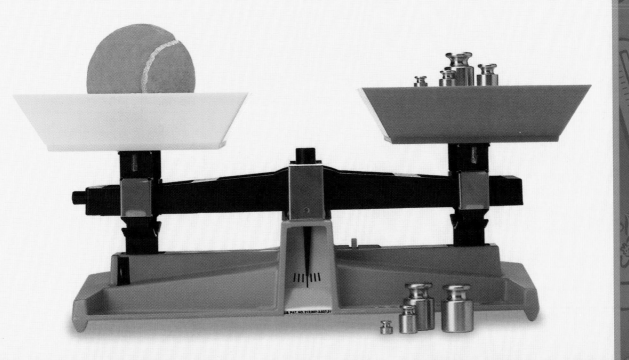

Making a Chart to Organize Data

A chart can help you keep track of information. When you organize information, or data, it is easier to read, compare, or classify it.

Classifying Animals

Suppose you are studying characteristics of different animals. You want to organize the data that you collect.

Look at the data below. To put this data in a chart, you could base the chart on the two characteristics listed— the number of wings and the number of legs.

My Data

Fleas have no wings. Fleas have six legs.

Snakes have no wings or legs.

A bee has four wings. It has six legs.

Spiders never have wings. They have eight legs.

A dog has no wings. It has four legs.

Birds have two wings and two legs.

A cow has no wings. It has four legs.

A butterfly has four wings. It has six legs.

Give the chart a title that describes the data in it.

Name categories, or groups, that describe the data you have collected.

Make sure the information is recorded correctly in each column.

Animals—Number of Wings and Legs

Animal	Number of Wings	Number of Legs
Flea	0	6
Snake	0	0
Bee	4	6
Spider	0	8
Dog	0	4
Bird	2	2
Cow	0	4
Butterfly	4	6

Next, you could make another chart to show animal classification based on number of legs only.

Reading a
Circle Graph

A circle graph shows a whole divided into parts. You can use a circle graph to compare the parts to each other. You can also use it to compare the parts to the whole.

A Circle Graph of Fuel Use

This circle graph shows fuel use in the United States. The graph has 10 equal parts, or sections. Each section equals $\frac{1}{10}$ of the whole. One whole equals $\frac{10}{10}$.

Of all the fuel used in the United States, 4 out of 10 parts, or $\frac{4}{10}$, is oil.

Of all the fuel used in the United States, 3 out of 10 parts, or $\frac{3}{10}$, is natural gas.

Of all the fuel used in the United States, 2 out of 10 parts, or $\frac{2}{10}$, is coal.

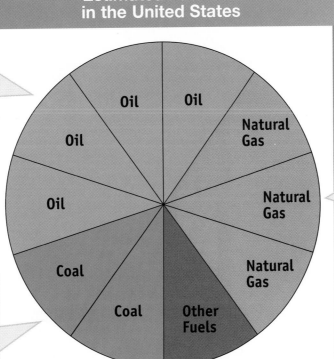

Estimated Fuel Use in the United States

Oil
Oil
Oil
Oil
Natural Gas
Natural Gas
Natural Gas
Coal
Coal
Other Fuels

Measuring Elapsed Time

A calendar can help you find out how much time has passed, or elapsed, in days or weeks. A clock can help you see how much time has elapsed in hours and minutes. A clock with a second hand or a stopwatch can help you find out how many seconds have elapsed.

Using a Calendar to Find Elapsed Days

This is a calendar for the month of October. October has 31 days. Suppose it is October 22 and you begin an experiment. You need to check the experiment two days from the start date and one week from the start date. That means you would check it on Wednesday, October 24, and again on Monday, October 29. October 29 is 7 days after October 22.

Monday, Tuesday, Wednesday, Thursday, and Friday are weekdays. Saturday and Sunday are weekends.

Last month ended on Sunday, September 30.

October

Sunday	Monday	Tuesday	Wednesday	Thursday	Friday	Saturday
	1	2	3	4	5	6
7	8	9	10	11	12	13
14	15	16	17	18	19	20
21	22	23	24	25	26	27
28	29	30	31			

Next month begins on Thursday, November 1.

Using a Clock or a Stopwatch to Find Elapsed Time

You need to time an experiment for 20 minutes.

It is 1:30 P.M.

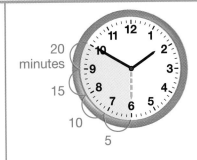

Stop at 1:50 P.M.

You need to time an experiment for 15 seconds. You can use the second hand of a clock or watch.

60 seconds = 1 minute

Start the experiment when the second hand is on number 6.

Stop when 15 seconds have passed and the second hand is on the 9.

You can use a stopwatch.

Press the reset button on a stopwatch so that you see 0:00oo.

Press the start button. When you see 0:15oo, press the stop button.

MEASUREMENTS

Volume
1 L of sports drink is a little more than 1 qt.

Area
A basketball court covers about 4,700 ft². It covers about 435 m².

Mass and Weight
A basketball has a mass of about 650 g. It weighs about 1½ lb.

Metric Measures

Temperature
Ice melts at 0 degrees Celsius (°C)

Water freezes at 0°C

Water boils at 100°C

Length and Distance
1,000 meters (m) = 1 kilometer (km)

100 centimeters (cm) = 1 m

10 millimeters (mm) = 1 cm

Force
1 newton (N) =
   1 kilogram x meter/second/second
   (kg x m/s²)

Volume
1 cubic meter (m³) = 1 m x 1 m x 1 m

1 cubic centimeter (cm³) =
   1 cm x 1 cm x 1 cm

1 liter (L) = 1,000 milliliters (mL)

1 cm³ = 1 mL

Area
1 square kilometer (km²) = 1 km x 1 km

1 hectare = 10,000 m²

Mass
1,000 grams (g) = 1 kilogram (kg)

1,000 milligrams (mg) = 1 g

Temperature

The temperature at an indoor basketball game might be 25°C, which is 77°F.

Length/Distance

A basketball rim is about 10 ft high, or a little more than 3 m from the floor.

Customary Measures

Temperature

Ice melts at 32 degrees Fahrenheit (°F)

Water freezes at 32°F

Water boils at 212°F

Length and Distance

12 inches (in.) = 1 foot (ft)

3 ft = 1 yard (yd)

5,280 ft = 1 mile (mi)

Weight

16 ounces (oz) = 1 pound (lb)

2,000 pounds = 1 ton (T)

Volume of Fluids

8 fluid ounces (fl oz) = 1 cup (c)

2 c = 1 pint (pt)

2 pt = 1 quart (qt)

4 qt = 1 gallon (gal)

Metric and Customary Rates

km/h = kilometers per hour

m/s = meters per second

mph = miles per hour

GLOSSARY

Pronunciation Key

Symbol	Key Words
a	cat
ā	ape
ä	cot, car
e	ten, berry
ē	me
i	fit, here
ī	ice, fire
ō	go
ô	fall, for
oi	oil
͡oo	look, pull
͞oo	tool, rule
ou	out, crowd
u	up
ʉ	fur, shirt
ə	a in ago
	e in agent
	i in pencil
	o in atom
	u in circus
b	bed
d	dog
f	fall

Symbol	Key Words
g	get
h	help
j	jump
k	kiss, call
l	leg
m	meat
n	nose
p	put
r	red
s	see
t	top
v	vat
w	wish
y	yard
z	zebra
ch	chin, arch
ŋ	ring, drink
sh	she, push
th	thin, truth
th	then, father
zh	measure

A heavy stress mark (′) is placed after a syllable that gets a heavy, or primary, stress, as in **picture** (pik′chər).

adaptation (ad əp tā'shən) A part or behavior that makes a living thing better able to survive in its environment. (C54) The spider's behavior of spinning a web to catch an insect, such as a bee, is an *adaptation* that helps the spider get food

air (er) The invisible, odorless, and tasteless mixture of gases that surrounds Earth. (E10) *Air* consists mainly of the gases nitrogen and oxygen.

air mass (er mas) A large body of air that has about the same temperature, air pressure, and moisture throughout. (E62) When warm and cold *air masses* meet, the weather changes.

air pressure (er presh'ər) The push of the air in all directions against its surroundings. (E31) You can see the effect of *air pressure* when you blow up a balloon.

amphibian (am fib'ē ən) A vertebrate that usually lives in water in the early part of its life; it breathes with gills and then later develops lungs. (C19) Frogs, toads, and salamanders are *amphibians*.

anemometer (an ə mäm'ət ər) A device used to measure the speed of the wind. (E39) The *anemometer* showed that the wind was blowing at 33 km/h.

atmosphere (at'məs fir) The blanket of air that surrounds Earth, reaching to about 700 km above the surface. (E12) Earth's *atmosphere* makes it possible for life to exist on the planet.

atom (at'əm) The smallest part of an element that still has the properties of that element. (B30) Water forms when *atoms* of the elements hydrogen and oxygen combine in a certain way.

axis (ak'sis) An imaginary straight line from the North Pole, through Earth's center, to the South Pole. (E78) Earth makes one complete turn on its *axis* in about 24 hours.

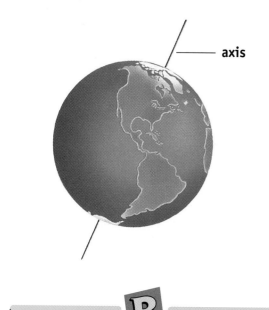

axis

barometer (bə räm'ət ər) A device used to measure air pressure. (E30) Scientists use a *barometer* to gather information about the weather.

bay (bā) Part of a sea or lake extending into the land. (A14) The ship sailed through the *bay* into the Atlantic Ocean.

behavior (bē hāv'yər) The way in which a living thing acts or responds to its environment. (C55) Purring, washing themselves, and hunting mice are three common *behaviors* of cats.

bird (bʉrd) A vertebrate that has wings, is covered with feathers, and hatches from a hard-shell egg. (C21) A *bird* is the only organism in the animal kingdom that has feathers covering its body.

boiling (boil'iŋ) The rapid change of state from a liquid to a gas. (B40) When water is *boiling*, bubbles of water vapor form.

carbon dioxide (kär'bən dī-äks'īd) A colorless, odorless gas. (E10) Plants use *carbon dioxide* from the air in the process of making food.

chemical change (kem'i kəl chānj) A change in matter that results in one or more different kinds of matter forming. (B56) A *chemical change* occurs when matter, such as paper, burns and forms gases and ash.

chemical formula (kem′i kəl fôr′my$\overline{oo}$ lə) A group of symbols that shows the kinds and number of atoms in a single unit of a compound. (B35) The *chemical formula* for carbon dioxide is CO_2.

chemical property (kem′i kəl präp′ər tē) A characteristic of a substance that can only be seen when the substance changes and a new substance is formed; describes how matter reacts with other matter. (B13, B56) A *chemical property* of iron is that iron can combine with oxygen to form rust.

chemical reaction (kem′i kəl rē ak′shən) The process in which one or more substances are changed into one or more different substances. (B57) A *chemical reaction* takes place when burning wood changes to ash.

chemical symbol (kem′i kəl sim′bəl) One or two letters that stand for the name of an element. (B30) The *chemical symbol* for gold is *Au*.

circuit breaker (sur′kit brāk′ər) A switch that opens or closes a circuit by turning off or on. (D52) When a circuit overheats, the *circuit breaker* switches off and the lights go out.

cirrus cloud (sir′əs kloud) A thin, feathery cloud made up of ice crystals high in the sky. (E57) *Cirrus clouds* often look like wisps of hair.

climate (klī′mət) The average weather conditions of an area over a long period of time. (E84) Some regions have a hot, rainy *climate*.

cloud (kloud) A mass of tiny droplets of water that condensed from the air. (E46) A dark *cloud* blocked the sunlight.

cold front (kōld frunt) The leading edge of a cold air mass that forms as the cold air mass moves into a warm air mass. (E62) Thunderstorms often occur along a *cold front*.

compass (kum′pəs) A device containing a magnetized needle that moves freely and is used to show direction. (D23) The north pole of the needle in a *compass* points toward Earth's magnetic north pole.

compound (käm'pound)
Matter made up of two or more
elements chemically combined. (B33)
Salt is a *compound* made up of
sodium and chlorine.

condensation (kän dən sā'shən)
The change of state from a gas to a
liquid. (B42) Drops of water form on
the outside of a very cold glass
because of the *condensation* of
water vapor in the air.

condense (kən dens') To change
from a gas to a liquid. (E46) Water
vapor from the air *condenses* on a
cold window.

conductor (kən duk'tər) A material through which electricity
moves easily. (D42) Copper wire is
a good *conductor* of electricity.

conifers (kän'ə fərz) Cone-
bearing plants. (C37) Pines and fir
trees are examples of *conifers*.

conservation (kän sər vā'shən)
The preserving and wise use of
natural resources. (A31) The *conservation* of forests is important to
both humans and wildlife.

controlled experiment (kən-
trōld' ek sper'ə mənt) A test of a
hypothesis in which the setups are
identical in all ways except one. (S7)
In the *controlled experiment*, one
beaker of water contained salt.

cumulus cloud (kyoo'myoo ləs
kloud) A large puffy cloud. (E55)
White *cumulus clouds* can often
be seen in an otherwise clear
summer sky.

delta (del'tə) A flat, usually triangular plain formed by deposits of
sediment where a river empties into
the ocean. (A12) The largest *delta*
in the United States is at the mouth
of the Mississippi River.

density (den'sə tē) The property
that describes how much matter is in
a given space, or volume. (B9, B11)
The *density* of air varies with its
temperature.

dicot (dī′kät) A flowering plant that produces seeds that have two sections. (C38) A trait of a *dicot* is that the veins of its leaves form a branching pattern.

electric cell (ē lek′trik sel) A device that changes chemical energy to electrical energy. (D60) A battery in a flashlight consists of one or more *electric cells*.

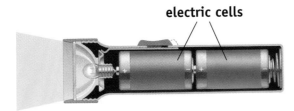

electric cells

electric charge (ē lek′trik chärj) The electrical property of particles of matter; an electric charge can be positive or negative. (D30) Rubbing a balloon with a wool cloth causes negative *electric charges* to move from the wool to the balloon.

electric circuit (ē lek′trik sur′kit) A path along which an electric current can move. (D41) We made an *electric circuit,* using a battery, wires, and a light bulb.

electric current (ē lek′trik kur′ənt) A continuous flow of electric charges. (D41) *Electric current* in wires allows you to run electric appliances, such as an iron or refrigerator, in your home.

electric discharge (ē lek′trik dis′chärj) The loss or release of an electric charge. (D33) A bolt of lightning is an *electric discharge.*

electromagnet (ē lek′trō mag nit) A magnet made when an electric current passes through a wire coiled around an iron core. (D70) A large *electromagnet* can be strong enough to lift heavy metal objects such as cars.

element (el′ə mənt) Matter made up of only one kind of atom. (B30) Iron, oxygen, and aluminum are three examples of *elements.*

energy (en′ər jē) The ability to cause change. (B39) Most automobiles use *energy* from gasoline to move.

environment (en vī′rən mənt) Everything that surrounds and affects a living thing. (C44) Desert animals and forest animals live in very different *environments.*

equator (ē kwāt′ər) An imaginary line circling the middle of Earth, halfway between the North Pole and the South Pole. (E78) The *equator* divides Earth into the Northern Hemisphere and the Southern Hemisphere.

erosion (ē rō′zhən) The gradual wearing away and removing of rock material by forces such as moving water, wind, and moving ice. (A10) Ocean waves cause *erosion* of the seashore.

evaporate (ē vap′ə rāt) To change from a liquid to a gas. (E46) Some of the water boiling in the pot *evaporated*.

evaporation (ē vap ə rā′shən) The change of state from a liquid to a gas. (B40) Under the hot sun, water in a puddle changes to water vapor through the process of *evaporation*.

exoskeleton (eks ō skel′ə tən) A hard outer structure, such as a shell, that protects or supports an animal's body. (C15) A lobster has a thick *exoskeleton*.

extinct (ek stiŋkt′) No longer living as a species. (C58) Traces of some *extinct* species can be found in fossils.

ferns (fʉrnz) Spore-forming plants that have roots, stems, and leaves. (C36) *Ferns* that grow in tropical places have very tall fronds.

filament (fil′ə mənt) A long, thin coil of wire that glows when electricity passes through it. (D48) The *filament* in an incandescent light bulb gives off light.

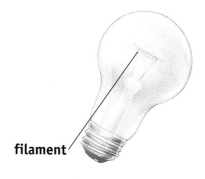

filament

fish (fish) A vertebrate that lives in water and has gills used for breathing and fins used for swimming. (C18) Sharks and tuna are kinds of *fish*.

flash flood (flash flud) A sudden, violent flood. (E67) Heavy rains caused *flash floods* as the stream overflowed.

fog (fôg) A cloud that touches Earth's surface. (E46) Traffic accidents often increase where *fog* is heavy.

fossil fuel (fäs'əl fyōō'əl) A fuel that formed from the remains of once-living things and that is nonrenewable. (A47) Oil is a *fossil fuel*.

freezing (frēz'iŋ) The change of state from a liquid to a solid. (B42) Water turns to ice by *freezing*.

front (frunt) The place where two air masses meet. (E62) Forecasters watch the movement of *fronts* to help predict the weather.

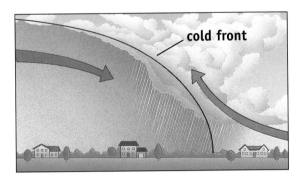
cold front

fuse (fyōōz) A device in a circuit that contains a metal strip, which melts when the circuit is overheated, thus breaking the circuit. (D52) The *fuse* blew because too many appliances were connected to the same electric circuit.

gas (gas) The state of matter that has no definite shape or volume. (B29) Helium is a very light *gas* that is used to fill some balloons.

generator (jen'ər āt ər) A device that changes energy of motion into electrical energy. (D58) The huge *generator* uses water power to produce electricity.

gill (gil) A feathery structure on each side of a fish's head that lets the fish breathe underwater. (C18) A fish takes in oxygen through its *gills*.

glacier (glā'shər) A huge mass of slow-moving ice that forms over land; glaciers form in areas where the amount of snow that falls is more than the amount of snow that melts. (A22) As it moves, a *glacier* changes the surface beneath it.

greenhouse effect (grēn'hous e fekt') The process by which heat from the Sun builds up near Earth's surface and is trapped by the atmosphere. (E15) Some scientists fear that air pollution may increase the *greenhouse effect* and raise temperatures on Earth.

hazardous waste (haz'ər dəs wāst) A waste material that dirties the environment and that can kill living things or cause disease. (A65) Some chemicals used to kill insects become *hazardous wastes*.

headland (hed'land) A piece of land that extends out into the water and usually slows down the flow of water that passes it. (A14) The lighthouse stood on a *headland* overlooking the bay.

high-pressure area (hī presh'ər er'ē ə) An area of higher air pressure than that of the surrounding air. (E33) Winds move from *high-pressure areas* to low-pressure areas.

horsetails (hôrs tālz) Plants that reproduce by spores and have underground stems. (C36) *Horsetails* are also known as scouring rushes because of the tough tip at the end of their bamboo-like stem.

humidity (hyoo mid'ə tē) The amount of water vapor in the air. (E47) Tropical climates have warm temperatures and high *humidity*.

hurricane (hur'i kān) A large, violent storm accompanied by strong winds and, usually, heavy rain. (E70) The winds of the *hurricane* blew at over 125 km/h.

hypothesis (hī päth'ə sis) An idea about or explanation of how or why something happens. (S6) The *hypothesis* about the expanding universe has been supported by evidence gathered by astronomers.

ice age (īs āj) A period of time when glaciers covered much of Earth's land. (E89) During the last *ice age,* glaciers covered parts of North America.

incineration (in sin ər ā'shən) Burning to ashes. (A60) You can get rid of trash by *incineration*.

instinctive behavior (in stiŋk'tiv bē hāv'yər) A behavior that a living thing does naturally without having to learn it. (C56) For a mother bird, feeding her young is an *instinctive behavior*.

insulator (in'sə lāt ər) A material through which electricity does not move easily. (D42) Rubber can prevent an electric shock because rubber is a good *insulator*.

invertebrate (in vur'tə brit) An animal that does not have a backbone. (C15) *Invertebrates* include jellyfish, sponges, insects, and worms.

landfill (land'fil) An area where trash is buried and covered over with dirt. (A59) In some places, towns decide to build recreation areas, such as parks, on the sites of old *landfills*.

learned behavior (lʉrnd bē-hāv'yər) A behavior that an organism is taught or learns from experience. (C56) Sitting on command, catching a ball, and jumping through a hoop are examples of *learned behavior* for a dog.

lines of force (līnz uv fôrs) The lines that form a pattern showing the size and shape of a magnetic force field. (D19) Iron filings sprinkled over a magnet form *lines of force* that show the strength and the direction of the magnet's force.

liquid (lik'wid) The state of matter that has a definite volume but no definite shape. (B29) A *liquid*, such as water or milk, takes the shape of its container.

litter (lit'ər) The trash that is discarded on the ground or in water rather than being disposed of properly. (A66) The children cleaned up the park by removing all the *litter* they could find.

liverworts (liv'ər wʉrts) Nonseed plants that lack true roots, stems, and leaves. (C36) The logs by the stream were covered with mosslike *liverworts*.

lodestone (lōd'stōn) A naturally magnetic mineral found at or near Earth's surface. (D22) A piece of *lodestone* will attract iron.

low-pressure area (lō presh'ər er'ē ə) An area of lower air pressure than that of the surrounding air. (E33) Storms are more likely to occur in *low-pressure areas*.

magnet (mag'nit) An object that has the property of attracting certain materials, mainly iron and steel. (D11) The girl used a horseshoe *magnet* to pick up paper clips.

magnetic field (mag net'ik fēld) The space around a magnet within which the force of the magnet can act. (D20) The magnet attracted all the pins within its *magnetic field*.

magnetism (mag′nə tiz əm) A magnet's property of attracting certain materials, mainly iron and steel. (D11) *Magnetism* keeps kitchen magnets attached to a refrigerator door.

mammal (mam′əl) A vertebrate, such as a cat, that has hair or fur and feeds its young with milk. (C22) Dogs, cats, rabbits, deer, bats, horses, mice, elephants, whales, and humans are all *mammals*.

mass (mas) The amount of matter that something contains. (B10) A large rock has more *mass* than a small rock that is made of the same material.

matter (mat′ər) Anything that has mass and takes up space. (B10) Rocks, water, and air are three kinds of *matter*.

melting (melt′iŋ) The change of state from a solid to a liquid. (B40) As the temperature of the air rises, snow and ice change to liquid water by the process of *melting*.

metric system (me′trik sis′təm) A system of measurement in which the number of smaller parts in each unit is based on the number 10 and multiples of 10. (B20) Centimeters, meters, and kilometers are units of length in the *metric system*.

mineral (min′ər əl) A solid, found in nature, that has a definite chemical makeup. (A41) Salt, coal, diamond, and gold are some examples of *minerals*.

mixture (miks′chər) Matter that is made up of two or more substances that can be separated by physical means. (B50) This salad contains a *mixture* of lettuce, cucumbers, celery, and tomatoes.

molt (mōlt) To shed an outer covering such as hair, outer skin, horns, or feathers at certain times. (C30) Snakes and insects *molt*.

monocot (män′ō kät) A flowering plant that produces seeds that are in one piece. (C38) About one third of all flowering plants are *monocots*.

mosses (môs′əs) Small nonseed plants that lack true roots, stems, and leaves. (C35) The leaflike part of *mosses* grows only a few centimeters above ground.

natural resource (nach′ər əl rē′sôrs) Any useful material from Earth, such as water, oil, and minerals. (A31) One reason that trees are an important *natural resource* is that their wood is used to build houses and to make paper.

nitrogen (nī′trə jən) A colorless, odorless, tasteless gas that makes up about four fifths of the air. (E10) *Nitrogen* is used by plants for growth.

nonrenewable resource (nän- ri nōō′ə bəl rē′sôrs) A natural resource that can't be replaced once it's removed. (A42) Minerals are classified as a *nonrenewable resource* because there's a limited amount of them.

nonseed plants (nän sēd plants) Plants that do not reproduce with seeds. (C35) Ferns are *nonseed plants*.

Northern Hemisphere (nôr′thərn hem′i sfir) The half of Earth north of the equator. (E79) Canada is in the *Northern Hemisphere.*

north pole (nôrth pōl) One of the ends of a magnet where the magnetic force is strongest; it points to the north when the magnet moves freely. (D13) *North poles* of magnets repel each other.

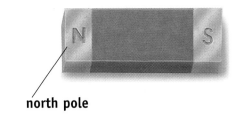

north pole

ore (ôr) A mineral or rock that contains enough of a metal to make mining that metal profitable. (A41) Gold, aluminum, copper, and tin come from *ores.*

organism (ôr′gə niz əm) A living thing that can be classified as belonging to one of several kingdoms. (C8) Animals and plants are *organisms.*

oxygen (äks′i jən) A colorless, odorless, tasteless gas that makes up about one fifth of the air. (E10) *Oxygen* is essential to life.

packaging (pak'ij iŋ) The wrapping and containers in which items are transported or offered for sale. (A75) *Packaging* protects products from damage but adds to their cost.

parallel circuit (par'ə lel sʉr'kit) An electric circuit having more than one path along which electric current can travel. (D51) Because the circuits in a home are *parallel circuits*, you can switch off one light and others will stay on.

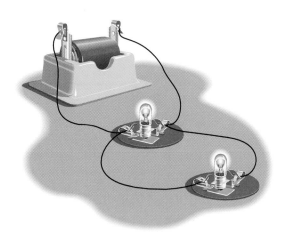

physical change (fiz'i kəl chānj) A change in size, shape, or state of matter in which no new matter is formed. (B48) Cutting an apple in half and freezing water into ice cubes are *physical changes*.

physical property (fiz'i kəl präp'ər tē) A characteristic of a material or object that can be seen or measured without changing the material into a new substance. (B12) One *physical property* of a ball is its round shape.

polar climate (pō'lər klī'mət) A very cold climate that does not receive much energy from the Sun. (E85) The Arctic has a *polar climate*.

pollutant (pə lo̅o̅t''nt) A substance that causes pollution. (A65) The exhaust gases from cars add *pollutants* to the air.

pollution (pə lo̅o̅'shən) The dirtying of the environment with waste materials or other unwanted substances. (A65) Water *pollution* can cause disease or even death in living things.

precipitation (prē sip ə tā'shən) Any form of water that falls from clouds to Earth's surface. (E46) Rain, snow, and hail are forms of *precipitation*.

property (präp'ər tē) A characteristic that describes matter. (B12) Hardness is a *property* of steel.

rain gauge (rān gāj) A device for measuring precipitation. (E47) The *rain gauge* at the weather station showed that 2 cm of rain had fallen in 24 hours.

recycle (rē sī′kəl) To process and reuse materials. (A72) Discarded newspapers are *recycled* to make new paper.

relative humidity (rel′ə tiv hyo͞o mid′ə tē) The amount of water vapor present in the air at a given temperature compared to the maximum amount that the air could hold at that temperature. (E47) A *relative humidity* of 95 percent on a warm day can make you feel sticky and uncomfortable.

renewable resource (ri no͞o′ə-bəl rē′sôrs) A resource that can be replaced. (A42) Water is a *renewable resource* because rain increases the supply of water.

reptile (rep′təl) A vertebrate, such as a lizard or a crocodile, that has dry scaly skin and lays eggs that have a leathery shell. (C20) *Reptiles* can be found in both deserts and rain forests.

river system (riv′ər sis′təm) A river and all the waterways, such as brooks, streams, and rivers, that drain into it. (A11) The Mississippi River and the many waterways feeding into it make up the largest *river system* in the country.

rock (räk) A solid material that is made up of one or more minerals and that may be used for its properties. (A41) Granite is a hard *rock* used in construction.

sand dune (sand do͞on) A mound, hill, or ridge of sand formed by the wind. (A21) *Sand dunes* are common in the desert.

sand dune

savanna (sə van′ə) A broad, grassy plain that has few or no trees. (C48) Nearly half of Africa is covered by *savannas*.

sediment (sed′ə mənt) Sand, soil, and rock carried by water, wind, or ice. (A12) The rushing water of the river deposited *sediment* along the riverbanks.

seed plants (sēd plants) Plants that reproduce with seeds. (C35) Corn and wheat are *seed plants*.

series circuit (sir′ēz sʉr′kit) An electric circuit in which the parts are connected in a single path. (D50) Electric current can follow only one path in a *series circuit*.

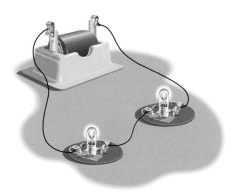

soil (soil) Loose material that covers much of Earth's land surface and is made up of three layers—topsoil, subsoil, and partly weathered rock. (A30) Plants, insects, and worms live in *soil*.

solar cell (sō′lər sel) A device that changes sunlight into electrical energy. (D64) *Solar cells* used in power plants can produce electricity without polluting the air.

solar energy (sō′lər en′ər jē) The clean and relatively low-cost energy from the Sun. (A50, D64) *Solar energy* is used to heat water in some homes.

solid (säl′id) Matter that has a definite volume and a definite shape. (B29) A *solid*, such as a rock, a wooden block, or an ice cube, has a definite volume and shape.

solution (sə lo͞o′shən) A mixture in which the particles of different substances are mixed evenly. (B51) Stirring sugar into water makes a *solution*.

Southern Hemisphere (su*th*′ərn hem′i sfir) The half of Earth south of the equator. (E79) The island continent Australia is in the *Southern Hemisphere*.

south pole (south pōl) One of the ends of a magnet where the magnetic force is strongest; it points to the south when the magnet moves freely. (D13) The *south pole* of one magnet attracts the north pole of another magnet.

standard unit (stan′dərd yo͞on′it) A unit of measure that everyone agrees to use. (B19) Scientists use the gram as the *standard unit* of mass.

state of matter (stāt uv mat'ər) Any of the three forms that matter may ordinarily take: solid, liquid, and gas. (B29) When ice melts, it changes to a liquid *state of matter*.

static electricity (stat'ik ē lek-tris'i tē)) Electric charges that have built up on the surface of an object. (D31) Walking across a carpet on a cold, dry day can produce *static electricity*.

stratus cloud (strāt'əs kloud) A low, flat cloud that often brings drizzle. (E55) Large sheets of very dark *stratus clouds* covered the sky on the rainy morning.

substance (sub'stəns) A class of matter made up of elements and compounds. (B34) Salt and sugar are *substances*.

switch (swich) A device that completes or breaks the path a current can follow in an electric circuit. (D41) In order to turn on the light, you must press the *switch* to complete the circuit.

temperate climate (tem'pər it klī'mət) A climate that generally has warm, dry summers and cold, wet winters. (E85) Most regions of the United States have a *temperate climate*.

theory (thē'ə rē) A hypothesis that is supported by a lot of evidence and is widely accepted by scientists. (S9) The big-bang *theory* offers an explanation for the origin of the universe.

thunderstorm (thun'dər stôrm) A storm that produces lightning and thunder and often heavy rain and strong winds. (E66) When the weather is hazy, hot, and humid, *thunderstorms* are likely to develop.

tornado (tôr nā'dō) A violent, funnel-shaped storm of spinning wind. (E72) The wind speed at the center of a *tornado* can be twice that of hurricane winds.

tropical climate (träp'i kəl klī'mət) A hot, rainy climate. (E85) Areas that are near the equator have a *tropical climate* because they receive the greatest amount of energy from the Sun.

troposphere (trō′pō sfir) The layer of the atmosphere closest to the surface of Earth. (E12) The *troposphere* reaches about 11 km above the surface of Earth and is the layer of the atmosphere in which weather occurs.

variable (ver′ē ə bəl) The one difference in the setups of a controlled experiment; provides a comparison for testing a hypothesis. (S7) The *variable* in an experiment with plants was the amount of water given each plant.

vertebra (vʉr′tə brə) One of the bones that together make up the backbone. (C14) Each knob in your backbone is a *vertebra*.

vertebrate (vʉr′tə brit) An animal that has a backbone. (C14) Reptiles and birds are *vertebrates*.

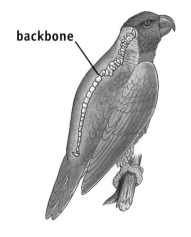

backbone

voltage (vōl′tij) The force of an electric current, measured in volts. (D63) Electric currents of high *voltage* travel through long-distance power lines.

volume (väl yo͞om) The amount of space that matter takes up. (B10) A baseball has a greater *volume* than a golf ball does.

warm front (wôrm frunt) The leading edge of a warm air mass that forms as the warm air mass moves forward into a cold air mass. (E63) Light rain often falls along a *warm front*.

water cycle (wôt′ər si′kəl) The movement of water into the air as water vapor and back to Earth's surface as rain, snow, or hail. (E46) The *water cycle* is powered by energy from the Sun.

water vapor (wôt′ər vā′pər) Water that is in the form of a gas. (E10) *Water vapor* from the air forms drops of water on cold glass surfaces.

weather (we*th*′ər) The condition of the atmosphere at a certain place and time. (E13) The *weather* today in Chicago is snowy.

weather forecaster (we*th*'ər fôr'kast ər) A person who makes weather predictions or reports weather conditions. (E61) The *weather forecaster* predicted rain for the next three days.

weather satellite (we*th*'ər sat''l īt) A human-made device in space that takes pictures of Earth and collects information about the weather. (E54) The *weather satellite* sent back pictures of clouds to weather stations in different locations on the ground.

weathering (we*th*'ər iŋ) The physical and chemical processes by which rock is broken down into smaller pieces. (A10) Cracks in rock produced by freezing rainwater or the growth of plant roots are examples of *weathering*.

wind (wind) The movement of air over Earth's surface. (E21) The strong *wind* lifted the kite high above the houses.

windsock (wind'säk) A device used to show wind direction, consisting of a cloth bag that is open at both ends and hung on a pole. (E38) The *windsock* showed that the wind was blowing from the north.

wind vane (wind vān) A device, often shaped like an arrow, used to show the direction of the wind. (E38) The *wind vane* on the roof of the weather station showed that the wind was blowing from the southwest.

INDEX

A

Adaptations, animal, C54
Air
  as matter, E10–E13
  moving, E21–E22
Air mass, E62–E63
Air patterns, E86–E87
Air pressure
  differences in, E31–E33
  measuring, E32–E33
  and temperature, E33
Algonquin moons, E74
Allis, Beatrice, B44
Alzheimer's disease, C34
Amphibians, C19
Anemometer, E37, E39
Anemones, sea, C28
Aneroid barometer, E32
Animal kingdom, C9, C10
Animals
  body parts, C54–C55
  needs, C44–C47
  of savanna, C48–C49
Archer, David, D26
Aristotle, C12
Arthropods, C30–C31
Atmosphere, E12–E13
Atom, defined, B30
Attraction
  electric, D31
  magnetic, D11
Auroras, D24
Avalanche, E45
Axis, of Earth, E78

B

Balance, B20
Barometer(s), E28*, E30,
  E32
Barrier islands, A14

Batteries, D43, D60
Bay, A14
Beaufort scale, E39, E70
Beaufort, Sir Francis, E39
Becquerel, Antoine H., B15
Begay, Fred, B24
Behaviors, animal, C55–C57
Bentley, Wilson A., E44
Birds, C21
Blood clots, C26
Blue-green bacteria, C11
Boiling, B40–B41
Bones, of bird, C21
Breezes, E22
Bronze Age, A38
Budgerigar (parakeet),
  C46
Butte, A21

C

Caloric theory, B41
Carbon, D49
Carbon dioxide, A49,
  E10–E11
Centipedes and millipedes,
  C31
Chalcopyrite, A34*
Chalk, A41
Chameleon, C20
Chemical change, B56
Chemical formula, defined,
  B35
Chemical properties, B13,
  B56–B57
Chemical reaction, B57
Chemical symbols, B30
Chilies, C34
Circuit breaker, D52, D76
Cirrus clouds, E56, E57
Classification, C21–C23

animals, C14–C15
  plants, C32–C33*,
    C35–C38
  time line, C12–C13
Climate, E84–E87
  controls, E86
  kinds of, E84
  past changes in, E88–E89
  world's, E84–E85
Clouds, E46
  kinds of, E55–E57
Coal mines, A49
Coastal beaches, A13
Cobb, Ray, D4
Cold fronts, E62–E63
Collage, B4
Communication devices, time
  line, D68–D69
Compass, D23
Compounds, B33–B35
  cooling, B38
  defined, B33
Condensation, E46
  defined, B42
Conductor, D38*, D42
Cones, C37
Conifers, C37
Conservation, A31
  time line of, A70–A71
Continental glaciers, A22
Contour plowing, A32
Corals, C28
Crocodile, C20, C56
Crude oil, B52
  changing state of, B52–B53
  products of, B53
Crust, Earth's, A40
Cumulus clouds, E55, E56
Cuvier, Georges, C12
Cyclamen plant, C38

D

Dam building, A33
Darrieus wind turbine, E40
Delta, A12
Density, B9*, B11
Dicots, C38
Doorbell circuitry, D72
Drizzle, E48
Dry cell, D61
Dung, as fuel, A46

E

Earth
  crust of, A40
  as magnet, D22–D24
  makeup of, A40
  poles of, D23–D24
  revolution and seasons, E80
  tilt of, E78
Edison, Thomas, D49
Electrical energy, D31
Electric art, D26
Electric cars, D73
Electric cells, D60
Electric charges, D30
Electric circuit, D37*, D41
Electric current, D40–D43
  producing, D58–D61
Electric discharge, D33
Electricity
  delivering, D62–D63
  from magnetism, D58
Electromagnets, D67*,
  D70–D72
Elements
  as building blocks, B33
  defined, B30
  symbols for, B30
Elephant, C54
El Niño, E87
Endangered animals,
  C59–C60
Endangered plants, C59–C60
Energy
  defined, B39
  from ancient sunlight, A48
  from sea water, A50

  See also Electrical energy;
    Gravity; Solar energy.
English system, B19–B20
Environment, of animals,
  C44–C45
Equator, E78
Erosion
  and weather as partners,
    A10–A12
  wind, A20–A21
Erratics, A23
Evaporation, B40, E46
Exoskeleton, C15
Extinct animals, C59
Eyewitness Living Earth
  (Smith), C37

F

Feathers, C21
  parts of, C50*
Ferns, C36
Filament, D48
Fins, C18
Fish, C18
Flash floods, E67
Flashlights, D42–D43
Flatworms, C29
Flood plains, A10
Fluorescent bulb, D48–D49
Fog, E46
Food
  for animals, C45
  savanna, C48
Force fields, D19–D21
Fossil fuels, A46–A50
  advantages of, A49–A50
  supply and demand, A47
  world sources of, A46
Fossils, and past weather,
  E89
4R's, A69
Foxglove, C34
Fractionating towers,
  B52–B53
Freezing, B42
Frog, development of, C19
From Glasses to Gases: The

Science of Matter
  (Darling), B31
Fronds, C36
Front, E59, E62
Fructose, chemical formula
  for, B35
Fuels, irreplaceable,
  A48–A49
Fungus kingdom, C9, C11
Fur, C23
Fuse, D52, D76

G

Garlic, C34
Gases
  defined, B29
  particles of, B31
Generator, D57*, D58
Gills, C17*, C18
Ginger, C34
Ginkgo, C34
Glacier grooves, A23
Glaciers, A18–A19*,
  A22–A24
GOES (Geostationary
  Operational
  Environmental Satellite),
  E54
Gold, B32
Graduated cylinder, B21
Granite, A41
Graphite, A41
Gravity, A22
  and air pressure, E31
Greenhouse effect, E14–E15
Gypsum, A34*

H

Hail, E48
Hair, C23
Halite, A41
Hazardous wastes, A65–A66
HDPE, A73
Headland, A14
*Hello! Hello! A Look Inside
  the Telephone* (Stwertka),
  D51, D72

Hematite, A34
HFCs, B38
High-pressure areas, E33
Hippopotamus, C44
Hoover Dam, D59
Horn, glacier-formed, A24
Horsetails, C36
Hosta plant, C38
Hot-air balloon, E20
Humidity, E47
Hurricanes, A15, E70–E71
Hydras, C28
Hydrocarbons, B52
Hypothesis, S6

I

I Can Save the Earth
    (Holmes), A42, A60
Ice ages, E89
Ice cores, E89
Incandescent bulb, D48
Incineration, A61
Industrial Age, A39
Information Age, A39
Inner core, Earth's, A40
Insects, C30
Instinctive behavior, C56
Insulator, D39*, D42
International System of Units
    (SI), B20–B21
Invertebrates, C15
Iron Age, A39

J

Jellyfish, C28
Jetty, A8–A9*, A15
Johnson-Allen, Martina, B4

K

Kangaroo rat, C46
Kingdoms, C8–C11, C13
Koala, C46

L

Land, steep, erosion of, A10
Landfill
    design of, A59

problems with, A60
Latimer, Lewis, D49
Learned behavior, C56
Leeches, C26
Leopard, C45
Levitation, D14
Light bulb, D48–D49
Lightning, D34–D35,
    E66–E67
*Lightning and Other
    Wonders of the Sky*
    (Pearce), E12, E47
Lightning rods, D35
Lines of force, D18*, D19
Linnaeus, Carolus, C12
Liquids
    defined, B29
    particles of, B31
Littering, A62*, A66–A67
Liverworts, C36
Living things, and
    environmental changes,
    C60
Lodestone, D22–D23
Low-pressure areas, E33

M

Macaw, C4–C5, C21
Maglev trains, D14–D15
Magnet
    defined, D11
    Earth as, D22–D24
    force field of, D20
    kinds of, D12
    properties of, D11–D13
Magnetic field, D18*, D20
Magnetism, defined, D11
Magnetite, A34
*Magnets: Mind-boggling
    Experiments You Can
    Turn Into Science Fair
    Projects* (VanCleave),
    D12, D17
Mammals, C22–C23
Mangroves, C46
Mantle, Earth's, A40
Margulis, Lynn, C13

Marie Curie (Fisher), B15,
    B51
Matter
    changes in, B48–B49
    defined, B10
    everywhere, B10–B11
    indestructible, B58
    properties of, B6–B7*,
        B12–B13
    states of, B29–B31
Matterhorn, A24
Measuring, time line of,
    methods, B18
Mejia-Zelaya, Adelina, D54
Melting, B40, B49
Mercury barometer, E30, E32
Mesosphere, E13
Metals, and pollution,
    A66–A67
Meterstick, B20
Metric ruler, B20
Metric system, B19–B22
    units of, B21
Minerals
    conservation of, A40–A42
    defined, A41
    through the ages,
        A38–A39
    uses of, A41
Mississippi Delta, A12
Mississippi River system, A11
Mixed media, B4
Mixture, defined, B50
Mole, C45
Molecule, B35
Mollusks, C30
Molting, C30
Moneran kingdom, C9, C11
Monocots, C38
Moraine, A23
Mosses, C35–C36
Mushrooms, C11

N

Natural gas, A47
Natural resource, defined,
    A31

Needles, conifer, C37
Negative (film), B59
Nitrogen, E10–E11
Nonrenewable resource, A42
Nonseed plants, C35
Northern Hemisphere, E79
Northern lights, D24
Nycander, Eduardo, C4

O
Oak tree, C10
Octopus, C30
Oil
   changes in state of,
      B52–B53
   and pollution, A65
One Day in the Desert
   (George), A9
Optical broadcasting wind
   indicator, E39
Ore, A41–A42
   processing, A43
Organisms
   classification of, C8–C11
   defined, C8
Outer core, Earth's, A40
Owl, elf, C47
Oxygen, E10–E11

P
Pacific Yew, C34
Packaging, A75–A76
Paper, and pollution,
   A66–A67
Parallel circuits, D47, D51,
   D52
Paramecium, C11
Particles, B30–B31
   and mixtures, B51
   speed of, B41
Peat, A48
PET, A73
Petroleum, A47
Photography, B59–B60
Physical change, defined,
   B48
Physical properties, B12

Plant kingdom, C9, C10,
   C35–C38
Plants, for medicine, C34
Plastics, and pollution,
   A66–A67
Polar climate, E85
Poles, magnetic, D13
Pollution, trash, A65
Power plants, D58–D59,
   D62–D63
Precipitation, E46
Prefixes, metric, B22
*Professor Fergus Fahrenheit
   and His Wonderful
   Weather Machine*
   (Groth-Fleming), E67
Property, defined, B12
Protist kingdom, C9, C11

Q
Quartz, A34

R
Radio signals, D72
Rain, E48
Rain gauge, E43*, E47
Rathje, William, A52, A60
Recycling, A72–A74
   aluminum, A74
   glass, A74
   machine, A72–A73
   new products from, A73
   newspapers, A77
   paper, A72
   plastic, A72–A73
Refrigeration, B38
Relative humidity, E47
Renewable resource, A42
Reptiles, C20
Repulsion
   electric, D31
   magnetic, D13
Resource(s)
   nonrenewable, A42
   renewable, A42
   supply of, A37*
River system, A11–A12

River valleys, A12
Rocks
   breakup of, A11
   description of, A41
   as source of minerals, A40
   uses of, A41
Rock salt, A42
Roddy, Leon, C13
Roker, Al, E4
Roundworms, C29
Rust (iron oxide), B57

S
Safety
   and electricity, D74–D76
   in storms, E68–E69
Salt grain, B34
Sand, A13–A14
   formation of, A12
Sand dunes, A20–A21
Satellite photographs, E70
Savanna, C48–C49
Scales, conifer, C37
Scientific methods ("Think
   Like a Scientist"), S2–S11
   controlled experiment, S7
   hypothesis, S6
   theory, S9
   variable, S7
Seasons
   changing, E78–E81
   and sun rays, E80–E81
Sea urchins, C29
Sea wall, A15
Sea water, to create energy,
   A50
Sediments, A12
Seed plants, C35
Segmented worms, C29
Seimon, Anton, E50
Series circuits, D45*, D50,
   D52
Shells, mollusk, C30
Shelter
   animal, C47
   savanna, C49
Shore areas, protecting, A15

Shoreline, changing, A13–A15
Silt, A12
Silver bromide, B59
Silver chloride, B59
Snakes and Other Reptiles (Elting), C57
Snow, A10, E44, E48
Snowfall, worldwide, E44–E45
Sod, A29*
Soil
  defined, A30–A31
  using, A31–A32
Soil profile, A30–A31
Solar cells, D64–D65
Solar energy, A47, A50, D64–D65
Solids
  defined, B29
  particles of, B30
Solution, defined, B51
Southern Hemisphere, E79
Southern lights, D24
Sphalerite, A34
Spiders, C31, C57
Sponges, C27
Spores, C35
Squirrel, C22
Standard air pressure, E32–E33
Standard unit, B19
Starfish, C29
States, causing change in, B40–B42
Static electricity, D30–D33
Stone Age, A38
Stratosphere, E13
Stratus clouds, E55, E56
Strip cropping, A32
Subsoil, A31
Substances, B34
  and mixtures, B50
Sunlight, and plants, C47
Switch, electric, D41

T

Tadpole, C19
Telecommunication, D68
Temperate climate, E85
Temperature
  animal, C45, C47
  and change, B48–B49
Terminal moraine, A23
Terracing, A33
Theory, S9
Thermometer, B21
Thermosphere, E12, E13
Third Planet, The (Ride and O'Shaughnessy), E79
Thunder, E66–E67
Thunderstorm, E66–E67
Timber wolf, C23
Topsoil, A31
Tornadoes, E72
Torop, Ellen, C40
Torricelli, Evangelista, E30
Traits, C8
Transformer, D63
Trash
  dumping in ocean, A64
  from packaging, A75–A76
  town's, A58
Trash disposal, A58–A61
  in the past, A59
Trash pollution, A65–A67
Tree rings, E88
Tropical climate, E85
Troposphere, E12, E13
Tungsten, D48, D49
Turtle, alligator snapping, C54

V

Valley, erosion of, A10
Valley glacier, A22
Veins (leaf), C38
Vertebrates, C14
Vibration, of particles, B30
Voltage, D63
Volume, defined, B10

W

Warm fronts, E62–E63
Water
  animal need for, C46
  chemical formula for, B35
Water cycle, E46
Water vapor, B42, E10
Waves, effect of, A13–A14
Weather, E13
  and clouds, E56–E57
  forecasting, E61–E63
  predicting by plants and animals, E60
Weathered rock, A31
Weathering, and erosion as partners, A10–A12
Weather maps, E61
Weather records, E90–E92
Weather satellites, E54
Weather sayings, E24
Wet cell, D60
Whales, C22
  killer, C45
Whittaker, Robert, C13
Wildebeests, C48
Wind, E21
  effect of, on land, A20–A21
Wind direction, E38
Wind farm, E41
  See also Windmill farm.
Windmill farm, A50
  See also Wind farm.
Windmills, E40–E41
Wind power, E40–E41
Windsock, E38
Wind vane, E35*, E38
Wolf pups, C23, C56
Wood, as fuel, A46
Worms, C28–C29

CREDITS

ILLUSTRATORS

Cover: Genine Smith.

Think Like a Scientist: 14: Laurie Hamilton. *Border:* Genine Smith.

Unit A: 11, 13: Susan Johnston Carlson. 13–15: Paul Mirocha. 22–24: Jim Turgeon. 23, 25: Skip Baker. 30–31: Brad Gaber. 32–33: Jim Salvati. 38–39: Dave Joly. 39: Eldon Doty. 40: Brad Gaber. 43: Terry Ravenelli. 44: Terry Boles. 46: Rodica Prato. 47: Martucci Studio. 51: Brad Gaber. 56: Jim Trusilo. 58–59: Robert Roper. 61: Ray Vella. 63: Michael Ingle. 64: Greg Harris. 65: Robert Roper. 68: Greg Harris. 69–71: Bob Ostrom. 71: Eldon Doty. 72–74: Scott MacNeil. 76: Ken Bowser. 77: Randy Chewning.

Unit B: 12–13: Nina Laden. 18: Dave Winter. 19: Terry Boles. 19–22: Mark Bender. 29–31: J.A.K. Graphics. 32: Susan Johnston Carlson. 33: Tom Buches. 34–35: J.A.K. Graphics. 38, 40–41: Ron Fleming. 43: J.A.K. Graphics. 49: Andrew Shiff. 53: Patrick Gnan. 59: Bob Doucet. 60: Dartmouth Publishing.

Unit C: 8–9: Lee Steadman. 12–13: Susan Melrath. 13: Linda Warner. 13: Eldon Doty. 14–15: Dave Barber. 18–20: Jim Deal. 30: Barbara Hoopes Ambler. 35: Wendy Smith-Griswold. 40–41: Phil Wilson. 44: Jackie Urbanovic. 44–47: Julie Tsuchya. 48–49: Linda Howard. 54–57: Richard Cowdrey. 59–60: Randy Hamblin.

Unit D: 13: Patrick Gnan. 15: Dan McGowan. 22: Brad Gaber. 30–31: Robert Roper. 35: *t.* Jim Effier; *m.* Andrew Shiff. 40: David Winter. 41: Hans & Cassady, Inc. 42–43: Dale Gustafson. 48: Patrick Gnan. 50–51: Hans & Cassady, Inc. 52: Robert Roper. 53: Hans & Cassady, Inc. 60–61: Robert Roper. 62–63: Geoffrey McCormick. 68–69: Vincent Wayne. 70, 72: Robert Roper. 74–76: Michael Sloan.

Unit E: 11, 13: Randy Hamblin. 14–15: Robert Roper. 20: Andy Lendway. 22: Flora Jew. 23: Robert Roper. 30: Susan Melrath. 31: Rob Burger. 32: Tom Pansini. 33: Rob Burger. 38–39: Pamela Becker. 46: Michael Kline. 49: Rob Burger. 55: Gary Torrisi. 56: Patrick Gnan. 60: Kristin Kest. 60: Thomas Cranmer. 61–63: Nancy Tobin. 62: Robert Roper. 66, 68–70: Tom Lochray. 71: Gary Torrisi. 72: Tom Lochray. 73: Gary Torrisi. 77: Josie Yee. 78: Mike Quon. 79: Josie Yee. 80–81: John Youssi. 84–85: Thomas Cranmer. 86–87: Uldis Klavins. 90–92: Julie Peterson. 93: John Youssi.

Math and Science Toolbox: *Logos:* Nancy Tobin. 14–15: Andrew Shiff. *Borders:* Genine Smith.

Glossary 17: *t.r.* Dan McGowan. *m.l.* Richard Cowdrey. *b.r.* Dale Gustafson. 18: Mike Quon. 19: Dale Gustafson. 20: Dan McGowan. 21,22: Dale Gustafson. 23: Robert Roper. 24: A.J. Miller. 26,27: Patrick Gnan. 28: Hans & Cassady Inc. 29: Dan McGowan. 30: Hans & Cassady Inc. 32: David Barber. 33: Patrick Gnan.

PHOTOGRAPHS

All photographs by Houghton Mifflin Co. (HMCo.) unless otherwise noted.

Front Cover: *t.* Superstock; *m.l.* Bill Brooks/Masterfile Corporation; *m.r.* Tim Flach/Tony Stone Images; *b.l.* Barbara Leslie/FPG International; *b.r.* Greg Ryan & Sally Beyer/Tony Stone Images.

Table of Contents iv: *l.* Harold Sund/The Image Bank; *r.* Cromosohm/Sohm/The Stock Market. viii: Stan Osolinski/The Stock Market. xiii: *t.r.* Brian Parker/Tom Stack & Associates; *b.l.* Tony Freeman/PhotoEdit; *b.m.* Buff Corsi/Tom Stack & Associates; *b.r.* Gary Withey/Bruce Coleman Incorporated. xiv: © 2000 Juha Jormanainen/Woodfin Camp & Associates. xv: *l.* NOAA; *r.* NOAA/NESDIS/NCDC/SDSD.

Think Like a Scientist: 2: *t. bkgd.* PhotoDisc, Inc. 3: *t.* PhotoDisc, Inc. 4–5: *bkgd.* Chip Henderson Photography.

Unit A 1: Kim Heacox/Tony Stone Images. 2–3: Kim Heacox/Tony Stone Images. 4: Mark Hopkins. 4–5: *bkgd.* Miriam Romais; *m.t.* Miriam Romais; *t.* Miriam Romais; *m.b.* Miriam Romais; *b.* Miriam Romais. 10: *l.* E.R. Degginger/Color-Pic, Inc.; *m.* C.C. Lockwood/DRK Photo; *r.* Cameron Davidson/Comstock. 12: *l.* Tom Stack & Associates; *r.* Manfred Gottschalk/Tom Stack & Associates. 13: Scott Blackman/Tom Stack & Associates. 14: *l.* E.R. Degginger/Color-Pic, Inc.; *r.* NASA/Corbis Media. 15: Bob Daemmrich Photography. 20–21: *bkgd.* Larry Ulrich/DRK Photo; *inset* Breck P. Kent Photography. 21: Breck P. Kent Photography. 22: *l.* E.R. Degginger/Color-

Archer/Space Art, San Rafael, California. 28: Grant Huntington for HMCo. 29: Grant Huntington for HMCo. 31: Grant Huntington for HMCo. 32: *t.l.* Grant Huntington for HMCo.; *t.r.* Grant Huntington for HMCo.; *b.* Grant Huntington for HMCo. 34: Ulf E. Wallin/The Image Bank. 36: Grant Huntington for HMCo. 37: *l.* Grant Huntington for HMCo.; *r.* Grant Huntington for HMCo. 39: Grant Huntington for HMCo. 40: *t.l.* David Young-Wolff/PhotoEdit; *t.m.* Tony Freeman/PhotoEdit; *b.l.* David Young-Wolff/PhotoEdit; *b.m.* David Young-Wolff/PhotoEdit; *b.r.* David Young-Wolff/PhotoEdit. 42: Grant Huntington for HMCo. 45: Grant Huntington for HMCo. 47: Grant Huntington for HMCo. 49: *t.* North Wind Picture Archives; *b.l.* The Granger Collection, New York; *b.r.* Stock Montage, Inc. 54: Adelina Mejia-Zelaya. 57: *t.* Ken Karp for HMCo.; *b.* Ken Karp for HMCo. 58–59: *t.* Tony Freeman/PhotoEdit; *b.* John Neubauer/PhotoEdit. 59: Peter Lambert/Tony Stone Images. 64: *t.* © 2000 Dewitt Jones/Woodfin Camp & Associates; *b.* © Lawrence Livermore/Science Photo Library/Photo Researchers, Inc. 65: *t.* Dan McCoy/Rainbow; *b.l.* Michael Newman/PhotoEdit; *b.r.* Ulrike Welsch/PhotoEdit. 66: *l.* Ken Karp for HMCo.; *r.* Ken Karp for HMCo. 67: Ken Karp for HMCo. 70–71: Deborah Davis/PhotoEdit. 71: Russ Kinne/Comstock. 73: *t.* © Mark Boulton/Photo Researchers, Inc.; *b.* Sipa Press. 76: *t.* Tony Freeman/PhotoEdit; *b.l.* Tony Freeman/PhotoEdit; *b.r.* Tony Freeman/PhotoEdit. 77: Russ Kinne/Comstock.

Unit E 1: Olaf Veltman/Creative Management Partners. 2–3: Olaf Veltman/Creative Management Partners. 4–5: *bkgd.* Michael A. Dwyer/Stock Boston; *inset* F. Scott Schafer/Outline Press Syndicate, Inc. 10: Richard Hutchings. 16: Grant Huntington for HMCo. 17: Grant Huntington for HMCo. 20: *l.* Tony Freeman/PhotoEdit; *r.* Wes Thompson/The Stock Market. 21: *t.* M.L. Sinibaldi/The Stock Market; *m.* Blaine Harrington III/The Stock Market; *b.* Jeff Gnass/The Stock Market. 24–25: *bkgd.* E.R. Degginger/Color-Pic, Inc. 26: Grant Huntington for HMCo. 27: Grant Huntington for HMCo. 29: *r.* Grant Huntington for HMCo. 31: Grant Huntington for HMCo. 32: Jeff Greenberg/PhotoEdit. 35: Grant Huntington for HMCo. 37: Grant Huntington for HMCo. 38: *l.* Daniel Brody/Stock Boston; *r.* © Jules Bucher/Photo Researchers, Inc. 39: *l.* Jan A. Zysko/NASA-KSC; *r.* © Stephen J. Krasemann/Photo Researchers, Inc. 40: *l.* Tony Stone Images; *r.* Mark Antman/Stock Boston. 41: Craig Aurness/Corbis. 42: Grant Huntington for HMCo. 43: Grant Huntington for HMCo. 44: *t.* Archive Photos; *b.* Fujifotos/The Image Works Incorporated. 45: *t.* © 2000 Juha Jormanainen/Woodfin Camp & Associates; *m.* © W. Bacon/Photo Researchers, Inc.; *b.* © 2000 Eastcott/Momatiuk/Woodfin Camp & Associates. 48: *t.r.* Jim Ballar/Tony Stone Images; *b.l.* © Syd Greenberg/Photo Researchers, Inc.; *b.r.* © Arvil A. Daniels/Photo Researchers, Inc.; *inset* © Photographics/Photo Researchers, Inc. 50: Courtesy, Anton Seimon. 50–51: *bkgd.* NASA; *inset* Courtesy, Anton Seimon. 53: Richard Hutchings for HMCo. 54: *l.* NOAA; *r.* NOAA/NESDIS/NCDC/SDSD. 55: Anthony Edgeworth/The Stock Market. 57: *l.* Gary Withey/Bruce Coleman Incorporated; *r.* Buff Corsi/Tom Stack & Associates. 59: Richard Hutchings for HMCo. 61: *l.* © NASA/Science Source/Photo Researchers, Inc.; *r.* © NOAA/Photo Researchers, Inc. 63: Ray Soto/The Stock Market. 65: Richard Hutchings for HMCo. 66–67: William Wantland/Tom Stack & Associates. 68–69: David Dennis/Tom Stack & Associates. 69: *l.* T.A. Wiewandt/DRK Photo; *r.* T.A. Wiewandt/DRK Photo. 70: *t.* NOAA/NEDIS/NCDC/SDSD; *m.* NOAA/NEDIS/NCDC/SDSD; *b.* NOAA/NEDIS/NCDC/SDSD. 72: *l.* Merilee Thomas/Tom Stack & Associates; *m.* Merilee Thomas/Tom Stack & Associates; *r.* Merilee Thomas/Tom Stack & Associates. 74–75: *bkgd.* Dewitt Jones/Corbis-Bettmann; *border* Morning Star Gallery; *r. inset* Superstock. 78: *l.* Terry Wild. 82: Richard Hutchings for HMCo. 83: Richard Hutchings for HMCo. 88: North Museum, Franklin & Marshall/Runk/Schoenberger/Grant Heilman Photography, Inc. 89: *l.* © James L. Amos/Photo Researchers, Inc.; *r.* © J.G. Paren/Science Photo Library/Photo Researchers, Inc. 90: *l.* William Johnson/Johnson's Photography; *r.* William Johnson/Johnson's Photography. 91: *t.* Anna E. Zuckerman/Tom Stack & Associates; *b.* © George Ranalli/Photo Researchers, Inc. 92: *t.* Cary Wolinsky/Stock Boston; *b.* Rob Crandall/Stock Boston.

Glossary 19: Buff Corsi/Tom Stack & Associates. 25: E.R. Degginger/Color-Pic, Inc. 31: Gary Withey/Bruce Coleman Incorporated.

Extra Practice

On the following pages are questions about each of the Investigations in your book. Use these questions to help you review some of the terms and ideas that you studied. Each review section gives you the page numbers in the book where you can check your answers. Write your answers on a separate sheet of paper.

Contents

Unit A Earth's Land R2

Unit B Properties of Matter R6

Unit C Classifying Living Things R9

Unit D Magnetism and Electricity R12

Unit E Weather and Climate R16

Unit A Extra Practice

Investigation 1 pages A6–A15

Write the term that best completes each sentence.

erosion	sediment	weathering

1. The process by which broken-down rock material is carried by moving water, wind, or ice is called ___.

2. The process by which rock is broken into smaller pieces is called ___.

3. Material that is carried by moving water is called ___.

Complete the following exercises.

4. Describe how a river valley becomes deeper and wider.

5. Why are shorelines the places most affected by erosion and weathering?

6. If you lived near a shoreline, how would you protect your home from the effects of erosion and weathering?

Investigation 2 pages A16–A24

Use the terms below to solve each riddle.

glacier	moraine	sand dune

7. I am a hill formed when wind deposits a pile of sand.
8. I am a huge mass of slow-moving ice.
9. I am rock material carried by a glacier.

Complete the following exercises.

10. How can wind erosion be prevented?
11. What are two ways in which glaciers shape the land?
12. What are some land features formed by the action of glaciers?

Investigation 1 pages A28–A33

Write the term that best completes each sentence.

conservation	natural resources	topsoil

1. Trees, coal, air, and water are examples of ___.
2. Another term for the wise use of natural resources is ___.
3. A mixture of weathered rock and humus is called ___.

Complete the following exercises.

4. Describe the properties of topsoil, subsoil, and weathered rock.
5. What is the greatest cause of soil loss?
6. Why is it important to conserve soil?

Investigation 2 pages A34–A43

Write the term that best completes each sentence.

minerals	ores	metals

7. Rocks are made up of natural solid substances called ___.
8. Rocks that can be mined for the minerals they contain are called ___.
9. Valuable substances from ores, such as copper and gold, are ___.

Complete the following exercises.

10. Identify two or more minerals.
11. How does a renewable resource differ from a nonrenewable resource?
12. Describe how a pure metal is mined.

Unit A Extra Practice

Investigation 3 pages A44–A50

Write the term that best completes each sentence.

peat	solar energy	fossil fuel

13. Energy from the Sun is called ___.

14. Natural gas, which is made from the remains of once-living things, is a ___.

15. A fuel that comes from the remains of ancient swamp plants is called ___.

Complete the following exercises.

16. Explain how the energy in fossil fuels can be traced back to the Sun.

17. What are some energy sources other than fossil fuels?

18. What are some of the advantages of using solar energy instead of fossil fuels?

Investigation 1 pages A54–A61

Use the terms below to solve each riddle.

ash	incinerator	landfill

1. I am a large hole that is filled, over time, with trash.

2. I am a place where trash is burned.

3. I am the material that results when trash is burned.

Complete the following exercises.

4. How are landfills better for the environment than trash dumps?

5. Why doesn't the trash in a landfill decay quickly?

6. Many cities and towns have laws against burning trash. Do you agree or disagree with such laws? Why?

Investigation 2 pages A62–A67

Write the term that best completes each sentence.

hazardous waste	litter	petroleum

7. Trash that is discarded on the ground or in water is called ___.

8. A pollutant that can harm the environment even in small amounts is called ___.

9. Plastic is made from a nonrenewable resource called ___.

Complete the following exercises.

10. What are some ways that litter in the oceans is harmful?

11. What problems can result from the improper disposal of motor oil, paint, pesticides, and other hazardous wastes?

12. Give examples of how littering can reduce natural resources.

Investigation 3 pages A68–A76

Write the term in each pair that correctly completes each sentence.

13. The processing and reusing of items is called (recycling, packaging).

14. Choosing products that are not overpackaged can help (increase, decrease) the amount of trash in landfills.

15. Pulp is a stage in the process of recycling (paper, plastic).

Complete the following exercises.

16. What is the meaning of the number code on the bottom of some plastic items?

17. What are some advantages and disadvantages of packaging?

18. What are some common objects you use that can be recycled?

Unit B Extra Practice

Investigation 1 pages B6–B13

Write the term that best completes each sentence.

density	mass	volume

1. The amount of space that matter takes up is called ___.

2. A measure of the amount of matter something contains is called ___.

3. The amount of matter in a given space is called ___.

Complete the following exercises.

4. What are physical properties?

5. Is the ability to burn an example of a physical property or a chemical property? Give reasons for your answer.

6. Choose an object in the room and tell about its properties. Explain how its properties would be affected by rotating the object.

Investigation 2 pages B14–B22

Write the term in each pair that correctly completes each sentence.

7. When all members of a group use the same objects to make measurements, they are using (metric units, standard units).

8. The metric system includes units such as (miles, meters).

9. Length can be measured using a (balance, meterstick).

Complete the following exercises.

10. Why is it important to use a standard unit to make measurements?

11. What is the difference between the metric system and the English system?

12. What tool would you use to measure the temperature outdoors? Would you use Fahrenheit or Celsius? Explain your answer.

Unit B Extra Practice

Investigation 1 pages B26–B35

Use the terms below to solve each riddle.

| atom | compound | state of matter |

1. I am the smallest part of an element that has the properties of that element.
2. I am a kind of matter made of two or more elements joined together.
3. I am a physical property of matter.

Complete the following exercises.

4. How do solids, liquids, and gases differ from each other?
5. How do a chemical symbol and a chemical formula differ?
6. A bottle of perfume is opened in one room and can be smelled in another room. Describe the theory of matter that explains why this happens.

Investigation 2 pages B36–B42

Write the term in each pair that correctly completes each sentence.

7. The change of state from a liquid to a gas is called (condensation, evaporation).
8. The change of state from a liquid to a solid is called (freezing, boiling).
9. The rapid change of state from a liquid to a gas is called (melting, boiling).

Complete the following exercises.

10. Describe the movement of particles in matter when that matter is heated and when heat is taken away.
11. In terms of the particles that make up water, describe what happens when a puddle of water dries up.
12. What makes HFCs well-suited to the task of keeping a refrigerator cold?

Investigation 1 pages B46–B53

Write the term in each pair that correctly completes each sentence.

1. Matter made up of two or more different substances is called a (mixture, solution).

2. A change in the size, shape, or state of matter with no new matter formed is called a (chemical change, physical change).

3. A fractionating tower is useful because each of the hydrocarbons in crude oil changes state at (the same, a different) temperature.

Complete the following exercises.

4. How are mixtures and solutions different?

5. Is the change from ice to water a physical change? Explain.

6. When water freezes and when water melts, it behaves differently from most other matter. Explain.

Investigation 2 pages B54–B60

Write the term in each pair that correctly completes each sentence.

7. The way vinegar reacts with baking soda is a (physical property, chemical property) of vinegar.

8. One or more different kinds of matter are formed during a (chemical property, chemical change).

9. The process that occurs when iron and oxygen combine to form rust is a (chemical property, chemical reaction).

Complete the following exercises.

10. How do physical changes and chemical changes differ?

11. Give examples of a slow chemical change and a fast chemical change.

12. What causes a chemical reaction on the film in your camera when you take a photo?

Unit C Extra Practice

 Investigation 1 pages C6–C15

Write the term that best completes each sentence.

| invertebrates | organisms | vertebrates |

1. Living things are also called ___.
2. Animals that have backbones are called ___.
3. Animals that do not have backbones are called ___.

Complete the following exercises.

4. How do organisms in the plant kingdom differ from organisms in the fungus kingdom?
5. How has the classification system for living things changed since Aristotle's time?
6. Give two examples of invertebrates and two examples of vertebrates.

Investigation 2 pages C16–C23

Use the terms below to solve each riddle.

| amphibian | mammal | reptile |

7. I live in water after I hatch; as an adult I can live on land.
8. I have dry, scaly skin and lay eggs that have a leathery shell.
9. I have hair or fur and feed milk to my young.

Complete the following exercises.

10. Name the five groups of vertebrates.
11. Identify one trait of each group of vertebrates.
12. Are all animals that live in the water fish? Explain your answer.

Unit C Extra Practice

Investigation 3 pages C24–C31

Write the term in each pair that correctly completes each sentence.

13. Clams and squids belong to the group called (arthropods, mollusks).

14. A tapeworm is an example of a (roundworm, flatworm).

15. Corals and sea anemones are kinds of (animals, plants).

Complete the following exercises.

16. How could you show that a butterfly's body has symmetry—that one side is a mirror image of the other?

17. Identify one arthropod that is an insect and one that is not. Tell one way in which these animals are alike and one way in which they differ.

18. Describe two traits of the group to which corals, hydras, and jellyfish belong.

Investigation 4 pages C32–C38

Write the term in each pair that correctly completes each sentence.

19. Mosses and liverworts grow in places that are (dry, moist).

20. Ferns have leaves called (fronds, spores).

21. Cone-bearing plants are called (conifers, horsetails).

Complete the following exercises.

22. Identify two types of nonseed plants. Choose one type and tell how it reproduces.

23. Give examples of a monocot and a dicot and explain how to tell to which group a plant belongs.

24. How are conifers and flowering plants alike, and how are they different?

Unit C Extra Practice

Investigation 1 pages C42–C49

Use the terms below to solve each riddle.

environment	savanna	shelter

1. I am everything that surrounds and affects an animal.
2. Animals need me for protection from enemies and from harsh weather.
3. I am a grassland found in tropical climates.

Complete the following exercises.

4. What are the basic needs of animals?
5. Give examples of how animals living in an African savanna meet their needs.
6. A lizard's body temperature changes with the temperature of its surroundings. How does such an animal keep its body temperature within a certain range?

Investigation 2 pages C50–C60

Write the term in each pair that correctly completes each sentence.

7. An elephant's tusks and trunk are examples of (adaptations, species).
8. Behaviors that living things inherit from their parents are (instinctive, learned).
9. A species that dies out is (endangered, extinct).

Complete the following exercises.

10. Choose an animal species and compare it to a similar, extinct species.
11. Give an example of an instinctive behavior and an example of a learned behavior.
12. Is the behavior of a newborn rattlesnake defending itself against attack an instinctive behavior or a learned behavior? Explain your answer.

Investigation 1 pages D6–D15

Write the term in each pair that correctly completes each sentence.

1. A magnet's property of attracting certain materials is called (gravitation, magnetism).

2. If you put the north pole of one magnet near the south pole of another magnet, the magnets will (attract, repel) each other.

3. The pole of a freely moving magnet that will point south is the (south pole, north pole).

Complete the following exercises.

4. How could a magnet help you determine if an object is made of of iron or not?

5. In what ways is a maglev train different from other trains?

6. How could you use a magnet with marked poles to find the north pole on a magnet with unmarked poles?

Investigation 2 pages D16–D24

Write the term that best completes each sentence.

magnetic field	lodestone	compass

7. In order to be attracted by a magnet, an object must be within the magnet's ___.

8. The naturally magnetic rock discovered more than 2,000 years ago is called ___.

9. A device containing a magnetized needle that shows direction is called a ___.

Complete the following exercises.

10. How could you show a friend a magnet's force field?

11. Name two properties of all magnets.

12. If you wanted to pick up a pile of paper clips, which part of a bar magnet would you use? Explain your answer.

Investigation 1 pages D28–D35

Write the term that best completes each sentence.

> electric charges   electric discharge   static electricity

1. The movement of negative charges can cause the buildup of electric charges on objects, or ___.

2. Tiny particles of matter can carry units of electricity called ___.

3. Lightning is an example of a/an ___.

Complete the following exercises.

4. How can an object become charged with static electricity?

5. What properties of positive and negative electric charges are similar to the properties of a magnet's poles?

6. Name two ways to stay safe during a lightning storm.

Investigation 2 pages D36–D43

Write the term in each pair that correctly completes each sentence.

7. A path along which electric charges can flow is called an (electric circuit, electric current).

8. A material, such as plastic or wood, that doesn't let electricity move easily through it is called (a conductor, an insulator).

9. A device that opens and closes an electric circuit is a (dry cell, switch).

Complete the following exercises.

10. Describe the parts of a simple electric circuit.

11. Why won't a bulb light in an open, or incomplete, circuit?

12. How could you set up a simple electric circuit in which you could easily control whether electric current flowed or didn't flow?

Investigation 3 pages D44–D52

Use the terms below to solve each riddle.

circuit breaker	parallel circuit	series circuit

13. I have only a single path for electric current to follow.

14. I have more than one path for electric current to follow.

15. I open a circuit by turning myself off.

Complete the following exercises.

16. In what ways are fluorescent bulbs better for the environment than incandescent bulbs?

17. What purpose do fuses and circuit breakers serve?

18. If you were going to build a house, would you use series circuits or parallel circuits? Why?

Investigation 1 pages D56–D65

Write the term that best completes each sentence.

generator	solar cell	electric cell

1. A device that changes light into electrical energy is called a/an ___.

2. A device that changes energy of motion into electrical energy is called a/an ___.

3. A device that changes chemical energy into electrical energy is called a/an ___.

Complete the following exercises.

4. How are magnets used to generate electricity?

5. What are transformers used for?

6. What are some advantages of using solar energy to produce electricity?

Investigation 2 pages D66–D76

Write the term in each pair that correctly completes each sentence.

7. A magnet that is made when electric charges move through a coil of wire wrapped around an iron core is called an (electric circuit, electromagnet).

8. Electric cars have rechargeable (batteries, magnets).

9. Refrigerators, hair dryers, and ceiling fans all contain (electric motors, dry cells).

Complete the following exercises.

10. Describe some of the developments in the field of telecommunication.

11. How is an electromagnet different from a permanent magnet?

12. Why is the statement "don't mix electricity and water" good advice?

Investigation 1 pages E6–E15

Write the term in each pair that correctly completes each sentence.

1. The lowest layer of the atmosphere is the (stratosphere, troposphere).

2. The condition of the atmosphere at a certain time and place is called (temperature, weather).

3. The blanket of air that surrounds Earth is the (mesosphere, atmosphere).

Complete the following exercises.

4. What is the greenhouse effect?

5. Identify the gases that make up air.

6. What two factors greatly affect weather?

Investigation 2 pages E16–E22

Write the term in each pair that correctly completes each sentence.

7. Wind is caused by the (even, uneven) heating of Earth's surface.

8. Materials tend to heat up faster if they are (dark, light) in color.

9. When air is warmed it (rises, sinks).

Complete the following exercises.

10. How does the pilot of a hot-air balloon make the balloon rise?

11. Why is a shoreline often a comfortable place to be in hot weather?

12. Would you wear dark-colored clothing or light-colored clothing in hot weather? Explain your answer.

Investigation 1 pages E26–E33

Write the term in each pair that correctly completes each sentence.

1. A device that measures air pressure is called a (barometer, thermometer).

2. The push of air against its surroundings is called air (pressure, temperature).

3. The first barometer, made by Torricelli, was (an aneroid, a mercury) barometer.

Complete the following exercises.

4. What are high-pressure areas and low-pressure areas?

5. Why does air pressure increase the closer you are to sea level and decrease the farther you are from sea level?

6. How does heating the air in a closed bottle and the air in an open bottle affect the air pressure in each? Explain.

Investigation 2 pages E34–E41

Use the terms below to solve each riddle.

anemometer	windsock	wind vane

7. I am a device that shows wind direction. Often I am shaped like a long arrow with a tail.

8. I show wind direction. I am a cloth bag that is narrow at one end and open at both ends.

9. I am a device that measures wind speed. I am made up of cups on spokes attached to a pole.

Complete the following exercises.

10. What is the Beaufort Scale?

11. How are windsocks and wind vanes alike? How do they differ?

12. Identify three benefits and one drawback of using wind power.

Investigation 3 pages E42–E48

Write the term in each pair that correctly completes each sentence.

13. Very fine drops of water are called (hail, drizzle).

14. Any form of water that falls from the air is called (humidity, precipitation).

15. The amount of water vapor in the air is called (humidity, relative humidity).

Complete the following exercises.

16. How do clouds form?

17. What causes rain?

18. At the same air temperature, would you feel cooler if the relative humidity was 10 percent or 100 percent? Explain your answer.

Investigation 1 pages E52–E57

Use the terms below to solve each riddle.

cirrus cloud	cumulus cloud	stratus cloud

1. I am a puffy cloud that forms when large areas of warm, moist air rise upward from Earth's surface.

2. I am a flat, gray cloud that forms when a flat layer of warm, moist air rises very slowly.

3. I am a cloud that looks like wisps of hair and I appear when air rises high enough for ice crystals to form.

Complete the following exercises.

4. What does the word part *nimbo-* mean in a cloud name?

5. How can clouds be used to predict weather?

6. How are weather satellites used in weather prediction?

Investigation 2 pages E58–E63

Write the term that best completes each sentence.

air mass	front	weather forecaster

7. Someone who makes predictions about the weather is a/an ___.

8. A body of air that has the same general temperature and air pressure throughout is called a/an ___.

9. A place where two types of air masses meet is called a/an ___.

Complete the following exercises.

10. What conditions do forecasters use to make predictions?

11. Describe how a cold front forms and how a warm front forms.

12. You hear that a low pressure area will move into your region by evening. What type of weather can you expect for that night?

Investigation 3 pages E64–E72

Write the term in each pair that correctly completes each sentence.

13. A storm that produces heavy rain, strong winds, lightning, and thunder is a (flash flood, thunderstorm).

14. A funnel-shaped storm of spinning wind is a (tornado, thunderstorm).

15. A large, violent storm that forms over warm ocean water is a (hurricane, thunderstorm).

Complete the following exercises.

16. What causes a thunderstorm?

17. Name one type of severe weather and identify some ways to stay safe during it.

18. Under what conditions is a storm called a hurricane?

Unit E Extra Practice

Write the term in each pair that correctly completes each sentence.

1. The imaginary line that circles the middle of Earth is called the (axis, equator).

2. The imaginary line that runs from the North Pole through Earth's center to the South Pole is the (hemisphere, axis).

3. The half of Earth below the equator is the (Northern Hemisphere, Southern Hemisphere).

Complete the following exercises.

4. How does the slant at which the Sun strikes Earth affect seasonal temperatures?

5. When the hemisphere in which you live is tilted away from the Sun, what season do you experience?

6. What season are people in the Southern Hemisphere having right now? How do you know?

Investigation 2 pages E82–E92

Use the terms below to solve each riddle.

| polar climate | temperate climate | tropical climate |

7. I am usually hot and rainy all year round.

8. I have warm, dry summers and cold, wet winters.

9. I am usually very cold.

Complete the following exercises.

10. Compare the climate of a place that is near a large body of water to that of a place that is far from a large body of water.

11. What are three methods scientists use to study climates of the past?

12. How does distance from the equator affect a region's climate?